The Versatile
Air Repair Ship
HMS *UNICORN*

Edgar Hibbert

ARTHUR H. STOCKWELL LTD.
Torrs Park   Ilfracombe   Devon
Established 1898
www.ahstockwell.co.uk

British Library Cataloguing-in-Publication Data.
A catalogue record for this book is available
from the British Library.

Arthur H. Stockwell Ltd. bears no responsibility
for the accuracy of events recorded in this book.

Dedicated to the fine work of the Fleet Air Arm pilots who flew off
under all sorts of conditions in inferior aircraft for most of the war.

ISBN 0-7223-3709-4
ISBN 978-0-7223-3709-7
Printed in Great Britain by
Arthur H. Stockwell Ltd.
Torrs Park   Ilfracombe
Devon

Contents

The RNAS, the Forerunner of the Fleet Air Arm

During the closing months of the Great War the RNAS (Royal Naval Air Service) led the world in pioneering the most advanced techniques in the art of landing an aircraft in one piece on a deck when the ship was steaming at sea. Also, they had built up a successful defence system, with bases all around our coastline. Defence squadrons of aircraft patrolled at dawn and dusk to seek out and bomb German U-boats, which would lurk at periscope-depth in large river mouths or estuaries and deserted bays. They would surface at nightfall to safely charge up their batteries under cover of darkness, all ready to slip out and pounce on some unsuspecting merchant ship to sink it as it headed for port or had just left harbour.

On April Fool's Day in 1918 the RAF (Royal Air Force) was formed out of the Royal Naval Air Service and the Royal Flying Corps, massacring the RNAS at a stroke, taking over 60,000 naval personnel and 3,000 naval aircraft, lock, stock and barrel, with all its bases around the coast. It was all handed over by the Admiralty to the Air Ministry who criminally neglected the defence bases and reduced the number of naval aircraft to barely 100 by 1920.

The only concession made by the Air Ministry was to insist that RAF personnel manned the few seaborne squadrons for use on aircraft carriers and a few float planes carried on several of the big ships for reconnaissance. They were under the dual control of the Admiralty and the Air Ministry, which caused many bitter arguments and resentment, as the Air Ministry believed in strategic bombing, which was all very well for plastering around a target, but not very accurate when aiming for the bull's-eye or against steaming ships.

Also, they let the efficient naval coastal defence system dwindle away to nothing, and, as they had full control of the purse strings, they spent a pittance on the Fleet Air Arm — making them do with ancient, patched-up, unreliable biplanes with torn holes in the fuselage and fabric wings. (They were patched-up with round linen patches with serrated edges cut out with pinking shears and then stuck on with dope.

The first small ship to be fitted with a flight deck was the *Campania,* which was closely followed by the *Argos*, both of which were used for training pilots to land on and take off from a small deck.

Also, the heavy cruiser, *Furious*, with a speed of 30 knots, had a deck built over her forecastle which, after several trials with a Sopwith Pup biplane, was found to be highly dangerous as one plane shot off the bows when the flight-deck party failed to stop it. (The pilot was drowned as they carried no Mae West life jackets or parachutes.) Later, another deck was added to the after part of the ship over the quarterdeck with two port and starboard passageways around a narrowed central bridge and funnel to connect the two decks.

When on trials, one of her aircraft shot down a German seaplane and destroyed two Zeppelins (L54 and L60). After this she went into reserve to be completely altered in Devonport Dockyard — a flush flight deck was built with six arrester wires slung across it, and the bridge and funnel were removed to the starboard side; also room was made to accommodate thirty-three aircraft.

She was then recommissioned to join the home fleet with a spell in the in the Mediterranean. In 1939, after war broke out, she patrolled the Atlantic.

The only other modification, made at a later date, was the fitting of an arrester hook to the aircraft to catch onto arrester wires, running across the flight decks, which paid out as the kite was brought to a halt. This eliminated the dangerous practice of the flight-deck party swarming around to drag the kites to a gradual halt.

Unfortunately some of the old salty admirals were blinded in favour of the old 15-inch-gun battleship, which had a range of twenty miles, and against the potential of an aircraft carrier plus aircraft, which had a combined range of thousands of miles to torpedo or bomb any target or act as an air umbrella for the fleet. Consequently they never supported the Fleet Air Arm, which ceased to be a world leader and was relegated to a third-class unit, being overtaken by the US Navy and Japan, and which slipped into the Air Ministry's hands without a fight.

During the ensuing period of the interwar years the budget for the armed forces was cut to the bone; so much so that naval pay was cut in 1926, causing a mutiny at Invergordon. Also there was no cash in the kitty for building new ships, especially battleships.

However, the Admiralty had recognised the importance of the Fleet Air Arm and had started converting several old suitable ships and cruisers into aircraft carriers. The first on the list to be added to the fleet was the *Eagle*, completed in 1920, with a speed of 24 knots, carrying twenty-two aircraft. Then came the *Hermes,* purpose-built in 1923, with a speed of 24 knots, to carry twenty aircraft; the *Furious* (already mentioned), to carry thirty-three aircraft; the *Courageous*, converted in 1924, with a speed of 30 knots, carrying forty-eight aircraft; and the *Glorious*.

During 1930 the Admiralty wanted to scrap all these vessels and build four new ones in their place but only managed to produce one, the *Ark Royal,* in 1939, originally designed for seventy-two aircraft, but only carried sixty owing to the size of our dry docks.

There had been many bitter arguments between the Admiralty and the Air Ministry over the dual control, and until 1937 having RAF personnel aboard ship working to naval routine and discipline, instead of having naval personnel. At this juncture the Air Ministry relented and handed back complete control of the Fleet Air Arm to the Admiralty, which had to start recruiting its own personnel to replace those from the RAF. They kept the shore bases and funds for new aircraft, making sure they had first pick of the latest models, leaving a small number of three unwanted types of aircraft for the Fleet Air Arm. The first one was the sturdy biplane, Swordfish, a torpedo bomber (1936 to 45); the second was the Gloster Sea Gladiator, a biplane fighter (1937 to 42); and the third was the Blackburn Skua, a low-winged monoplane dive-bomber (1938 to 41), which was quite good but was spoilt by a ha'p'orth of tar as the Air Ministry refused the cash to develop the bombsight. All these models were fitted with arrester hooks to stop them on landing on a flight deck.

So, at the start of the war in 1939, the Fleet Air Arm were equipped with obsolete aircraft and were third-rate compared with the Japanese (whose aircraft were based on German designs) and American aircraft. However, when conditions were right, our pilots achieved some splendid results with their kites.

The Fairey Swordfish was a sturdy biplane (affectionately known as a stringbag) with a small 690-h.p. Bristol Pegasus radial engine with a top speed of 100 knots or 138 mph, with twin open cockpits and a crew of three. It carried a 1,605-pound torpedo with a 200-pound warhead (which was no use against the heavy armour of a battleship) or eight depth charges or six rockets, and was the only kite able to take off or land in a heavy Atlantic swell owing to its slow stalling speed. It was a maid of all types of work, such as protecting convoys against U-boats with depth charges. It had numerous successes in the Mediterranean protecting convoys, in particular, Operation Judgement, when Swordfish from HMS *Illustrious* launched a surprise torpedo attack on Taranto, hitting three battleships and sinking one for the loss of two kites. Also, two Swordfish from *Ark Royal,* under terrific gunfire, valiantly hit the battleship, *Bismarck,* aft, causing her steering gear to jam so she could only move in a large circle, so she could not escape from the terrific gunfire and was sunk by the home fleet.

Unfortunately, the slow approach of the Swordfish when launching a torpedo attack at 900 yards made them vulnerable death traps when facing the massive power of anti-aircraft gunfire from ships. This happened in the English Channel (on 11 to 13 February 1942) when the *Scharnhorst* and *Gneisenau* made a dash up the Channel, homeward bound. Heroically a squadron of Swordfish made a torpedo attack which failed to stop them — the pilots and crews forfeited their lives in vain.

The Gloster Sea Gladiator was an outdated fighter biplane with a 756-h.p. Bristol Mercury radial engine and a top speed of 257 mph (three of them were christened, *Faith, Hope* and *Charity*). They were put to great effect in the defence of Malta by the RAF. When radar gave them a few minutes' warning of approaching German or Italian bombing raids, they would climb to their maximum altitude then dive down on the enemy at high speed, gained in the dive, to break up their attacks.

Also there was the Blackburn Skua, a light two-seater low winged monoplane with a small 830-h.p. Bristol Perseus engine. It was a dive-bomber, carrying one 500-pound bomb, which performed quite well at dive-bombing. It sank the small German cruiser *Konigsberg* but its bomb load was too light to attack the battlecruiser *Scharnhorst* (they bounced off the armoured deck). Also, its bombsight was never developed and its landing speed was too high to land on a carrier, so the hooks were often torn off. Consequently it soon lost its favour and was scrapped.

The Fairey Albacore, a three-seater enclosed biplane, was built to replace the Swordfish and was powered by a Bristol Taurus 1130-h.p. engine and carried a 1,605-pound torpedo or 2,000 pounds of bombs. It had three machine guns mounted for defence and did some good work but never became popular.

The Fairey Fulmar was a poor two-seater fighter with a speed of only 272 mph. It was replaced by the Seafire (a modified Spitfire with a hook). It arrived on the scene when the RAF had an improved model, but it was a useful kite with a Rolls-Royce Merlin engine of 1,470 h.p. and a top speed of 352 mph. However, it performed well in the Italian invasion on 9 September 1943 in Operation Avalanche, when the British X Corps And American VI Corps stormed Salerno. Several squadrons from *Unicorn* and auxiliary carriers formed an umbrella for the fleet and landing craft whilst the landings took place.

The Fairey Barracuda was an ungainly looking aircraft with massive air flaps to slow it down whilst dive-bombing. It arrived too late on the scene to make full use of its useful diving performance; also it was powered by a small 1,640-h.p. Rolls-Royce Merlin engine with a speed of only 228 mph instead of having a more powerful Rolls-Royce Griffon engine, which would have given it a much better performance. It carried a crew of three, had two machine guns and could carry a 1,620-pound torpedo or 1,500 pounds of bombs or 4,150 pounds of depth charges. It put up an excellent performance when bombing the battleship, *Tirpitz*, putting her out of action for three months. It also bombed and severely damaged the oil refineries at Palembang, Sumatra, which cut off the Japanese oil supplies. However, it was soon ditched when the more powerful Yankee Avenger torpedo bomber became available. It had an all-round better performance (except for dive-bombing). Also a small number of Martlets (or Hellcat fighters) were supplied.

The Fairey Firefly, was a two-seater fighter bomber powered by a Rolls-Royce 1,730- or 1,990-h.p. Griffon engine, with a speed of 300 mph. Its much-improved performance replaced the underpowered Fulmar, as it carried four 20-mm cannons with a bomb load of 2,000 pounds of bombs or eight rockets. It performed well with the Barracudas on its sole attack on the oil refineries of Sumatra.

Through the war the Fleet Air Arm put up a remarkably fine performance considering the third-rate antiquated low-speed death traps they had to use. Although fairly reliable, they were no match against the German and Italian land-based aircraft, or the numerous dual-purpose Japanese aircraft, which were used from land or from their large aircraft carriers.

However, by 1943, as the RAF were being supplied with more powerful Rolls-Royce engines, leaving a surplus of smaller Merlin engines which were dumped then snapped up by the Fleet Air Arm. They were much needed to supply extra power to improve the performance of their later models.

The Fleet Air Arm pilots had much to contend with as they had to be trained to land on a small space, about 350 feet long, and to obey the orders of the batsman who indicated the drop in height so that the aircraft's hook would catch on one of the arrester wires to stop it. If the aircraft bounced and missed the hook it would end up in the crash barrier. Also, if the pilot cut the speed too much on the final turn, the aircraft was liable to stall and slide sideways into the sea. Only the old Swordfish, with its slow stalling speed, could operate in the rough stormy Atlantic weather. When the bows were dipping into a huge trough causing the waves to part and break over the flight deck, the take-off of an aircraft had to be timed so the bows lifted high out of the water so it was airborne as it reached the end of the deck.

In 1941 a new type of escort carrier appeared, being made from a converted merchant ship, with a flat top, to protect the Atlantic convoys which were rapidly depleting.

By 1944 the Fleet Air Arm was much better equipped to face the Japanese in the Pacific Ocean with a mixture of our own and American aircraft. The Americans also had superior aircraft carriers which would stand up to the Japanese bombing.

Fate of the Aircraft Carriers

Courageous was the first aircraft carrier to be sunk in the Western Approaches on anti-U-boat patrol when the captain foolishly sent his two escort destroyers on a false sighting of a U-boat. They should have been in attendance when the ship sped into the wind to land-on her aircraft, which had to circle around to land one at a time. This took everyone's attention, as all eyes were on deck watching the aircraft land instead of being on the lookout for the lurking sub (U-boat 29), which slammed three torpedoes into her.

10

Glorious was sunk in the evacuation of Norway by the two battlecruisers, *Scharnhorst* and *Gneisenau*, shortly after landing-on a squadron of RAF Hurricanes, which clogged up the flight deck. They prevented their own Swordfish being armed up and used because the Hurricanes could not be struck down in the hangar out of the way because they had fixed wings instead of folding ones.

Ark Royal (commissioned late 1939) had sixteen 4.5-inch guns, forty-eight 2-pounder (40-mm) pom-poms, thirty-two 0.5-inch (12.7-mm) machine guns and armour-plated lower hangar and upper and lower decks, also all-or-nothing side belt armour. She had two hangars and a crash barrier so that aircraft could land-on whilst others could be catapulted off on the two catapults at the same time. Also, she had three lifts and the deck was illuminated by two rows of lighting for landing in fog or night flying, making her one of the most advanced aircraft carriers of her time.

She served with distinction in the Mediterranean, but her biggest success was when two of her Swordfish squadrons attacked the *Bismarck* with two torpedo hits in a vital spot — the steering gear — so she was unable to steer in a straight line and run for port, which enabled the *Rodney* and *King George V* to give her a massive pounding before she sank.

Unfortunately, the *Ark Royal* was sunk in 1941, some thirty miles off Gibraltar by one torpedo. It should have been possible to save her as she was not terribly badly damaged and still had most of her machinery undamaged, but she sank next day through some internal weakness and poor effort from her damage-control parties.

Illustrious was the first of the new carriers (commissioned on 21 May 1940). She carried thirty-six aircraft and was attacked on convoy duty to Malta after her successful raid on Taranto. At Taranto, her two squadrons of Swordfish attacked the Italian fleet, sinking one battleship and damaging two, after which the Germans came to the Italians' aid. They tried to annihilate her with their crack Fliegerkorps X on 10 January 1941. Fifty Stuka dive-bombers hit her with six 1,000-pound bombs, which crashed down on her armour-plated deck that prevented her sinking. Although badly damaged and on fire with her steering damaged, she managed to limp into Valletta Grand Harbour, Malta, where she lay at anchor. She was attacked daily from 10 to 23 January, while her temporary repairs were completed. Then at night she slipped out, making good her escape through the Suez Canal before landing up in Norfolk Navy Yard, Virginia, USA, for a refit. She joined the Pacific fleet and was hit by a kamikaze aircraft which did some damage but did not put her out of action; but soon after, as her machinery was worn out, she returned home to Devonport.

Hermes was sunk on 9 April 1942. Operating in the East Indian fleet, Ceylon, it was sunk just after dawn by D3A Val dive-bombers from Admiral Nagumo's fast carrier-striking force by aircraft from *Akagi, Hiryu* and *Soryu,* which obtained forty hits and sank the small carrier in ten minutes in the Bay of Bengal.

Eagle was sunk on 11 August 1942 after delivering a load of Hurricane aircraft to Malta, during a massive convoy known as Operation Pedestal; her luck ran out and she was hit by four torpedoes fired from U73 and quickly listed to port and sank within four minutes.

Formidable, commissioned on 24 November 1940, successfully served in the Mediterranean and Battle of Crete and the invasion of North Africa and Italy. Then, in 1945, she served with the British Pacific fleet and was hit by two kamikaze aircraft. One bounced off her armour-plated flight deck and the other caused a bad fire, which was quickly brought under control by the damage-control parties. She finished up with some clumsy clot accidentally firing a kite's machine gun in the hangar, causing a terrific explosion which damaged thirty aircraft and badly strained her hull. However, all was not lost and she took part in the final onslaught against Japan, flying-off a few aircraft.

Victorious, commissioned on 15 May 1941, carried fifty-four aircraft and launched a torpedo attack against the battleship *Bismarck*, and obtained one hit on her thick side armour, which exploded but did little damage. Later, she was used by the British Pacific fleet along with *Illustrious,* with air strikes on Sabang and oil refineries at Palembang, before joining Task Force 57 with the main British Pacific fleet force against the Sakishima-Gunto island chain in 1945.

Indomitable was commissioned on 1 October 1941, and saw a

great deal of action during the war. She carried forty-eight aircraft, and along with *Formidable* provided air cover for the troops landing at Salerno, Italy, flying 214 fighter sorties in three days without accident during 1943.

Indefatigable was completed with many improvements on 3 May 1944, and *Implacable* on 24 August 1944. Both carriers had their capacity of kites increased to eighty-one by the use of outriggers and deck parks. All six carriers finished off by serving in the Pacific and survived the hits by the kamikaze bombers.

Furious was the oldest carrier to survive the war and carried on doing the good work.

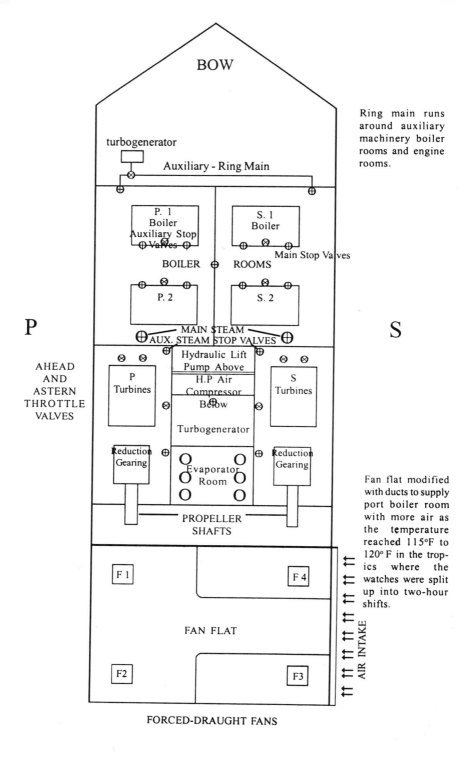

BOW

turbogenerator

Auxiliary - Ring Main

Ring main runs
around auxiliary
machinery boiler
rooms and engine
rooms.

P. 1
Boiler
Auxiliary Stop
Valves

S. 1
Boiler

Main Stop Valves

BOILER   ROOMS

P. 2

S. 2

P

S

MAIN STEAM
AUX. STEAM STOP VALVES

AHEAD
AND
ASTERN
THROTTLE
VALVES

Hydraulic Lift
Pump Above

P
Turbines

H.P Air
Compressor
Below

S
Turbines

Turbogenerator

Reduction
Gearing

Evaporator
Room

Reduction
Gearing

PROPELLER
SHAFTS

Fan flat modified
with ducts to supply
port boiler room
with more air as
the temperature
reached 115ºF to
120º F in the trop-
ics where the
watches were split
up into two-hour
shifts.

F 1

F 4

FAN FLAT

AIR INTAKE

F2

F3

FORCED-DRAUGHT FANS

HMS *Unicorn*

General Description

The *Unicorn* had been laid down as a liner on 29 June 1939, launched on 20 November 1941 and completed on 12 March 1943. Her original displacement was to have been 14,530 tons with a draught of nineteen feet; but was increased in the building to 16,530 tons with a draught of twenty-four feet.

She was a unique treble-purpose ship designed to serve the Fleet Air Arm in any part of the world, as a repair ship-cum-depot ship, also as an aircraft carrier or a fast transport to keep the fleet carriers up to full strength in men and equipment.

She had a total complement of 1,094 officers and men, when carrying her Fleet Air Arm repair staff and her three complete squadrons with thirty-six kites with crews to fly them and bods to maintain them.

Her two engines produced a total of 40,000 s.h.p. at the top speed of 23½ knots (on trials). She had a range of 11,000 nautical miles at an economical speed of 13½ knots, when the tanks were full up with 3,000 tons of oil fuel. As in all cases of depot ships she was underpowered with exactly half the power of a heavy cruiser (which had four 20,000-s.h.p. engines, or 80,000 s.h.p. in all). The idea was that the smaller the engines and boilers the less space they would take up, leaving more space for the huge stocks of Fleet Air Arm spares, magazines and workshops.

She was lightly armed, with her main armament being eight 4.5-inch high-angle anti-aircraft guns mounted in twin turrets in the four quarters of the ship at flight-deck level. She also carried two eight-barrelled pom-poms (two pounders) around the ends of the island structure, plus thirteen small 20-mm short-range anti-aircraft armaments around the flight deck and island.

Owing to the wartime shortage of material her engines had been scraped from the bottom of the barrel after being hidden away in some obscure corner of the shop. The labyrinth gland seals on the 2-h.p. turbine shafts did not conform with Admiralty specifications as their tolerances were slightly above the permitted size. This meant the steam seals were not quite up to standard, making it easier for the atmospheric pressure to seep through the glands so that more steam was required to maintain the vacuum at 29.8 inches in the condenser to obtain the high efficiency of the turbines. Also the extra steam tended to heat up the bearings a little further along the shafts.

Also there was a shortage of plumber-block bearings for the long prop shafts for the propellers which should have been supported by two bearings on each shaft instead of one. This caused the shafts to sag and run out of true.

However, she was a maid of all work and served the Fleet Air Arm well. She was used for training Fleet Air Arm pilots on deck landings and take-offs; patrolling with the home fleet from Scapa Flow along the Norwegian coastline; providing an air umbrella for the fleet at the Salerno landings along with some Woolworth carriers; repairing all Fleet Air Arm aircraft in the Far East at Trincomalee; then finally joining the fleet train from Sydney to Leyte in the Philippines to supply new aircraft and repair damaged kites for the fleet carriers (being the fastest supply vessel up to 20 knots).

She greatly differed from the original HMS *Unicorn,* which was a 46-gun wooden frigate sailing ship, launched in 1824 from Dundee Shipyard, where she was built along with Scott's ship *Discovery* (both vessels are still afloat together in Dundee Harbour).

Unlike the *Illustrious* class of aircraft carriers that had a 2½-inch armour-plated box around the top of her single hangar, the *Unicorn* had a 2-inch nickel chrome armour-plated flight deck with a complicated system of armour-plating around her magazines of 2 inches for'ard and 2½ to 3 inches aft, with 2-inch armour-plating for the two bulkheads which contained the engine-room machinery compartments.

The flight deck was set out as follows: a broken white line ran the whole 646 feet down the centre of the deck and two rows of specially protected landing lights ran either side of it along the flight path. A catapult of over 100 feet long was positioned from the bows about a third of the distance across from the port side edge with an attachment added when in use; it was used when the ship could not generate enough wind to lift the kite off the flight deck with its short runway, or when the ship was stationary in harbour facing into the wind. It was controlled from a box which was slung over the port side at deck level, where the control valve for the steam jet was also housed. It was positioned on the centre line with four different angled white lines marked off running from it on each side to indicate at what angle the ship's bow was steaming into the wind. Next came the windbreak which was also controlled from the same box. It consisted of several multi-holed (2-inch) plates which lay together thwartships (looking for all the world like flattened kitchen colanders), which were raised about eight feet to form a fence to give shelter to the repair and deck handling parties as they worked on the kites from the air current formed by the for'ard motion of the ship.

The for'ard and aft lifts were situated towards the starboard side with the island in between them. The for'ard one was forty-six by thirty-three feet in area and the aft one was slightly smaller (forty-six by twenty-four feet) and they were positioned between the arrester wires. They could each handle loads up to 20,000 pounds to and from the flight deck to each hangar, and they were both worked by Weirs turbo hydraulic pumps. Each structure weighed about 40 tons.

The island was an irregular narrow shape, at least 100 feet long, which lay for'ard of the centre on the starboard side and carried out the same functions as a normal ship's bridge, but pivoted to one side only with a narrow control platform and wheelhouse facing to the fore. The mainmast, radar mast and funnel stuck up above it and its usual waste pipes for the safety valves and twin steam sirens were mounted on each side of it. The island contained four decks which housed the captain's sea cabin, communicating offices, wireless office, radar office, signalling platform with searchlights and all the various pigeonholes for the different flags and pennants to be flown above. Also, facing the flight deck, perched up aloft was Fly Co's control platform with a bird's-eye view of the deck below and his office behind it, where all the orders came from for the pilots and flight-deck staff when the ship was at 'fllying stations'. Also there was a briefing and waiting room for the pilots on the flight-deck level below. The island also had a small number of anti-aircraft lightweight guns mounted all around it, as well as two multi-barrelled pom-poms for protection for'ard and aft around the base. The flight deck was rounded at the bows, with a longer rounded section aft. There was about 600 feet length by ninety-six feet in places of workable space. There were four twin-turret 4.5-inch anti-aircraft guns mounted at deck level to give them a larger arc to turn in. A special barge for transferring aircraft to the fleet carriers was slung under the deck aft, tucked away in a cutaway section. The aft section of the deck had hydraulic wireless masts positioned alongside which were dropped to the horizontal position when flying.

Also there were six arrester wires, which were evenly spaced, crossing over thwartships from port to starboard; they were mounted on two large pulley wheels, which lay flat at the sides and which were designed to pay out steadily for 50 to 100 feet when the aircraft hook caught hold of one. They were mounted over two long round springs which were positioned evenly (from the centre line, which was marked in white along the whole length of the deck) about one third of the breadth from each side. When aircraft were taking off, or being handled by the flight-deck party, the springs were held down flat on the deck by a hydraulic system so that the aircraft could easily be pushed over them. When aircraft were landing the cables were raised an inch or two by freeing the springs so they rose up to lift them thus ensuring the dangling hook from the tail of the aircraft would catch onto one of them.

For'ard of the arrester wires lay two crash barriers with three loosely connected cables, which were only raised when an aircraft missed all the wires. They were worked by the engine-room staff from a small control box slung over the port side from where the raising and lowering of the arrester wires and the wireless masts were controlled.

On the for'ard section of the deck there was a windbreak which lay flat on the deck until required to be raised about eight foot. It was full of holes of an inch diameter something like a flattened kitchen colander, and was used when the wind was gusty to break up its force whilst work was carried on behind it. In front of it, in the deck centre, was mounted a small steam jet used for keeping the ship heading into the wind.

On the port side for'ard of the flight deck a rail about 100 feet long was sunk into the deck about three yards from the side. A large catapult eyelet was mounted onto it and this was driven from underneath by a compressed-air piston. When the bogie was suddenly hurled forward it dragged the aircraft fast enough to become airborne at the end of its travel. The bogie was rapidly forced back to its starting position by hydraulic pressure acting on the back of the piston pumped by a large Weirs steam-turbo hydraulic pump which was left ticking over, then it suddenly screamed into action shoving the piston back in less than a minute.

When in harbour at weekends, or when no flying was due to take place, the arrester wires were generally disconnected by a pin being removed from the port side so the cables could be coiled up on the starboard side out of the way. They were reconnected when flying was due to take place.

Two strong springs were positioned about a third of the breadth of the ship across from both sides. They sprang up and down being controlled hydraulically, and were held down whilst the deck handling party moved kites in position at all times except when landing-on was taking place.

On both hangar decks there were special flat fasteners which had been welded into position to strike down the kites securely when they had been struck down in the hangars. Also around the hangars were several sumps with scuppers to allow any flooding or spillage to drain overboard through a pipe with a flap valve to prevent seawater flooding back. Around the sides and on the deck close to them were various supply lines, such as high- and low-pressure air lines and aviation-spirit fuel lines, and electric battery chargers in boxes on wheels to start up some of our kites.

The for'ard section of the lower hangar was used mostly for weekly cinema shows when possible. The projector was housed behind the bulkhead and holes were cut through to show the film.

For'ard of the lower ranger lay the fo'c's'le, which was partly enclosed, where the electric capstans worked to raise or lower the anchors.

For'ard of the upper hangar lay the engine test bed in a compartment which ran thwartships from port to starboard. It had large rectangular holes cut into it and was fitted with thick wire-mesh screens to allow a good air supply for the engine on test. Also there was the coppersmith's shop and the catapult machinery.

Aft of both hangars there was a cutaway section to hold a large aircraft lighter, powered by twin Ford V8 engines for ferrying newly repaired or damage aircraft around the fleet or to transport repair parties with spares to repair the job.

19

Below this section lay the captain's cabin and the main keyboard flat, which was manned by a royal marine. Below this was one of the most important pieces of machinery in the ship, which was the Hasties (steering gear). This consisted of four massive hydraulic rams, which worked on the tiller which moved the large rudder from midships to port or starboard as required to steer the ship.

The boiler rooms contained four Admiralty three-drum water tube boilers which supplied superheated steam at a pressure of 300 lb/in^2 for two sets of Parsons geared turbines.

The two units lay together on the port and starboard sides of the ship, with the boiler rooms having their two boilers facing one another. They were for'ard of the engine rooms, with the auxiliary compartments positioned in between them, and they contained the after turbogenerator, the steam hydraulic pump for the lifts, a small electric hydraulic pump for stowing the lifts, a high-pressure air compressor (compressing up to 4,000 pounds) and two sets of three large drum evaporators which by boiling up the seawater produced fresh water for the boiler feed and for drinking.

Above the two boiler rooms there was a fan flat containing eight turbo-driven fans with louvres. All the air intakes faced the starboard side, towards the main intake and the funnel ducts which joined together. The purpose of the fans was to suck vast quantities of air in to create a pressure in the boiler rooms to aid combustion of the oil fuel in the furnaces.

Next along the deck were the two barriers, which lay flat across the deck from the island. They were operated from another small box slung over the port side directly in line with them, which also controlled the wireless masts and the arrester gear.

Each barrier consisted of three stout steel cables spaced out about a foot apart and loosely held together by several steel strops strung out at intervals over the whole length. They were held in position between the tops of two rising legs, which could be raised to about six feet above the deck.

The latticework wireless masts were spaced out in two sets of four along each side, towering vertically above the flight deck until flying was about to commence, then they were lowered hydraulically on their pivots until they lay horizontally in their outboard position.

Behind the barriers lay eight arrester wires, which had two long springs positioned either side of the flight path to hold the wire up about six inches, from the deck in between them, and to allow the trailing hook to latch onto the wire. This gradually paid out some fifty feet or so before bringing the kite to a sudden halt.

When the hook was disconnected the wire slowly slithered back over the deck tightly into position thwartships like a snake uncoiling, operated by an unseen clever system of hydraulic air cushioning. When at flying stations the springs were drawn down tightly to the deck. This lowered the wires for the kite's wheels to run over them when being moved about by the flight-deck party, or when taking off.

When there was no flying the wires were unpinned, then neatly rolled up on the starboard side out of the way.

The port and starboard cranes were based on sponsons at a level with the upper hangar deck so when not in use the framework was stowed neatly out of harm's way, lowered to the deck. They were electrically driven and were capable of lifting large loads of stores and gear from awaiting boats or jetties below onto the flight deck. They were conveniently placed to serve the after lift. Also they could lift out the motor boats which were tucked away neatly around them.

The hangars were twin ones on top of each other, being rather short (about 400 feet long) and 16 feet 6 inches high to accommodate the tallest float planes with their wings folded.

Both hangars were divided up into three sections when two modified fire curtains when lowered. They were made of fireproof material instead of small hinged sections of steel which were found to be deadly killers on HMS *Illustrious*: a bomb bounced down the lift shaft bursting in the hangar, which caused the metal curtains to shatter treacherously like a broken pane of glass into thousands of slivers. They were razor sharp, which created havoc by killing or maiming any unfortunate man who happened to be standing in their way. They also ripped large holes into the fuselages and wings of kites, ripping them to ribbons, and cut into ammunition boxes containing belts of bullets which started firing off in all directions. Some fuel tanks that had recently been filled burst into fireballs of flame, also some tyres were slashed which burst suddenly with a terrific bang. It all added up to a ghastly scene of carnage in the hangar.

The hangars were floodlit by groups of lights suspended from the deckhead, where also hung a sprinkler system to spray and quench a fire. It was supplied with water from the fire main which also fed

21

hydrants throughout the ship, including the hangars and flight deck. Also, some special foam-making twin hoppers with drums of chemicals were secured alongside to produce a continuous supply of foam to carpet each section of the hangars when the fire curtains had been dropped to isolate any fire damage to one section.

Drafted to *Unicorn*

Monday 6 July 1942 — A small party was assembled in Devonport Barracks, consisting of several stokers; chief and petty officers; chief ERA Fred Crate (a fitter and diver); ERA Joe Anning (an enginesmith); ERA Ted Perkins (a boilermaker); ERA Taff Gunney (a fitter and turner) and myself, Ed Hibbert (a fitter).

We had all had an early shake then lashed up our hammocks before washing and shaving. Then we dressed in the rig of the day before going to the mess for breakfast. After this we collected our gear, which consisted of hammocks, kitbags, cases, attaché cases and tool boxes, then loaded them up onto the handcart. We then took them down to the barracks station, then went to the galley to collect our packed meal. After this we returned to the station to muster to answer the roll call. We then boarded several carriages which took about thirty of us to North Road Station, where our carriages were left in the sidings to be coupled up to the train for Bristol Temple Meads Station.

When we arrived there we were shunted off into a siding to await the train from London to Stranraer. Soon we were coupled up once again, passing through my hometown of Stockport, then stopping at Manchester, Preston, Lancaster and Kendal. After this the train approached Shap Fell, which had a steep climb of about 1,200 feet. The engine began to falter owing to the poor quality of the coal, which quickly burnt away from a bright fire to a dull one. The stoker was kept busy trying to keep a full head of steam, as pressure was being lost through the piston packings, the steam injector and several other leaking joints. Suddenly the engine lost power causing the driving wheels to slow down then lose traction. They spun around with the engine overspeeding and with a rapid huffing and puffing of exhaust steam up the chimney, bringing the train to a sudden halt. Before the driver could ease down the regulating valve and sand the rails, the train started to gather speed, alarmingly hurtling backwards down the slope. The driver slammed on the brakes and simultaneously shut off the steam.

It took a few anxious minutes for the squealing brakes to grip on the wheels then bring the train to a grinding halt.

As the train had to await the banking engine, the stoker raked out the ash, clinker and dust, then spread the dying embers over the firebox. He shovelled the coal evenly on top of it, to get a roaring fire to bring the steam pressure up to the red mark at 225 pounds.

After what seemed like ages, the banking engine approached from the rear. A shrill blast from the whistle gave the driver up front warning of its approach. He opened his steam regulating valve steadily and eased off his brakes until free. He also opened his sanders to allow a trickle of sand to fall on the rails to give the driving wheels a grip as they started to turn on the smooth track. Then the banking engine gave the guard's van a massive shove. A terrific jolt and bang reverberated throughout the train as each set of buffer springs cushioned the effect by fully compressing on each carriage in front, so that they all jumped forward one after another allowing the driving wheels of the front engine to start turning then take up the drive.

Soon the weary engine gradually gathered speed as both drivers adjusted their throttles to move the train, together with a double huffing and puffing, with the extra power from the two engines; soon they had reached the brow of the hill where the banker dropped behind, returning to its shed whilst our train gathered speed downhill and was soon passing through Penrith.

The train then struggled on to Carlisle where it arrived at 23.00. The engine was disconnected, leaving the carriages at the platform whilst it was driven on to the shed. The firebox was emptied out, just leaving enough fire in the far corner to be built up with a few shovelfuls of coal whilst the ash pan below was being emptied into the ash pit. Whilst the tender was being refilled with coal and water, the shed fitter quickly renewed the two piston-rod packings. Then the fire was carefully spread out with more coal added to raise steam as quickly as possible. We stretched our legs, pacing the platform before joining a long queue for a weak cup of railway tea and a margarine butty. We were thirsty owing to the fact that at Preston the train began to move off before many had been served from the tea trolley. Some of the lucky ones had managed to get back into their carriages before it moved, but others spilt their tea in the mad rush to scramble through the carriage doors, which left most of us very thirsty.

Within the hour a new driver and fireman had taken the engine over, and raised a full head of steam ready for coupling up to take us on the last leg of the journey. The fireman spread the coal evenly to get a good roaring fire with the safety valves lifting, so the engine had plenty of power to complete our journey, which was in the region of 150 miles. We all settled down bleary-eyed. The engine was much more lively as it passed through Gretna Green, then had several stops at Annan, Dumfries, Castle Douglas and Castle Stuart, picking up numerous goods on the way to be shipped over.

It was about three and a half hours later when we reached Stranraer Harbour. We were rudely awakened as the train hit the buffers with a sudden jerk, throwing the forward-facing passengers off their seats. Then we all piled out into the draughty atmosphere of the cold sea breeze, before searching for a truck in the dark to unload our gear onto. Then we reported to the RTO who was responsible for our passage on board the ferry. The first thing he did was to take us to the canteen for a hot drink and a snack. He then looked after the loading of our baggage on board. He also made a note of our travelling warrant that covered all our fares. Then he issued each of us with a boarding card to be shown to the officer manning the gangway.

As we climbed aboard, the cattle and sheep were being driven off. Their stowage quarters were hosed down, but the strong farmyard smell still lingered. We gazed over the handrail while the vessel completed her loading. As dawn was breaking the docks were a hive of industry, with the dockers working in the gloom pierced by the occasional group of lights, unloading the trucks and vans that had been brought in by our train. There was a vast assortment of goods to be unloaded, such as empty milk churns, and refilled oxygen and acetylene bottles. They clanged together as they were placed on large cargo nets to be lifted down the hold by whirring cranes and then stowed away by stevedores. Also, goods such as barbed wire, wire netting and bags of nails and bolts were emptied from the vans by the dockers to be lifted aboard along with small and large packing cases. Large boxes were slung up separately; so were drums of oil hoisted by steel strops. Metal grips fitted over their rims and gripped securely so that they could be lowered down the hold where stevedores upended them to prevent them rolling about as the ship moved.

As each railway van was emptied, the doors were shut and fastened before being winched out of the way amidst the squeaking, banging and rattling, with another van taking its place. Finally, the dockers opened up the mail vans which were the last to be dealt with. They were full of hundreds of mailbags, which were piled up onto a train of trucks and towed alongside with a small tractor. They were loaded on board last so they could be the first to be unloaded. The ship was then prepared for sea with the hatches being battened down with large balks of timber (square wooden beams) which fitted one against another to fill in the hole. This was covered by a large tarpaulin, then wedged and lashed down to keep any rough sea out. Also the sea doors were shut then bolted tightly into position. Now all that remained to be done was to drive several army trucks and private cars (which were a rarity) onto a special framework to be hoisted aboard as deck cargo. Suddenly, the ship's siren bellowed forth a warning for everyone not taking passage to clear off the ship. The gangway was then removed and dropped on the jetty, with the guard rails being fastened back into place.

Promptly at 06.30 the mooring ropes were cast off for the ship to leave harbour. With another blast of the siren she steamed down Loch Ryan with the gentle hum of her turbines rising from below. We were all herded aft with the steerage passengers. We were hardly able to move. It was even worse in the seating space down below where we had to queue for about fifteen minutes for a cup of tea.

Fortunately the crossing was like a millpond and we were soon steaming into the North Channel where the ship increased her speed to 15 knots. This was shown on the log aft which was worked by a long trailing cable with a small propeller on the end to spin it and drive the mechanism. We could hear the rumble of the propeller thrashing in the water and could see when a movement was made by the rudder from the mechanical tiller mounted on the deck. After being at sea for two hours we could see the coast of Northern Ireland. Then about half an hour later we reduced speed having completed the thirty-nine-mile trip across the water. There was still a chill in the air but as it had been raining it gave the small fields of Larne grass an extra-bright shade of fresh emerald green.

As we approached the jetty the log rope was drawn in, then carefully coiled up before the ship's side was cleared. The ropes to be thrown across so the ship could be tied up when at last it arrived with a bump on the rubbing strake which hit the jetty. The engines were stopped then we went astern to stop the weigh of the ship, which was quickly secured alongside. The guard rail was dropped then the gangway was run up into position.

We collected our gear from the hold, then made several trips with it, trudging back and forth over the gangway, loading it onto several station trucks to pull it onto the platform. An RTO awaited us to check our travelling warrant then show us to the carriages reserved for our party. We piled our gear into a goods van, then had to wait for the engine to be coupled up. We had to wait for the steam heating to warm up the compartments as the carriages had stood in the cold sea breeze all night. We then had to await for the train to be loaded up with newspapers, letters and a host of other items before the guard waved his green flag, blew his whistle, then stepped back into his van. The driver responded by blowing his engine whistle then waited for the signal to change from red to green before starting off. We skirted the coastline down the right-hand side of Belfast Lough, stopping at Whitehead, Kilroot, Carrickfergus (where an old small castle stands on guard at the water's edge), then on to Greenisland, Whitehouse and Greencastle, passing by several small whitewashed cottages surrounded by lush green fields on the way. Often there was an old-fashioned handpump nearby for drawing water from the well. We continued running by the water's edge until we entered the outskirts of the city. We soon ended up at York Road Station, Belfast, the terminus for the LMS Northern Lines Railway.

The train stopped and we all disembarked then unloaded our kit, stowing it directly onto an old awaiting bus. This was under the charge of a killick seaman who had come to meet the party. He was responsible for taking us to the pay and supply offices of HMS *Caroline* (an old sea-cadet training ship down in the harbour), which had all naval personnel working in Belfast and Harland & Wolff on its pay books.

A good-looking smart young Wren with dark black hair and brown eyes with a small light-blue killick's badge on one arm and a pale-blue W on the other arm (indicating that she belonged to the writer's branch) took our names, ranks and numbers from our pay books, entering them in a large ledger. Then she issued us all with civilian ration books. She then gave the leading seaman, who was in charge of the bus, a list of the various billets allocated to us and also passed on the order for us to report to the chief down on the ship in the afternoon.

We all clambered aboard the bus, which started by dropping off bods with billets nearest to the city centre, then gradually worked towards the outskirts. About half a dozen bods were dropped off. Then Holy Joe (nickname for Joe Anning because of his religious beliefs), who was an enginesmith from the West Country, was dropped off at Mrs Hamilton's a few streets away from where we were dropped off at Mrs MacCracken's — 80 Bloomfield Avenue, off Newtownards Road, Belfast. There were three of us — Taff Gunney, Ted Perkins and myself. We climbed out, then collected our gear and stowed it up in the bedrooms before meeting our landlady. To her we handed over our ration books, which only entitled us to small quantities of meat, fat, sausage, margarine, jam, tea, a slice of bacon and one egg per week. Then we all sat down for a cup of tea and a rest. We had a good wash and shave before joining a long queue for fish and chips at the local chippy. We all came away with meagre portions which we ravenously devoured before setting off in search of the ship.

We caught a tram down the Newtownards Road to stop at Queens Bridge, where we alighted, then walked back making our way along Queens Quay where piles of household coal was being dumped from two Kelly's coal boats. They were discharging the coal by means of two large grabs which kept opening their jaws wide then closing them with large amounts of coal in their buckets. This they dropped directly into awaiting horse-drawn coal carts or lorries. We next passed by the drab-looking station building of the County Down Railway, which had been running at a loss for years. We then bore right down Queens Road which was at least a mile long, running straight through Harland & Wolff's shipyard, which was situated an the right-hand bank of the River Lagan.

On one side of the works toward the river lay the Abercorn Basin dry docks, slipways, wharves and jetties; whilst on the other side of the road lay the engineering works, which included the plate and rib shop where all the rolling into shape was done. The pieces were drilled then bolted together before being riveted to form the keel, ribs and hull of a ship on one of the numerous slipways near

28

the water's edge. Then there was the engine shop where some massive-looking steam and diesel reciprocating engines and turbines with large helical driving wheels were being assembled, and the pipe shop where many of the smaller pipes were bent and shaped to all different lengths and sizes of the templates then had flanges welded or brazed on the ends. Also, blocks of administrative offices lay in between. The tram track ran through the whole length of the works to Queens Island where all the ships lay for fitting out. We walked nearly to the top of Queens Road in search of HMS *Unicorn*. We eventually found her alongside the fitting-out basin, as yet unnamed, bearing the works number 725 on her side.

She was riding high out of the water, looking more like a wrecked rusty old hulk than a brand-new ship. She had a massive freeboard of some sixty-odd feet above water level with the added island structure, its large funnel and mainmast towering another fifty feet above the flight deck. Along her sides a number of sponsons jutted out to support the gun platforms, the cranes' mountings and the wireless masts, which were already fitted into place. Along both sides of the ship there were about a dozen large oblong rugged holes cut out at upper-deck level, some with fairleads and bollards at the edge for cables to be slipped through then secured; whilst others allowed entrances aboard for the gangways to be hoisted on. My first impression of the ship was that of sheer terror as she looked to be top heavy, causing me to imagine she would turn turtle in the first gale we encountered, but happily my thoughts proved to be wrong. However, there were huge weights yet to be added which would greatly reduce the freeboard — particularly the flight-deck gear, including the two lifts and the catapult, and also much of the auxiliary machinery, the steering gear, electrical gear (including the generators), the evaporators for producing tons of fresh water daily, freezing machinery, air compressors and hydraulic pumps.

There was a vast array of piping with various diameters, lengths and shapes, with curves and half curves, to be installed section by section as each one was completed to the shape of the templates. There were suction and discharge for the following uses: for seawater into the condensers, oil coolers and fire main, which ran into most compartments throughout the ship; for freshwater pipes from the evaporators to the boiler feed tanks and freshwater supply tanks for the hot and cold water around the ship; and for oil-fuel pipes from tanks to furnaces. There was also a host of large, medium and small pipes for steam and water for the boilers and engines, the forced-lubrication (FL) copper pipes around the engines and the auxiliary superheated and saturated in compartments away from the engines and boilers. There were also pipes for high- and low-pressure air lines, plus a host of others down to the sink drains.

There were literally miles of various sizes of electric cables, especially for lighting and ventilation motors; and various pipes for plumbing in the galleys, bathrooms, heads, sickbay and cabins. Also there were over 1,000 lockers for the troops, cots for the sickbay, mess, tables and stools; a complete telephone system, tannoy and wireless for broadcasting; and radar and signalling equipment — not to mention thousands of other items required to finish the ship off.

Many of the compartments were in pitch-black darkness, except where gangs of men were working under strings of electric bulbs. Also, sometimes, when the supply of components dried up, a gang of men would waste no time huddling around an improvised table for a game of cards, until the foreman chased up more work for them, or more components arrived.

Eventually we found both the port and starboard boiler rooms. Each contained two boilers already mounted on their sliding feet facing one another, so that they could be controlled by one watch of men. All the control valves were grouped together so that they could be easily adjusted.

We then went to visit both engine rooms at the bottom of two extra-steep creaking ladders in deep airy spaces which lay aft of the bulkheads. They were already having holes cut in them to allow pipes from the boiler rooms to run through, most with valves to be attached.

Both sets of high- and low-pressure astern turbines had been mounted on their beds and were being secured at one end with large bolts and held with sliding feet at the other. Two large condensers were slung below them. Each set of turbines was coupled up to two double-helical pinion gearwheels which were meshed into the main gearwheel. All were housed into a gear case which was bolted down aft of each set of turbines. Each main gearwheel was connected up to a prop shaft through a Michelle thrust block, with each shaft being supported in the centre by a plumber block. (Note: the prop shafts would need realigning once the ship was complete with all the weight added.)

The beds for all the auxiliary machinery through the boiler and engine rooms were in the process of being welded together, then riveted to the framework.

By this time we were all becoming weary after such a long journey, so Taff suggested we should climb out of the gloom into the sunlight, then make our way back to our new quarters. We made our way to the nearest tram stop only to find there was a restricted service until after the rush hour, owing to wartime economy, so we had to wait another twenty minutes for a tram. When it came it dropped us two stops past our destination as we were unfamiliar with the area, so we had to stagger back down the road, reaching our digs in a completely knackered state.

We sat in the parlour until teatime when we were joined by Mrs MacCracken's daughter, Sarah, a secretary, whom we christened Spitfire (because of her quick fiery temper). Her brother, Sam, was away from home at the Masonic boarding school in Dublin. After tea we had a short discussion, then retired early to get our heads down, being completely worn out.

The following day we climbed the steep gangway in search of the chief ERA. We looked from stem to stern, high and low, from the hangar deck to the hold, through rough holes, then down wooden ladders, through gloomy passages to various spaces which were lit up with men working. To get aft from the lower decks we had to walk two thirds of the way along the main deck, which was blocked off as there was no through way in the engine-room department. We had to climb up to the upper deck, then climb down the next hatch before continuing aft down below.

At every well-lit area, where there was a gang of men working, we asked if anyone had seen the chief, also enquiring how long they thought it would take to complete the ship. Then after a good long search we climbed back down the gangway onto the jetty where we joined Chief ERA Crate and Joe Anning. They were waiting for Chief ERA Rodgers who was standing some distance away talking to Commander E. Oliver, the chief engineer of the ship and also the Fleet Air Arm.

Shortly afterwards he ambled over, took our names, then led us to a small hut which was furnished with a desk in front of a large window, and two chairs and a long stool. This was to be our base for the next few months. He also supplied us with pencils and notebooks to jot down any useful information appertaining to the job and to make sketches of the numerous pipelines and ring mains running around the ship. We also made copies from nine tatty well-worn blueprints of the layout of each deck, starting from the hold (at the bottom), followed by the platform, lower, main and upper decks and lower hangar, lower platform, upper hangar, upper platform (with the flight deck on top) and several small decks in the island structure, which was an important part of our job during the stand-by period.

We were told to muster daily outside the hut (which was kept locked all night) at 8.30 to be detailed off to take note of the various constructions and installations being carried out in various parts of the ship; or sometimes muster downtown at the offices of HMS *Caroline*, as we were on her pay books. We also mustered for slops, for an issue of Tickler tobacco (for rolling into cigarettes), for medical treatment or seasonal leave passes, etc. Most of the time we were free to roam about the ship to get to know it thoroughly; also to note where all the pipelines ran (they passed through the bulkheads or sometimes deckheads, which made them hard to trace), and to learn where all the numerous valves were positioned in the various compartments.

So we were left to our own devices. Then Taff, Ted and myself decided to take a quick look around the engine-room department which was situated in the mid-length of the ship. The boiler and engine rooms were positioned on the port and starboard sides of the ship with the auxiliary machinery rooms in between them. We picked our way through dimly lit passages, through rough holes cut through the bulkheads and decks, then down rickety wooden ladders to the decks below. Many of the decks had large holes in them where the plates had been left off to allow pipes and machinery to be lowered down, then secured into position.

We then returned to our digs.

The next morning we were still soundly asleep when it was time to get up, so we needed an extra-hard shake to stir us from our slumber. We all scrambled to get dressed and shaved at the double, then hastily swallowed a mug of tea and a piece of toast and marmalade before beating a hasty retreat. We found the trams were few and far between after the rush hour, then had to wait for what seemed like ages for the next one. We finally arrived at our meeting place after 09.00, being over half an hour adrift, but fortunately nothing was said when the chief came over from the engineer's office where he was in charge — fortunately naval discipline was lax.

We decided to carry out a thorough search of the ship, visiting every compartment and nook and cranny which was lit up, to get a general picture of the state of the ship, of how much work had been done and of how much more there was to do to finish her. We asked the fitters, boilermakers, pipe fitters, etc., or anyone else working around the ship, in order to get a good general picture of the situation. One of the longest jobs being tackled was the welding up of all cable carriers to the bulkheads and deckheads through the ship from the generating and switchboard rooms (to carry cables from about 3 inches diameter to ½ inch diameter) for lighting in every part of the ship.

We found that the ship had already been in dry dock to have her rudder fitted, along with two manganese bronze screws which had been attached to the prop shafts. They had been inserted into lignum vitae hard wooden bearings and through the glands and were resting on the plumber blocks' bearings before the ship was launched. Also many holes had been cut out of the ship's hull for all the seacocks, blowdown valves, sluice valves and various suction valves, with most of the discharge valves positioned along the ship's side well above sea level so that all valves could be mounted over the holes on the inner side of the ship's hull.

The work of sandblasting was well under way, having been started immediately after launching to remove all the rust from the numerous plates which formed the ship sides, the deck, deckheads or sides of each compartment, as well as hangars and stores throughout the ship, which would take several months to complete. The machinery spaces, where there was much work to be done, were cleaned out first. When we arrived the boiler and engine rooms were clean, with the auxiliary rooms being in the process of being cleaned, but work would continue until every cabin, mess, office, store, galley and sickbay, etc. had been completed.

There were about forty port and starboard double-bottom oil-fuel tanks formed by adding tops in between the framework. Some others were for fresh water and reserve feed tanks for the boiler water; also a large main feed-water tank was constructed in each engine room. All the tanks had the necessary holes cut in their sides at the base for suction valves to be fitted, and holes were cut in the tank tops where necessary for filling and dipping pipes to be

33

connected. Some tanks, including the MF tanks, had sight glasses fitted.

The two engine-room lubricating-oil tanks were installed in the bilges aft of the gear cases. Six special tall round storage tanks for aviation spirit had been installed in the bowels of the ship, standing upright on the hold deck, evenly spaced out from one another.

Other tanks installed were for diesel oil for the two emergency diesel generators and motor boats. A smaller tank was installed for a supply of petrol for the crane (Jumbo), the Clark Cat (forklift) and the two Ford V8 engines used to power the aircraft lighter.

We started off for'ard where the two Clark Chapman capstans were beginning to be assembled. Their driving posts were standing upright through the deckhead glands to turn the capstans on the fo'c's'le. They would eventually raise or lower the anchor chains through the hawse pipes to or from the cable lockers. They were driven by worm and pinion gearing from two large electric motors with brakes to stop them turning instantly.

Next we climbed up several lots of ladders to the flight deck which was littered with all manner of packing cases and gear waiting to be used down below. The catapult run had been installed for'ard along with the windbreak. Work had just started on installing the heavy components of the two lifts into position leaving two unguarded holes in the deck which made one quite dizzy when looking down. The two sets of raising-barrier legs had been pivoted to the deck along with the sheaves that guided the wires. Also the sheaves for the arrester wires had been mounted on the port and starboard sides of the deck. They would eventually guide wires below to a mechanism which allowed the wires to draw out steadily when in use.

Then we climbed several flights of ladders in the rusty island structure to the open bridge and wheelhouse on the deck below. They were both bare, but eventually all orders would be issued from the officer of the watch on the bridge to the quartermaster via a voice pipe. He could then turn his wheel on the required course to steer the ship without much effort. The orders were transmitted by two small-bore copper pipes which ran aft to the steering compartment below the captain's flat supplying hydraulic pressure on one pipe at a time. They operated on two reversible electric hydraulic pumps which acted on four massive great rams which turned a double tiller connected to the rudder. This turned on its pivots from midships up to 45° either port or starboard according to which way the wheel was turned to set the ship on course.

Then we made our way down via the platform decks until we reached the upper deck, which was exposed on both sides by a series of oblong ragged holes which ran up from deck level, stretching from stem to stern. These holes were to gain access to the deck — to tie up the ship through her fairleads onto the bollards, for boarding ship via the gangway, or for tying up lighters and tankers for supplies or fuelling, etc. The deck also had scuppers at the edge to drain any water away. We made our way down through the keyboard flat, passing by the captain's quarters to the deck below where the massive Hasties (steering gear) was about to be lowered into position.

We made our way midships through gloomy passages through the bulkheads and hatchways, having to tread cautiously as some of the deck plates were still missing to allow some of the long pipes, etc. to pass through for installing. Also, there were electric welding cables, windy drills and chisels, air hoses with distributors at the end for attaching windy drills, chisels, caulking tools, rivet guns, grinders and small portable furnaces for heating up the rivets. Also acetylene bottles with long hoses were scattered about along with other bits and pieces. We went up and down a series of rickety ladders, making a brief visit to numerous compartments to get to know our way about. Only those areas being worked in had staging around them to get at the job and to see what the men were doing. The rest of the places were dimly lit with daylight creeping in or in complete darkness.

We found several auxiliary machines had been lined up then secured by bolting them to their beds, waiting to be coupled up to their numerous pipes and cables.

After a busy forenoon of walking and clambering all over the ship and along passages, stepping over numerous obstructions to acquaint ourselves with the bowels of the ship, we returned to the hut for a sit down before queuing for a tram, which was an old one. It rattled and shook along a well-worn track up the Newtownards Road, until at last we reached our stop at Bloomfield Avenue, which was a long walk from our digs.

We all felt knackered with all the extra exercise we had had. It made us ravenously hungry, so we soon devoured our dinner without knowing what it was. We retired to the parlour for a good long rest.

We were not required to clock on as one of us could be found in the hut during the afternoon. Then I went in search of a packet of fags, being desperate for a smoke.

Eventually we caught a tram to return to our hut, where we started looking at well-worn and tatty thumbed blueprints of the different decks. We took it in turns to copy one, which we had to scale down from about a four-foot copy, into the 7x4-inch notebook we had been provided with. We had to complete the drawings within the first month.

As none of us were much good at sketching, our first efforts at drawing were too small to print in the space, so we left them until the next week to try again. I decided to draw half the deck on each page so that there was room for over 100 compartments. This allowed me to print the letters larger, which aided me to locate each compartment more easily.

We did not pack up work until 17.00, only to find that we had got caught in the city rush hour. The trams were full up and some workers were even hanging on to the back, so we had to wait for half an hour before catching the next tram. The conductor shouted, "Pass along the car, please." So we ended up being squeezed like sardines in a tin, and were annoyed when the tram halted at our stop, then started off again before we could group up to force our way out. We got off at the next stop.

After tea we all went for a short walk around the area to get to know it, before returning to listen to the wireless and discuss the news, which was still as grim as ever.

We retired to bed early that night, drawing the blackout curtains tightly across the window to prevent any chinks of light showing on the outside, or else an extra-keen air-raid warden would be knocking on the door to tell us to adjust the curtain.

Before going to sleep I reviewed the new situation on the *Unicorn*. It was an infinitely better situation compared with the sinking of my last two ships, HMS *Edinburgh* and *Trinidad*, which were at the bottom of the Barents Sea with many of my shipmates.

Little did I realise that there was far worse to come in the bitter cold Arctic Ocean on the run to Murmansk in summer, where there was daylight for twenty-four hours a day, and brilliant sunshine glistening on the sea and ice packs most of the time. Once the course of a convoy had been established on its way to Russia by a Jerry Focke-Wulf Condor (which encircled the convoy constantly until relieved by another) the ship was doomed to be sunk. This happened in the case of PQ17, when all but five ships out of a total of forty-six that set sail to relieve the seige of Leningrad.were sunk with valuable armaments.

After about ten minutes I was completely exhausted and fell fast asleep, completely oblivious to any sounds from our new surroundings.

We all slept soundly until after a great deal of trouble Mrs Mac woke us up next morning. Eventually we all crawled out of bed, had a hasty shave and washed in a hurry before going down for a cup of tea and an Ulster fry. This consisted of soda bread, fried bread, treacle bread, potato bread and one egg and one slice of bacon per week. An occasional sausage or tomato was sometimes added to our meagre rations. Sometimes we would have porridge, toast and marmalade or a fried kipper.

Eventually we all left to catch the next tramcar to the dockyard. We impatiently waited on the Newtownards Road for five minutes before an old boneshaker turned up. It had hard reversible slatted seats, unlike the later ones with blue padded seats. As we paid our fare the conductor asked if we wanted to go to Queens Island, which was near the ship, so we booked our tickets to there as it saved us a long trek up Queens Road. The tram was very rickety. It set off down the track rattling and constantly stopping with a screech of brakes to let passengers off before rumbling onward.

However, on reaching the turning point at Queens Quay, the driver stopped to allow the conductor to switch over the points to swing round into it, but much to everyone's amazement the tram charged on straight ahead over the bridge towards Castle Junction in the city centre. Apparently the points were badly worn and sometimes failed to work. The driver had to stop and take his control handles to the other end of the tram, then reverse it back over the points so the conductor could wedge a for'ard bogie wheel to guide it onto the curved lines to the right. Then the driver returned to the front to drive the tram onto the quay. He stopped for the wedge to be picked up, before starting up and curving round into Queens Road. We trundled along until we arrived at the terminus where the tram suddenly ground to a halt with a shudder and a jerk, which shook us from our seats before we all trooped out.

We met Chief ERA Rodgers (a boilermaker) down in the fan flat where he was watching the first of the four Allen turbo-driven large forced-draught fans being installed — there being two fans for each boiler room. Their job was to create an air pressure as required in each of the rooms to mix with a fine spray of hot oil. There were up to nine sprayers on each boiler, which would combust with a terrific roar to maintain a pressure at 300 pounds to keep the finger on the red mark through the range of the movements to full speed.

We visited both port and starboard boiler rooms, which were laid out in a similar manner with both boilers facing one another. The airlock cabins both had two doors, which were designed to allow one to pass through when any number of fans were running to build up a pressure inside the room and on the inner door. This would not open until an equal pressure had built up on the other side in the cabin with the outer door shut.

He showed us the position of the various bulkhead valves and cross connections already mounted so we could note them when sketching the main steam line, the auxiliary superheated and saturated ring main and lines.

All the boiler mountings had been bolted into position and the auxiliary equipment had been recently lowered into position, all ready to be lined up then bolted down to their beds. Both the feed heaters for both rooms had been secured aloft on the ship's side. They were fed with the condensate pumped back from the engine rooms by the main feed pumps, entering the boilers via the robot valves and main feed checks to maintain the water at half a glass in the sight glasses.

The chief explained that both boiler rooms supplied each engine room as separate units; also, that most of the auxiliary machinery was duplicated, so in the case of a unit failing the ship could always limp home on reduced power.

The watch below in each boiler room consisted of a chief and stoker PO, along with two stokers. The chief stoker had all his control valves towards the outer side, in between the two boilers, so he could operate them from the checker plate platform below. He had to perform the juggling act with the hot-oil temperature and pressure, along with the room air pressure. The nine sprayer manifold valves on each boiler were operated by a separate stoker, who would turn on then flash up the number of sprayers (or shut them off when ordered) so the fine sprays of oil fuel, mixed with the air pressure, formed roaring balls of fire in the furnaces without blowing off or making black smoke up the funnel.

The stoker PO would be perched up on the gratings keeping an eagle eye on the water level, which should keep bobbing up and down in the sight glasses at half a glass. If for any reason it disappeared the PO would take his finger out, then blow through the sight glasses and robot to make sure there was no obstruction or sticking. Then, if no water appeared, he would rush down the ladder like greased lightning, then across the plates to start up the auxiliary feed pump on reserve feed tank suction, which discharged through the auxiliary feed check valve into the boiler which the chief had opened. This routine was essential, especially if the main feed pump in the engine room had tripped out and stopped. The evaporation rate of boiler water was so great, especially at high speed, that the top drum and first few fire rows of water tubes would be empty within three minutes, causing the tubes to distort and melt, and causing the boiler to become completely useless and unfit for service.

Then we met up with our other messmates, who had been standing by the ship for several months, as the chief was going to allocate various parts of the ship for us all. First was Chief ERA Bungy Williams, a West Country bloke, who was put in charge of both engine rooms. ERA Hookey Walker (late of the destroyer HMS *Fearless*, which was sunk in the Mediterranean) was given the outside machinery to look after, consisting of steering gear, wheelhouse, engine telegraphs and sirens. ERA Ginger Evans had the most unusual job of looking after all the electrical gear, motors, starters, switch gear for lights, fans and pumps in the engine-room department. They each showed us around their parts of the ship in turn during the next week.

The chief gave the rest of us different parts of ship. Chief ERA Crate and ERA Perkins (both Cornishmen) were to be in charge of all the flight-deck gear — the lifts, catapult, windbreak, crash barriers, arrester wires and wireless masts (all being installed by Weirs of Cathcart, Glasgow). ERA Joe Anning was to assist Chief ERA Rodgers (a boilermaker) down the boiler rooms, whilst ERA Taff Gunney was to look after the installing of the Weirs evaporators and the two Peter Brotherhood high-pressure air compressors along with a Revell low-pressure air compressor.

I was detailed off to watch the installing of the two Weirs refrigerating compressors, cold and cool rooms, the two identical turbogenerators and two English Electric diesel generators for emergency.

By now the forenoon was nearly over so we spent a short time discussing our new parts of ship, then dispersed for dinner. Afterwards I left in a hurry, having run out of fags. My tin of Tickler tobacco was finished and there was not another issue of this rolling tobacco until the end of the month. My shattered nerves began to twitch badly under my eyes and my hands were still shaking from my two abandon-ship experiences in the Arctic, causing me to become desperate for a fag. On my way back to the ship I asked in half a dozen shops for my favourite brand of Player's Medium, but soon found that most shopkeepers saved the best brands for their regular customers. All that could be obtained was two or three of the harsh brands from each shop. I eventually acquired about fifteen cigarettes, which I resolved to spin out by having a few drags, then stubbing it out and not having another drag for at least an hour. The situation was so bad I decided that if anyone lit up a fag near me I would pluck up the courage to ask them to sell me one.

On reaching the ship I went in search of the machinery that had been allotted to me and moved through the rough-cut holes in the deck intended for hatches, down numerous rough old ladders of all sizes then through the CO_2-bottle storage room and doorway into the refrigerating compressor room where two condensers had been recently mounted on the ribs of the ship side with the main components already lowered into position. The electric motors were already lined up to the compressors on their beds, which were bolted down with the driving belts adjusted and the guards fitted in place. The two seawater circulating pumps were bolted down in position; also the inlet and outlet manifold valves and scale traps were secured to the inner side of the room, with the cold-water tank and ice tank being secured into position.

Then climbed out of the compartment and down a passage to the adjoining refrigerated cold and cool rooms, which were still bare, rusty and without any lighting, and I went on to the Ford turbogenerator directly below. It was a self-contained unit (made by Fraser & Chalmers of Erith, Kent) and was a 400-kW set producing 1,600 amps at 230 volts DC. It was resting on its bed waiting for a start to be made on it. I then located the after turbogenerator, which was exactly the same model, also awaiting a start to be made on it. It was situated in the auxiliary compartments which housed the hydraulic lift pump, the high-pressure air compressor and the evaporators, all resting on their beds waiting for work to commence.

I also located the two emergency diesel generators, which had been lowered down then left in isolated compartments to be completed at a later date. At around 16.30 we must have had enough tramping about the ship, constantly climbing up and down ladders, as we all returned to the hut and decided to call it a day. We departed to our new abode, catching an early tram before the rush hour.

In the evening we had a good long rest in the parlour before having a good walk around before turning in.

We were all refreshed after a good night's sleep, and made our way down to the ship in a leisurely fashion. We spent the forenoon about the decks, discussing the work being carried out, taking notes and also finding out what was going on around the city. Then, during the afternoon, we grouped together and caught a tram down to the pay office for HMS *Caroline* in Queens Square, opposite the customs house on Donegal Quay, to line up for our weekly pay and 35/- a week lodging allowance. We saluted the lieutenant pay bob as he handed us our pay packets whilst a young Wren noted the amount down in her ledger.

We had a wander around the shops, first having a look around Robinson and Cleavers (the largest shop) but we found out their fancy prices were beyond our slender pockets, so we soon made a quick exit then had a look in Woolworths where the prices were much more reasonable.

As Saturday was a half day we went down until dinner time. Later on I caught a tram to Castle Junction, then had a wander around Donegal Place, Chichester Street and City Hall (which was built in white stone similar to the town hall in my hometown, being designed by the same architect), and finished up in Bedford Street at the Classic Cinema where Joseph Seal was playing at the organ. Afterwards I found a small café to obtain egg, sausage, and chips.

Sunday was a relaxed day, so we enjoyed an extra-long lie in bed. Then, after breakfast, we went in search of the Sunday papers, which did not arrive until 11.00 or later. We joined a long queue and each got a different copy so that they could be read from cover to cover then swapped. The news was not encouraging! U-boats had sunk fifteen ships around Trinidad in the West Indies during the last two months; Lancaster bombers had made their longest daylight raid on the U-boat yards in Danzig; and the Russians were regrouping their forces to defend Leningrad which was under siege. Later in the day we took a tram and had a long walk around Knock and

41

Dundonald as far as Stormont (the Parliament building).

On Monday morning we discovered that by waiting a few minutes longer we could catch a trolleybus instead of a tram, which was much quicker and far more comfortable. Also, we found a short cut halfway down the road which knocked off ten minutes from our journey, so we waited for it to turn up. Ted and Taff were the first to board it. Then, just as I had gripped the pole with my left hand with my left foot on the platform, the conductor rang the bell causing the driver to start off with a jerk which nearly pulled my arm out of its socket as the bus sped down the road causing me to be dragged off my feet. Fortunately I was able to bring my right hand up to grip the pole, otherwise I would have been thrown on the hard surface of the road, probably being flung flat on my face. Fortunately I managed to get my feet, which were flying in the air, down on the platform, which saved a nasty accident. We were no sooner on than it was time to get off. I did not complain about it, not having worked up enough courage to do so (being very nervy and timid); also, my left arm had not started to ache much.

We passed down a street of terraced houses in which the gable of the end house had a painting of King Billy mounted on a white horse (indicating that it was a Protestant area). Then we crossed over the railway on a latticework bridge, which was only a few minutes from our final destination. By this time my arm had become quite sore, so I mentioned it to the chief who told a foreman who happened to be passing. He told me to go down the road to the first big block of buildings to locate the first-aid post in the rear.

There had been a spate of accidents that morning so my arm had a long wait while the nurse and her assistant dealt with all the other cases. The first victim was a chap who had stepped backwards only to find himself falling on the deck below, which knocked him out. So he landed up on a stretcher unconscious. Another casualty was grinding the edge of a rusty plate without any goggles on, so he got a speck of grit in his eye, which looked uncomfortably inflamed. Another person had his fingertips crushed whilst meshing two gearwheels together. But the worst of the lot was a man with long hair who was drilling and omitted to use the safety guard. He leaned over the drill which caught hold of a dangling lock of hair, tearing a clump out along with a piece of scalp, leaving a bloody area uncovered and letting out a howl of agony.

My complaint was nothing compared with this lot of accidents.

42

Although it was quite painful I felt like leaving as several of the cases had to wait for an ambulance. As I had nowhere special to go so stayed all morning until the nurse could examine my arm, which she found to be slightly swollen. She dressed it with a cold compress, then put my arm in a sling. As she was brewing up she gave me a weak cup of tea with some sugar in it. I thanked her, then left for dinner.

After dinner I returned to the hut for a sit-down (not being able to do much with one arm). As no one else turned up to talk to, the time started to drag, so climbed up the gangway onto the upper deck and got talking to a fitter. He was waiting around to install a fire and bilge pump replacement for one that had got damaged in the port engine room. He was being held up by a handrail and a piece of platform that was in his way. He could have easily removed them himself, but the demarkation line in the ship, which he dare not cross, made it part of a boilermaker's work. The ruling on this line was strict without any flexibility, and it greatly added to the total cost of the ship as it often occurred that one tradesman waited ages for another type of tradesman to remove something first. He told me he had already been waiting two days and he had sneaked out to the cinema the day before to watch a film then returned in time for clocking off. I then managed to scrounge a well-thumbed cowboy book off him, which helped me to pass the evening after returning to my digs.

After a restless night my arm still felt sore, so decided to amble around on the flat, resting my arm in the sling without using it climbing ladders. I spent my time visiting the various workshops to see how everything was made. The first shop I came across was the boiler shop where the boilers for the *Black Prince* had all been completed. They were three-drum Admiralty water tube boilers with all the flanges standing proud for the mountings to be attached to the top dish-shaped ends. All drums had a manhole riveted into position. There were men caulking the seams on another boiler to make them steam-tight. The boiler shop also made all the handrails around the ship and engine rooms, the working platforms around the machinery and catwalks (made of checker plates which had a lumpy surface to prevent slipping), the ladders and the gratings.

The next place of call was the coppersmith's shop. Here all the large to small pipes were bent to the shape of templates, then hoisted up into position in the ship before the flanges were brazed on at each end so the holes could be mated up with other already-fitted flange holes.

I went on to the rolling shop where all the ribs and frames were stretched out to shape on the shop's floor, then carefully rolled out into matching pairs to numerous shapes and sizes to form the rounded tapering bows and the bulging holds (which included the engine-room and boiler-room spaces as well as the awkward shapes around the shaft passages, or passage if a single screw). The large plates that formed the outer skin had to be individually shaped until each one fitted on to the contours of the frames, which called for a great deal of skill. They had to be re-rolled several times until the exact shape had been formed.

A visit to the engine shop revealed a couple of massive Burmeister & Wain diesel engines, which were in the final stages of construction. One was being started up for the very first time. A sudden hiss of compressed air from a large bottle forced down the pistons in turn to start the engine slowly moving around until it began to fire. It then settled down to a steady dull thumping diesel knock. After about ten minutes the engine was stopped and reversed (astern). The note suddenly altered as several sounds merged together. It was entirely different to the hum and whine of a turbine, which was quite a pleasant sound. I did not linger in this part of the shop as the obnoxious smell of diesel oil and exhaust fumes pervaded the atmosphere.

So carried on to another part of the shop where several turbines were being assembled with their numerous banks of blades stepped up in stages to allow for the pressure drop in the steam. This also allowed for its expansion with the rotor blades, which turned in between them with very little clearance between the tips of the blades.

Also, there was a large variety of medium and small turbines, and small reciprocating engines for small coasters and naval corvettes, sloops and minesweepers.

There was a set of double-helical single reduction gears being bedded into their gear-case bearings, which were for the light cruiser, *Black Prince,* to slow the turbine speed in the area of 6,500 rpm to the prop-shaft speed of about 320 rpm.

Finally I visited the machine shop which turned out a vast array of objects, from small nuts and bolts to studs and flanges. The men were cutting teeth in gearwheels; using machinery for a vast variety of casting (small and large) which they were assembling together; drilling holes that had been marked off; milling squares on valve spindles or metal into various other shapes. A large planing machine was working to and fro taking half-inch cuts with a hard-tipped tool off the tops of six cast-iron cylinder castings set up in a row. They were clamped down until they were machined flat, then they were turned over to be machined on the other side. There were automatic machines for drilling tapping hexagon bars, then parting them off as nuts or turning the bar to size then screwing it and parting it off to make a bolt for the nut to be screwed on — mass producing them one after another. Then I wandered around asking the odd question here and there about how things were made, and also of anything of interest I could think about. I soon found the day had quickly slipped by.

On returning to the hut, I found it empty so eventually called it a day, packed up and returned to my quarters for a read and a good night's sleep.

Next day my arm was greatly improved — a little sore but no longer painful — so I decided to make a start on the sketches of the various decks, which were completed by Friday morning. (They were rough and ready but clearly showed where the compartments lay.)

During the afternoon we all trooped down to the pay office, then had a wander around before finding a small café, called Anne's Pantry, where we had tea and scones with plum jam (the usual strawberry jam had become a rarity). We then returned to our digs to give Mrs Mac the weekly lodging allowance.

On Saturday we turned to on the ship until 12.00 then had the unexpected luxury of having our weekend off.

After dinner we split up, going our separate ways. I caught a tram downtown, then had a wander around Smithfield Market, which was full of bric-a-brac, old beds and furniture, gramophones, wireless sets, watches, silver, leather and nails for shoe repairs and old second-hand books, from which I bought several novels. Tomatoes were being rationed out on the fruit stall so I joined the queue to get two nice tasting tomatoes, which were a treat.

On Sunday Mrs Mac took us out on a picnic to Craigavad on the Bangor line from the old County Down Railway Station. We visited some friends of hers and joined in a game of rounders with the children. It turned out to be quite a pleasant change.

During the third week the ship became a hive of industry as the assembly work changed into top gear. Various groups of men started to finish off numerous jobs. Platers and riveters started to plate over all the holes in the deck where the heavy machinery had been lowered through. Scuttles were cut out of the ship's side in rows for the messes, offices, cabins, sickbay and island by oxyacetylene cutters. Then they were drilled and countersunk so that heavy brass frames could be riveted, for the thick toughened-glass windows and deadlights which formed the portholes. Holes of varying sizes were drilled into the deckheads and bulkheads to fit watertight electric-cable glands through all the compartments. There was a terrific din of rat-tat-tat from the rivet guns and the whirr of the windy drills.

Work also started on smoothing all the large oblong holes along the ship's side. The rough holes for doorways and hatches were having coamings fitted and welded on to carry the doors.

Work started on lining up and bolting down all the auxiliary machinery in the boiler and engine rooms. Then all double-bottom tanks had all the necessary work done — fitting the filling pipes from the upper deck along with the sounding tubes for dipping the oil-fuel tanks (to check oil level). Then from their base suction valves the pipe fitters started to arrange two networks of piping, making templates to connect up each pipe to form the oil suction lines for the port and starboard oil pumps with a cross-connection valve to join up the two systems. The feed and freshwater tanks were dealt with in a similar manner. The boilermakers completed the air duct for the fan flat and the ducts from the secured high-speed fans with louvres into both boiler rooms as well as the four boiler flues joining to the funnel. The eight boiler blowdown cocks were connected to the seacocks and the four steam-driven fire and bilge and two electric pumps were mounted on their beds around the ship.

At the weekend I joined Ted and Taff and went to a dance and would have liked to have taken up dancing as a pleasant relaxation, but although I tried a few times with an occasional partner my nerves were so tensed up that I could not follow the rhythm; also my legs were wooden so they refused to function properly. After the second week I ended my visits, and then called it a day and packed up, being too self-conscious.

Next day we took a tram up York Street passing by Gallaher's tobacco factory, then through Shankill Road to Antrim Road and got off at Cave Hill to visit the zoo, which was short of animals owing to the lack of special food for them because of wartime rationing.

The days passed by quickly, so it was soon Friday which was the end of the month and was able to draw a tin of Tickler tobacco as well as my pay (with the aid of a couple of packets of Rizla papers was able to roll my own cigarettes).

The two superheated-steam main and auxiliary self-closing valves had been mounted on each boiler front along with the saturated-steam valve and the two sight glasses (they were always kept showing half a glass of water owing to the rapid evaporation of water in the boilers, which would soon run dry if the water stopped bobbing in the glass). Robot valves were mounted on the top drums of the boilers to maintain the water level which controlled the amount flowing through the main feed check valves when the ship was steaming.

In harbour, when only one boiler was steaming auxiliary, the auxiliary feed pump, which took its suction from the reserve feed tank, was used to discharge the water into the boiler by the auxiliary feed check valve.

At sea, once all the power had been extracted from the steam flowing through the turbines, it entered the condensers where there was a vacuum of 29.8 inches which helped the numerous rows of cooling pipes to change the steam back into condensate so it could be used again. It collected in the bottom of the condensers and was maintained at half a glass in the sight glasses by the contraflow valves working to and from the main feed tanks by the extraction pumps. These pumps also supplied water to the main feed-pump suctions mounted above before being discharged through the feed heaters to the main feed check valves on the boilers. All this piping for the closed feed system had been completed.

Large copper cooling pipes had been fitted to the sluice valves for the main condenser cooling via the circulating pump.

The forced-lubrication system (referred to as the FL system), which had all its copper pipes connected around the main turbine and gearing bearings along with the main thrust bearing from the oil tanks through the filters and FL pumps to the coolers then back to the tanks, had been completed.

The working platforms had been constructed up from the bilge frames with checker plates to walk on in both engine and boiler rooms, around which all the controls had been grouped. The boiler-room airlock cubicles, with their two doors, had been installed to contain the air pressure. The inner doors led to a runged grating with short ladders down to the next grating to operate all the various valves on the boiler fronts. From there short ladders ran down to the main working platforms where the chief stokers and their two assistants controlled the steam pressure.

The eight running down valves (to bilge) had been fitted to each of the bottom boiler drums, along with the eight blowdown valves which had been coupled up to the seacocks with pipes. These pipes were periodically blown down to remove all the sediment and solids that had built up in the feed water).

Four steam-driven fire and bilge pumps, along with two electric ones around the ship, had their suction pipes coupled up to small round sumps in the bilges, which gathered all the slopping bilge water before it was discharged overboard. The seacock suction pipes were coupled up to the pumps.

As the different compartments were gradually cleaned out by sandblasting, work commenced an the numerous multi-hole cable carriers, starting off from the turbogenerator rooms to the switchboards, to carry 2½-inch cables which would pass through gland holes at the top or bottom of bulkheads, decks and deckheads. They were welded up the sides then over the top so as to keep the cable well clear of any other installations along its path. From the switchboards smaller cable carriers were used to carry 2-inch cables to the junction boxes in numerous compartments and passages. From them the cables were reduced in sizes, from about 2-inch down to 1½, 1 and ½-inch. The larger size was used for the degaussing gear to carry the cables which were wrapped round the inside of the hull (to generate a magnetic field to counter the magnetic field of any mine laid on the bottom to spring up then sink the ship).

Other carriers were welded on in between more junction boxes and fuse boxes for the two for'ard capstan winches and the one aft; the steering motors; the port and starboard cranes; the auxiliary electric motor for the lift pump, motors for the refrigerating compressors, circulating pumps and evaporator pumps; the two high- and two low-pressure air compressors; the two electric fire and bilge pumps; the two emergency diesel generators; and the galley dough mixers, spud peelers and electric ovens.

Once these carriers for the larger cables had been completed the smaller sizes were welded from numerous fuse boxes to starter boxes for the air trunking supply, exhaust motors and electric lighting for the engine and boiler rooms, all auxiliary compartments, messes, cabins, sickbay and dentist, offices and stores, magazines, passages, working spaces, locker flats, bathrooms and heads; then upward into the hangars for group lighting and battery charging; then onto the flight deck for the landing lights; then finally into the island structure for illuminating and ventilating cabin spaces — also for working the radar, wireless, signalling and steaming lights, etc.

This work took several months to complete, but once started it was quickly followed up by threading huge drums of cable through the glands which were fitted into holes drilled in bulkheads, deckheads and decks wherever they were needed. Once the cables had been threaded through the glands they were made watertight. Then each cable was neatly clipped to the carriers about a foot at a time, owing to its heavy weight which had to be supported whilst the clips were bolted to the carrier. The cables were laid from the generators which were the source of the power to the switchboards which distributed it. Once each cable was laid into place the two ends were bared then connected up to the terminals. Work gradually progressed from the switchboards outward, with the cables being connected up with the junction boxes, then on to further junction boxes and then fuse boxes until all the heavy cables were connected up to the large starter boxes and electric motors. Once completed the smaller cables were connected up to smaller starter boxes and motors mostly for the ventilation fans and circulating pumps. Once all the motors had been wired up there were hundreds of light switches and fittings to be installed (enough to light up a small town).

By the end of the month considerable progress had been made in each of the boiler rooms. The oil-fuel suction network of pipes along with cross-connection valves for both the port and starboard double-bottom tanks led from their numerous tank suction valves to each of the boiler rooms' oil-fuel pumps, through the discharge valves to the strainers. They then passed through the heaters (which thinned the oil down), and on to the manifold oil-fuel control valves mounted on each side of the boilers' fronts to supply the sprayer nozzles with thin oil. This would fan out into a large spray of fine vapour, which mixed with the forced-draught air to form a large roaring fireball when the boilers were steaming.

Work was also started on the steam and water pipelines to connect up each of the two port and two starboard boilers, then extend them to the two engine rooms. Both main steam lines were started first by four sets of pipes from the four self-closing main stop valves on each set of boilers. They swept upwards to be married together to form single pipelines which passed through the aft bulkhead to an emergency trip valve (this could be shut off instantly by pulling a lever). They led on to a branch line for a valve to main steam, to auxiliaries, then on to two throttle valves and the main turbines in both of the main engine rooms.

The two auxiliary superheated-steam stop valves were connected with a pipeline supplying each boiler and engine room's auxiliary machinery. Later, cross connections and bulkhead valves were added to form the ring main around the ship.

The two saturated-steam stop valves were joined together to supply each engine and boiler room along with cross-connection valves and bulkhead valves to be extended upwards for the sirens, etc.

The main and auxiliary feed check valves on each pair of boilers were connected together to be fed from their own main or auxiliary feed pump.

The two exhaust steam lines from the auxiliary pumps to the feed heaters were eventually completed.

All the sea cooling pipes to and from the various pumps, condensers and lubricating-oil coolers were started on.

Before any of these pipes could be made, templates had to be made in sections to carry the pipes around various obstructions or sometimes on a different level to pass through the bulkheads. All these pipes had flanges welded on at the ends, and were bolted together with an insertion in between the faces to make steam-tight or watertight joints (longer lengths of straight piping were used where possible).

The main and auxiliary superheated joints were mated together with a face-to-face joint with a smear of red lead and copal varnish. The saturated-steam-pipe joints were made with corrugated brass rings or steam jointing material, such as Permanite, which was also used for hot-water-piping joints. Cold-water and seawater joints were made from rubber insertion sheeting which was knocked out by hammering around the outer and inner edges of the bore as well as the bolt holes. As each pipe was bolted on to the line it was supported from above or below according to its need. Also most pipes were grouped together towards the top of the bulkheads, making it difficult to sort out which one was which in the compartment on the other side.

Both of the engine-room hatches were completed with the door hinged on extra-high coamings welded around the holes above the deck level, and long ladders with broad iron treads and handrails which went down to both port and starboard working platforms (made up of checker plates to prevent slipping). They had been installed to control the engine throttles from. Also, there was a short runged ladder from each of the platforms, which led below to narrow checker-plate catwalks to gain access to the auxiliary machinery mounted down below.

By now we had settled down to our new routine quite well, but were being severely rationed with minute quantities, obtained on our civilian ration book, of meat, offal, ham, bacon, sausages (which were mostly stuffed with breadcrumbs) and margarine, etc. We often felt a little hungry, so we made up with bread or Ulster potatoes, which were baked in their skins then mixed up with a drop of milk and margarine. The bulk was made up with cabbage, turnip, and carrots, etc.

Some days we would have an Irish stew for dinner made from one pound of mutton ribs, two pounds of potatoes, three or four onions, pepper and salt with a pint of water and a sprinkling of chopped parsley if obtainable. The potatoes were layered in thin slices and the contents of the pan were allowed to stew for two and a half hours. The quantities were increased a little to feed five or six of us. It was the one meal we always looked forward to.

One morning, as I was wandering by the ship's side, some dirty beggar on the flight deck urinated down below, splashing and staining my white cap cover, which made me furious. I had stepped back out of sight before being able to shake my fist or let out a string of violent lower-deck oaths. Fortunately there was not much damage done so the incident was soon forgotten.

The regulating-steam valves for the oil heaters, pumps and forced-draught fans were mounted in position, having their valve spindles lengthened, being brought down to working level from the foot plates. The auxiliary suctions from the reserve feed tanks had been coupled up to the auxiliary boiler feed checks.

The boiler saturated-steam stop valves had been coupled up to a rambling pipeline to the evaporators, oil-fuel heaters and oil-fuel tank heating, then up as far as the bug binder on the upper gallery deck, the steam jet on the flight deck and the sirens mounted on either side of the funnel.

The Weirs draughtsman and fitter, Norman, turned up to start work on the refrigerating system, with the outside contractors who had arrived to insulate the cold-room and cool-room spaces, walls, deck and ceiling, with large thick slabs of dark-brown cork. This was bonded together with boiling-hot bitumen, which gave off a pleasant fresh smell. It had to be put around the lugs with holes in which would hold bolts to carry the evaporator grid's pipes, which would contain the refrigerant; also the rails, racks and shelves for the meat contents (offal and fats).

A carpenter then lined the room with wood throughout. The floors were also lined with lead. Then he hung several thick insulated doors to their jambs, so that each one swung easily into the framework, sealing it with two dogs to keep it airtight. They each had hasps so that they could be kept securely locked. He also fitted temperature tubes for thermometers to be inserted. This insulation was vital to keep the cold in the rooms and the heat out, especially as there was a hot turbogenerator room directly below along with the superheated-steam ring main which supplied it. The surrounding temperature (which would rise to 120°F in the tropics) and the room's insulation had to contain a temperature down to -18°F of frost.

Also in the boiler rooms the checker-plate platforms had been installed along with the steel ladders and gratings above from the airlocks. (These had both been completed with their two doors, which had been hung in position halfway down on a level with the boiler mountings.)

Down both engine rooms the 2½-feet-diameter condenser pipes had been installed between the sluice valves, the Drysdale circulating pumps and main condensers, the closed feed system (using recycled boiler feed water from the condensers), extraction pump via the contraflow valves to main feed tanks and pumps, then through the feed heaters to the boilers via the robot valves and main feed check valves had also been installed. The lubricating-oil system had been connected up on both port and starboard sets of engines from the supply tanks in the bilges through the suction filters and Weirs circulating pumps to each turbine bearing. These had a siphon breaker attached so in the event of oil failure enough oil would be left in each bearing housing to run the turbine for several minutes until the fault was rectified. Also, each breaker had a lit-up sight glass so that one could observe a golden rod of oil flowing through it. The oil was then pumped around the gears and thrust block, back through one of the coolers, to be returned into the tanks.

During our second month the auxiliary superheated-steam ring main was completed along with the cross-connection and bulkhead valves from each of the boiler self-closing valves. It was arranged to be split up in two sections when the ship was steaming at sea, so that the port and starboard sides of the ship were totally separate units. The two port boilers supplied steam to the port main engines and auxiliaries, which consisted of four forced-draught fans, the oil-fuel pumps, the auxiliary feed-water pump and a fire and bilge pump in the boiler room. Down the engine room it was connected to the main steam-to-auxiliary valve, the air ejectors, the gland steam, the main feed-water pump, the extraction pump, the circulating pump, the lubricating-oil pump and the fire and bilge pump, with a similar arrangement for the starboard unit.

All these pumps had recently been connected up to the closed exhaust system, which worked with a back pressure of up to 15 pounds, and was used to heat up the boiler feed-water heaters or be used through a spring-loaded valve on the 10th expansion of the low-pressure turbines. It could also be used to boil up the brine in the evaporators, or finally when in dock it could be put up the funnel waste pipe which had been installed in the funnel along with the waste pipe for the safety valves.

There was exactly the same kind of arrangement for the starboard unit, which had also been completed, except in the case of the two turbogenerators which could work from steam supplied from either side. If one side failed the load on the other machine could be quickly altered to supply the steering gear and the main working spaces. The turbo hydraulic lift and catapult pumps could be supplied with steam from either side of the ring main according to what suited best.

This unit system was devised in case of contaminated oil fuel, bad steam leak or explosion causing loss of pressure. The ship could limp back to port on one engine, and one turbogenerator to provide power, especially for the steering gear and main working spaces.

Work had commenced on the port and starboard main superheated-steam lines to the engines, beginning at the four main stop self-closing valves on each of the two boilers. Templates were made in sections for the pipe fitters to shape their pipe before marrying the sections together to converge into a single pipe. This passed through the bulkhead and trip valve, then branched off to the main-to-auxiliary steam valve, before carrying on to the main engines' ahead and astern throttle valves to the main turbines.

As each section was made, the flange joints had to be mated together, face to face, by a fitter who made the joint and added a smear of red lead and copal varnish, before bolting them together to withstand a pressure up to 300 pounds. As each section was added it was suspended from above to take its weight.

Both port and starboard main steam lines were completed in a like manner after several weeks' work. Walter, the Fraser & Chalmer's fitter, arrived to install the two turbogenerators. He started off by lining up both beds then bolting them down so the turbo could be aligned with the gearing and the generators. He then coupled up both sets of throttle valves to the auxiliary steam line, after which he assembled each self-contained unit separately by coupling up the three pumps driven off the same shaft.

They were all coupled up to their various suction and discharge pipes. The extraction pump was coupled up to the condenser to draw out the condensate from the bottom then discharge it into a large drain tank (to be recycled again with the boiler feed water). The circulating pump drew seawater from a seacock through a trap (to prevent seaweed, etc. blocking up the pump) and discharged it into the condenser through a large bank of small-bore tubes to cool it and transfer the heat overboard via another seacock. Finally, the piping was connected up for the lubricating-oil pump, which drew its oil from a large sump beneath the unit through a filter to the turbo and gearing bearings, then on back through a cooler to the sump. This system also had a small handpump attached to build up the oil pressure when starting up the turbo. The fitter then coupled up the gland steam pipes which sealed the two labyrinth packing glands on the ends of the turboshaft which, along with the air ejector (connected to the steam supply and the suction pipe to the condenser), helped to maintain the vacuum of 29.8 inches in it to keep it cool. He also connected up the vacuum valve from the condenser to the throttle valve (which shut the set down should the vacuum drop below 20 inches). Then all that remained to be done was to connect up the various small pipes and gauges to the instrument panel, for steam, oil, circulating water, extraction-pump pressure, as well as two pilot lights which glowed when the generator started producing a current. He also coupled up a few steam drains around the unit. Once completed, Walter and his assistant continued working on the aft set.

The other makers of auxiliary machinery began installing their plant. Norman, the Weirs fitter, along with his mate, Jock, started installing the evaporators which lay aft of the auxiliary rooms. They consisted of six large upright drums with about a dozen double copper heating coils at the bottom to boil up the brine. A baffle with a steam vapour valve at the top was connected to the condenser. There were two sets of three drums which operated independently; each had its own condenser, steam supply and three electric pumps — one for cooling the condenser, one for maintaining the level of seawater surrounding the copper coils, and one for returning the brine to the sea. They secured all the plant in position, then completed all the necessary pipe work, before leaving Harland's to install the details like the ventilation and electrics, and paint out, etc.

After this, Norman and Jock started installing the pipe grids in the two cold rooms and the cool room. A grid consisted of straight lengths of pipe bent around at the ends to run parallel with one another, so there was about a dozen pipes one above the other; each grid connected to the next one alternately at the top or bottom. Each pipe was screwed at the ends to allow a flat flange with holes to take two ¾-inch bolts. The ends of the pipe were tapered inward to take a thick diamond-shaped copper washer between them when the two flanges were bolted together. They could withstand pressures up to 1,800 pounds per square inch (at that pressure the safety disc would burst). Once all the grids around the three rooms had been assembled and joined together the two cold rooms had an extra set of grids hung from the top.

Once completed, the thick galvanised bars to hang the meat hooks on were installed along with some shelves in the cool room.

Then templates were made for pipes to couple up the ten manifold inlet and return valves to and from the grids, the ice tank and the cool-water tank. They were shipped across the water to Cathcart, Glasgow, so the first lot of coupling-up pipes could be made then returned within the week. All the manifold valves could be connected up to form what was called the evaporator side of the system, where the liquid CO_2 gas passed the regulating valve at high pressure. The gas was allowed to expand in the grids, changing its state into freezing vapour as the pressure dropped.

Whilst the pipes in the rooms were completed, more templates were made down the CO_2-compressor compartment from the compressor discharge valves to the condensers; then on to the regulator to the inlet manifold; then from the return manifold through two scale traps back to the suction side of the compressors. These also had extra suction valves connected to the pre-cooler mounted nearby with a connection into the system (to be used in the tropics to add to the efficiency of the plant).

Also templates were made for the circulating water from seacocks to the two electric pumps through the traps, then through the condensers overboard via two more seacocks.

Whilst Norman and Jock waited for the lengths of piping to be delivered, they had the welders down to fasten some girders to the deck to form a framework to mount the electric starter boxes for the compressor and circulating electric motors. Also they had the bottle storage room completed with forty racks to stow the spare CO_2 bottles (each weighing 180 pounds and holding 40 pounds of gas). Also in the middle of the deckhead a hook was welded to hang a weighing machine used for telling if a bottle was full or empty.

Once the pipes were returned they soon had their flanges screwed on, and, with the copper joints inserted, they then bolted them up to make the joints and complete the system.

The seawater pipes were soon jointed together with rubber insertion joints. Then Norman and Jock went to help in installing much of the equipment for the flight deck.

As the ship was nearing completion, Joe Anning and myself were sent over to Rosyth for a firefighting course. We went downtown to draw the necessary papers and tickets from the HMS *Caroline* pay office then caught the Burns Laird night ferry from Donegal Quay. It pulled away from the side at 21.00 into the narrow channel way of the River Lagan. We had a quiet trip until approaching the Firth of Clyde when the foghorn sounded, causing the ship's engine to slow down to slow ahead as a heavy fog had formed obscuring the coastline for miles around. Eventually we arrived at the Broomilaw in Glasgow several hours late.

As we were not due to arrive for training until the next forenoon we spent the afternoon wandering around Paisley where we stopped at Joe's home for the night. We caught the early train to Edinburgh next morning, then crossed over the Forth Bridge to Rosyth to attend the firefighting school at 09.30, to be instructed in the basic art of firefighting on board ship. Fire can be a deadly hazard at sea if not tackled immediately.

Fire consists of three items — combustible material, oxygen, and heat above flashpoints. Remove any one of the items and there is nothing else left to support the fire.

On board ship, if the mess deck became too hot and full of fumes to be worked in, the firefighters could close down all hatches and air vents to exclude the vital air supply with its oxygen to keep the fire burning. Then the surrounding bulkheads and deckheads could be sprayed to cool the space off. It could then be left until it was convenient to open up the deck again to be entered by one man wearing a special mask with a long hose attached so he could breathe in fresh air whilst he went down to remove any overheated smouldering material liable to burst into flames again. Also, a portable fan was lowered down to extract all the fumes so that the working party could be sent down to clear away the damaged gear to be ditched overboard.

A simple example is an oil fire in a household chip pan: the housewife answers the doorbell and is detained whilst the oil overheats above flashpoint, then sets on fire creating thick black smoke. The first thing to do on her return would be to shut off the gas flame below; then soak a towel with water and spread it out, then drop it carefully over the pan, away from where she is standing, so that the flames don't shoot out and burn her; then shut all doors to allow the oil to cool down; then remove the pan so it doesn't spill on the floor to rekindle the fire, causing much greater damage.

We were told the safety of the ship was everybody's responsibility, and anyone discovering an outbreak of fire should shout out, "Help! fire!" to attract the attention of anyone passing by or within earshot to enlist their aid. The various hand extinguishers, along with sand and water buckets could be used to tackle the fire whilst someone else alerted damage control as to the position of the fire. A fire party could then be mustered to ensure the fire was properly extinguished (otherwise it was liable to rekindle and develop into a raging inferno within minutes, getting totally out of control).

We were shown how to use the water extinguisher. It was started by banging the knob on top, then it could be used to spray small petrol or oil fires and also to jet smouldering wood or cloth material to damp it down. As for the sand, it was useful for smothering material — oil or petrol and possibly electric fires — but on no account was water to be used on electric fires, as one was liable to be electrocuted or a short circuit might occur and black out the ship.

A special type of gas container was used to extinguish electric fires. Also, there were sprinkler systems in the hangars and magazines, which could be used to keep the cordite cool should it overheat.

A foam extinguisher was best for small petrol and oil fires, and we had a try at operating one to put out a small tray full of burning oil by directing the jet of foam on the small bulkhead behind it. The foam ran down until it completely covered the fire, which went out due to lack of oxygen. Then it was kept covered until the oil temperature had dropped below its flashpoint.

As a hose needs the strength of several men to direct the spray into the heart of the fire, we were split up into several parties to put out a fire in a large structure representing a compartment of a ship. We entered behind a large spray of water, which we directed into the centre of the fire, advancing towards it as the spray changed into steam, which reduced the oxygen content in the space. The spray acted as a barrier, protecting us from the flames, smoke and fire only a few feet away. Within five minutes we were able to bring the fire under complete control so it could be prepared for the next party to have a go.

It was pointed out that a solid jet of water would not give us any protection against the fire or fumes. Also it would only cool a small area of the fire as it passed through the flames, causing the water to build up and flood the compartment. In case of an oil fire, the burning oil would still float on top then eventually the ship would sink, as happened several times in Liverpool Docks.

Sometimes, the ship would have steam extinguisher in the boiler room, with a whistle blowing as a warning when in use. It could only be used to smother an oil fire if the fan intakes and airlock doors were shut (also the watch had to be evacuated).

We all had an exercise in two rooms representing two compartments in a ship. We were in complete darkness, it smelt of smoke and was quite eerie. We had to enter by a bulkhead door, shut it behind us, then grope our way forward until we found a handrail with a ladder to climb down. We then groped our way across the compartment and skirted around several objects until we came to another bulkhead door. We passed through, then closed it behind us. We crossed over the compartment until we located the final ladder, which led up to a platform with a bulkhead door to get out into the daylight once again and shut the door behind us. It was then all ready for the next person to have a go. The object of the exercise was to give us some idea what it was like down below if the lights went out suddenly.

On our return to Belfast I picked up the threads where they had been left off. The fag situation was becoming intolerable as the shopkeepers severely rationed them to three or four a day and would not sell me a full packet. This caused me to scour around two or three different areas, taking up two or three hours per day and ending up with only seven to ten cigarettes, which were smoked in no time at all. This left me nervy and irritable for the rest of the day, especially if anyone lit up nearby and I would be forced to ask if they would sell me one.

So to make them last out the day the only thing to do was to use what little bit of willpower I possessed to eke out the few fags obtained to use in the forenoon, afternoon and the long evenings when there was little to do. So to make them last longer they were lit up, then snuffed out after three drags. Using each fag three times helped to ease the craving a little, but it was only a stopgap measure and failed to satisfy me (having reached the limit of my endurance).

At the end of the month I drew my last ration of Tickler tobacco, plus some Rizla papers to roll my own fags, and resolved that every time the urge got strong to light a fag I would resist it for as long as possible by using autosuggestion to tell myself I had stopped smoking.

At last the final day arrived and I had no fags, and had to convince myself that I had stopped smoking. Every time anyone lit up nearby, especially when the urge was at its strongest, I would make for the fresh air. After a long struggle through the day I managed to go to bed without smoking one.

As each day passed, the urge to smoke melted away but left me with long evenings after the 6 o'clock news. I filled in the time with more reading of books from the library and long strolls about town and in the country nearby.

Several incidents occurred whilst on my jaunts. The main one happened whilst passing by some houses where a housewife came out screaming that her chip pan was on fire. It was no trouble for me to enter the kitchen, turn off the gas and shut the inner door then smother the fire with a damp cloth, and told her not to move the pan until it had cooled down, then left with her thanks. Another time, when passing by, a farmer was struggling to change a wheel on his truck and was unable to unscrew the four wheel nuts so was able to help him by using my foot on the spanner and exerting a greater pressure on the nuts, causing them to be removed easily so that the wheel could be replaced by the spare one, which was soon screwed up into position. The farmer was so pleased that he gave me half a dozen fresh eggs (which were on ration). The third incident occurred in the centre of a country road where a tiny bleating lamb had lost its mother. I picked it up carefully and pushed it through a hole in the hedge where it gambolled off towards its mother.

After a few weeks had passed, I noticed Taff and Ted went to the local hop, so decided to have a few dancing lessons in the evenings at John Dossor's, where a large crowd of young people gathered to enjoy themselves.

After several sessions I began to feel embarrassed and nervy. After taking several wrong steps, I had a mental block so that I could not think. My mind went completely blank and my legs became completely wooden. Somehow I managed to stagger off the floor, acutely embarrassed, and sat down to watch the remaining dances, by which time my confidence had returned.

As everyone left in a hurry, surging down the steps outside the hall to catch their last bus or tram, I bumped into a party that was going in my direction. We caught a tram from Castle Junction over Queens Bridge, where we alighted to walk to the station where Ellen caught her train to Donaghadee. Before she left we arranged for a further meeting at the weekend. She became my regular girlfriend, so from then on we spent much of our spare time together, visiting various picture houses and various places around Belfast, Bangor and Donaghadee.

I looked forward to the weekend and had been invited down to Donaghadee. So after finishing in the dockyard at noon, then returning for my dinner and getting spruced up, I made my way to the station to catch the 13.30 train to the Dee and joined a long queue at the booking office to purchase a return ticket, then filed past the barrier, showed my ticket, then passed by an engine that was as clean as a new pin. (It differed greatly from the ancient rolling stock, which was in its own old brown-paint livery with the County Down coat of arms painted on each carriage.) The third-class seating accommodation had hard slatted seats. Eventually the compartment filled up and the porter shut all the doors. The guard blew his whistle and waved his green flag, then stepped back into his van. The driver responded with two hoots on his steam whistle then opened up the steam regulator. The wheels started to grind around, then rat-tat-tatted over the line joints and points and the carriages swayed, rattled and groaned with the forward motion.

The train sped on its way, stopping at several halts as well as the main stops of Knock, Dundonald (passing nearby to Stormont), then on to Comber, Newtownards and Millile Halt before reaching the Dee (short for Donaghadee), a pleasant little seaside town standing on the North Channel twenty-two miles east of Belfast. Opposite was Portpatrick, seven miles across the water on the Scottish coast, which could be seen clearly on a clear day.

Ellen awaited my arrival outside the station. As it was a bright sunny day we wandered around to the Free harbour, which was full of fishing boats. The lifeboat strained at her moorings in deep water, ready to slip out to answer an emergency call. Also, there was room for a small Kelly's coal boat alongside the jetty to unload enough household coal for the surrounding district and the local gas plant. Several fishermen sat about mending their nets or repairing their lobster pots. We then passed by some neat little whitewashed cottages with one pump to provide water for several of them. Also their occupants paid a peppercorn rent of one shilling a week. We walked to the right until we faced the Copeland Isles. They lay out to sea off the small village of Groomsport, which was on the Bangor Road (eight miles long), then we returned to Ellen's house to meet the family for tea.

Afterwards we went to the small local cinema to see the latest Gaumont Graphic news and a golden oldie selection of Charlie Chaplin films. Then we had to make our way through the streets with all the houses blacked out and unlit street lamps, until we reached the station which was faintly lit up with gas lamps (just enough to see one's way along the platform). Ellen saw me off and each of us went our separate ways. The train was ready with the engine attached, but several men had to operate a weird and wonderful acetylene-gas producer at the end of each carriage (a container where the gas was made by controlling dripping water

61

onto carbide). The gas was then piped to each compartment to a gas mantle which had to be lit by a man carrying a lighted taper, then turned down so as not to show through any chinks in the drawn blinds once the doors were shut. It seemed a long hour's journey back to Belfast without being able to look out of the windows. However, I was feeling contented and looked forward to our next meeting.

By now I was beginning to get to know the various compartments quite well and had gained a general picture of how all the machinery worked. On visiting the aft turbogenerator room I found Walter and his assistant had almost completed their task and all that remained to be done was to have the two tool racks welded to the inner walls for both sets before leaving the ship to work on another across the yard.

By the end of the third month all the auxiliary machinery had been installed, mostly by their makers. Also the two steam turbo hydraulic pumps for the lifts and the catapult had been installed and completed. All the heavy primary electric cables had been laid from the switchboard and junction boxes to the various compartments ready for connecting up as the machinery was installed. So the position was that the degaussing gear was completed along with the two emergency diesel generators. The large electric motors had been coupled up for the capstans, steering gear, auxiliary electric lift pump, the two high- and two low-pressure air compressors, the refrigerating compressors, the two electric fire and bilge pumps and the evaporator pumps. Power was laid to the guns, the paravane and lighter winches, and also to the galley and for the hangars, flight deck and island structure to be connected up when all the equipment was installed.

As Norman and Jock had almost completed their task an the refrigerating and evaporating machinery, all that remained to be done was to fix the pressure-gauge panels to finish off the plant. Then as all the auxiliary machinery had been completed Harland's started off finishing all the various rooms one by one, by adding doors and working platforms where necessary, fitting supply and exhaust fans with motors (and starters) to the trunking from the upper deck, along with the lighting and switches. Then the compartment was cleaned out ready to paint the bilges or deck with red lead paint, with the walls and deckhead done in white or aluminium paint.

The quarterdeck and port and starboard waists had been laid and secured with the usual teak planks with long seams in between caulked with oakum, which was stuffed then hammered tight, leaving room on top of it to be filled in with boiling-hot pitch, poured into the gap to make each seam watertight. This was scraped off level with the wood decking.

Work started on all doors with handles and dogs for the bulkheads and hatches with watertight joints. Usually six dogs were used to fasten them tight to withstand the thrust of seawater pressure in the event of flooding. Other types of doors, such as wooden ones for messes, cabins, offices, working places and stores, etc., began to appear around the ship. Metal ladders with steady chains started to replace the rickety wooden ones down the hatches and up to the gallery and flight decks, then on up the island structure.

Many rows of holes were drilled or cut out on the flight deck for landing lights, for the steam jet and for the arrester wires which ran over springs to keep them up about six inches above deck in the centre. These springs here long round bars which were arched in the centre, and secured at one end with a flattened eye bolt running through the deck attached to hydraulic gear to pull them down flat against the deck when there was no flying or when aircraft were being manoeuvred into place or taking off. They were also along the edges of the deck where the arrester wire came through around sheaves pivoted to the deck for both the arrester wires and the barriers.

Saturated-steam lines were extended to the oil-fuel heating tank coils (for clothing in Arctic weather conditions), the calorifiers (for hot water), then upward to the bug binder (to sterilise dirty hammock sheets), the sirens and the flight-deck steam jet to complete the system.

Steam drains were fitted to the cocks to all boiler and engine rooms, main steam lines, auxiliary steam lines and exhaust pipelines. The pipes were led away in groups of up to six into pig's ears where they were to be inserted so that the hot water could be run down to large drain tanks, then pumped back again into the feed system for further use.

The two Peter Brotherhood four-stage high-pressure compressors (at 4,000 pounds) were installed in the for'ard and aft part of the ship; each had a set of six reservoirs with valves and pipelines along with hoses to be installed in various parts of the ship.

Also two Revell low-pressure compressors at 150 pounds were installed fore and aft, each with their own reservoirs with the pipelines to be installed in various places where necessary. Each compressor had its own water cooling system for the cylinders and air coolers which were yet to be installed.

The telephone exchanges were installed; followed later on by leads running to phones (or blowers as we called them!) to numerous places — the bridge, engine-room department, offices, some cabins, wardroom, sickbay and galleys, plus a host of Fleet Air Arm departments and various other places.

Direct emergency phones with their own generators were installed direct to the bridge, damage control, wheelhouse, engine and boiler rooms, auxiliary rooms (including the turbogenerators and switchboards), the aft steering position, plus several other places.

The two emergency (E.E.C.) diesels were completed with exhaust pipes, electric cables, oil-fuel tanks and pipes, and water cooling pipes.

Fan trunking with electric fans and starter boxes, and louvres were installed throughout all the machinery spaces for supply and exhaust air. They'd all their doors fitted, then had been cleaned and painted, with working platforms installed where necessary.

The freshwater and oil-fuel filling pipes came through the centre of the wooden decking in both the port and starboard waists on the upper deck to brass fittings which had screwed watertight brass caps mounted flush with the level of the deck. The caps were removed for filling so a large brass T piece could be screwed in to be attached to one or two hoses as required.

The brass aviation-spirit valves were mounted nearby in both waists, but were set well back against the superstructure.

Both oil-fuel filling lines ran through to the main deck below to the port and starboard manifold pipes. These had branches off to each of the separate filling valves, which had pipes running into long funnels at the top of each filling pipe to let the air escape. Also nearby was a sounding pipe with a cap which was removed to dip the tank with a long steel tape. This tape had a graduated weight at the end, to show the depth of oil in inches and feet (similar to a dipstick in a car's oil sump).

By now the hangars and many of the compartments had been cleaned out by sandblasting so that work could commence on fitting them all out: It was a most unpleasant job removing the rust from all the plates that formed the deck, the deckhead and sides and doors. The atmosphere was filled by a thick brown choking dust, so the two operators had to be clad in protective clothing and masks. Once all the rust had been removed the place was swept out ready for everything to be installed then painted out.

At the side of the wooden decking on the quarterdeck and waists, room had been left for drainage channels along the ship's sides. These had a series of oblong scupper holes cut into them so that any waves that happened to slop over, or water used for swabbing or hosing down the decks, would be able to drain away.

The superheated-steam ring main was extended upwards through the decks for'ard to the upper gallery deck to the turbo-driven hydraulic pump for the catapult, with the pipeline being secured to the bulkheads and deckheads where necessary.

One Saturday afternoon I caught the train on the County Down railway from Belfast (which was a small diesel twinset) and passed through Marina, Craigavad, Sydenham, Holywood (which ran alongside Belfast Lough) and Carrickfergus (with its castle on the other side), then arrived at Bangor, a small seaport and seaside town situated twelve miles from the city centre to do a spot of courting with Ellen, who was waiting at the station.

We spent a pleasant afternoon together on the sandy beach watching the ferry and boats pass up and down, also watching the burnt out hulk of the *Georgic* swinging at anchor in the bay awaiting major repairs. We also walked around the town then managed to get a cup of tea and some fish and chips from a small café. We then visited the local cinema, which showed one of the many repeat films (which was not too bad). By then the time had slipped by, causing us to rush for our transport. Both left at 21.30 so we bid one another a hasty farewell and agreed to meet the next week.

The following week we met in the city centre to pay a call to Smithfield Market as I wanted a spare valve for the wireless set, which had conked out through old age. We found the stall crammed full of spare parts. It would have taken us all day to sort through but fortunately the stallholder was able to put his finger on a suitable replacement in a few minutes. He found a small cardboard box to put it in then charged me ten bob. (Later, when it was installed, we were delighted to hear the set working again so we could hear the news, music, and several interesting or funny programmes.) Whilst we were there we joined a long fruit-stall queue for a couple of tomatoes and apples to supplement our meagre diet.

We caught a tram from the terminus at Castle Junction. It went up the Shankill Road then on up the Antrim Road. We alighted at a stop near Belfast Castle, which was not an ancient structure but used for offices. We had a walk around the grounds before paying a visit to Ellen's aunt for tea as she lived nearby. Afterwards we paid a short visit to her grandma down the road towards the city centre. She kept quite fit despite her age and small rations.

We ended up at the pictures where Joseph Seal was playing popular tunes an his Wurlitzer cinema organ, which had all kinds of sound effects. We then caught a Ballymacarrett tram back the station before making arrangements for the next week.

One evening I caught the train to the Dee and got comfortably seated in the carriage. An old chap sat down opposite me, then proceeded to pull out his pouch and pocketknife to cut an inch of twist from a short black coil (it was a tobacco of local manufacture, made at Gallaher's). He rubbed it carefully in the palms of his hands before stuffing it into the bowl of his pipe and returning the pouch and knife to his pocket. He produced a box of matches to light up with, then started puffing away, filling the small space with a cloud of foul smoke which made us all cough. Then much to everyone's disgust and amazement he spat out with deadly accuracy, aiming into a gap in the door where the window drops down.

At the first stop along the line all the irate passengers dived out of the compartment, seeking other seats along the train, and left him to enjoy his horrible cloud of smoke.

Many of the famous White Star liners had been built here on the slipways. The coal-burning *Oceanic* of 17,274 tons, the *Celtic* of 20,900 tons and the ill-fated *Titanic*. The *Titanic* was reputed to be unsinkable but on her maiden voyage unfortunately the captain wanted a record crossing and threw caution to the wind. He ignored the iceberg warning and rammed one at full speed, which rubbed off the rivet heads. These were iron instead of the modern ones of steel. This allowed six side plates to spring open, and the water flooded into the first six compartments in the bows to gradually fill up and sink the ship.

They later built the prewar liners, powered by diesel or steam turbines, such as the *Andes* (Royal Mail Line) of 26,435 tons and 30,000 s.h.p. at 21 knots, with 950 passengers and crew; the *Reina del Pacifico* (Pacific Steam Navigation Co.) of 17,702 tons and

22,000 s.h.p. at 18 knots, with 888 passengers; and the *Edinburgh Castle* (Union Castle Mail Steamship Co.) of 27,489 tons and 35,000 s.h.p. at 22½ knots, with 669 passengers. They also built Royal Navy Ships: the aircraft carrier *Formidable* of 23,000 tons and 110,000 s.h.p. at 30½ knots with a complement of 1,392 men; and the heavy cruiser *Belfast* of 10,000 tons and 80,000 s.h.p. at 32 knots, with a complement of 850 men. These were just a few ships amongst a host of others, mostly 10,000- or 7,500-ton merchant cargo and tanker ships and smaller ones.

For building the ships it was necessary to have full-sized drawings showing the shape of each pair of frames in the vessel. The form of each drawing was transferred to bending slabs where cherry heated frames were pressed into shape. On the floor of the moulding loft a full size of the body plan was drawn on black board and cut out using a knife so full-sized templates and moulds could be made of each piece. The templates were sent to the steel maker along with large moulds for the stem, sternposts, rudder and other heavy forgings. The bar keel was laid along in blocks positioned in the centre of the slipway. The bars are about 12 inches deep by 3 inches thick, and are joined together by scarf joints (long tapered joints) and rivets. Large ships have their keel inside the plating so it does not protrude. The keel ran the whole length of the ship. Made from special steel forgings for the stem and sternpost, which has a special boss to allow a single propeller shaft to run through with a space for the propeller to turn in, it also has forged pins all ready to let the rudder pivot on. This is for a single-screw ship; two-, three- or four-screw ships have a different arrangement.

The frames are erected across the keel and adjusted in their correct position and secured by ribbands and shores. Beams, stringers and keelson are fitted into place, then secured by rivets. The rivets on the framework were secured, then flattened by a large hydraulic press similar to a large jaw, which fitted over them whilst two prominent stumps, similar in function to teeth biting, closed on both sides of a rivet, flattening it into position.

Rivets were made of high-tensile steel to withstand high stresses up to 38 tons per square inch.

A destroyer which is a medium-sized ship of about 300 feet long would have in the range of 200 frames. Other ships would have more or less according to length and type.

Frames on small ships would be pitched at 20 inches in midsection with an increase up to 33 inches on larger vessels. Also the gap was slightly reduced on the for'ard section, slightly more than the after section.

The outer bottom plating and side plating formed the shell of the ship with the primary function of keeping the water out. The inner bottom plating was used to form spaces for fuel or water tanks called DBs or double-bottom tanks which prevented flooding should the ship strike a rock. These floor plates were stiffened by an intercostal keelson forming part of the ship's longitudinal framing.

All vessels had a collision bulkhead not less than one twentieth of the vessel's length from the bows. Also, they had watertight bulkheads at each end of the machinery space. Watertight compartments and bulkheads were used to a great extent on Royal Navy ships to protect against explosion damage.

In merchant ships, subdivision corresponds to watertight compartments, which are very few and far between, greatly adding to the cost. Consequently extra ones are only used in special ships such as tankers and liners, etc. Beams were strung thwartships across from port to starboard frames at intervals to support the deck plates, which were secured by countersunk rivets.

I spent one afternoon wandering around the three shipyards of Harland and Wolff on the right-hand bank of the River Lagan. The first yard was a small one for small- to medium-sized vessels which backed onto the Abercorn Basin where there was a limited area of 727 feet long by 646 feet broad (small for launching new ships). There were a host of small ships being built on the six slipways (two at a time on most), such as frigates, corvettes, sloops, minesweepers and also small coastal vessels. Some of them had bare frames or ribs reminding me of a skeleton of a prehistoric monster turned over on its backbone.

Then I passed on over a long wharf with sheds containing moulding lofts where the whole ship's structure is drawn out, being cut into black board so as to make accurate patterns.

Then on to the next yard downriver with three long slipways where the large ships were being built. The hull of the *Black Prince* was rapidly taking shape and was nearly ready for launching. Also there was a 10,000-ton merchant ship under construction and a large tank-landing craft was nearly completed.

A little further downriver was a small works with four medium-sized slipways occupied by a variety of craft, then a jetty and a wharf where several ships were tied up for a refit.

Cranes on gantries ran along the whole length of the slipways, which lay in such a position to back onto a rail track where a steam or diesel engine pushed or pulled a truck or trucks from the shops on the other side of the road. Loaded with the necessary frames and plating, etc., they could be unloaded by crane directly on to the slipways.

The plates arrived already drilled and countersunk where necessary in rows around their edges before being manoeuvred. They were then clamped into position on the frames where they were re-drilled through the holes into the frames, then bolted temporarily for being reamed through the frames. This ensured they were accurately mated so the rivets could be pushed through easily.

The driller worked a windy air drill, putting weight on from a drilling post clamped to the plate. As it whirred and buzzed slowly around, the drill cut long bright spirals of steel swarf from the rusty plating until it suddenly speeded up as the point of the drill burst through the other side of the frame, causing the driller to shut off the air suddenly. Then he reamed out the hole before setting the drill and post for the next hole. This was tediously repeated throughout the day.

When all the holes were drilled they were completed by the riveters who rapidly filled them all in again. Then the bolts were removed and the holes re-drilled, then reamed, then riveted up so the plate was finished and ready to be caulked round the edges with a windy hammer with a single-edged caulking tool to make it watertight.

The slickness of the riveting team was a joy to behold. The rivets were heated up by a coke furnace blown up by wind from the low-pressure air line. When the rivet glowed a cherry red it was plucked from the fire with a long pair of tongs. Then the first man skilfully tossed up the heated rivet to the second man who caught it in a pair of asbestos gloves before quickly inserting it into the hole. Then he held his dolly against it whilst the man at the other side of the plate with the windy gun opened it up with a rat-tat-tat until the rivet had swelled out sufficiently.

The sound of the rivet gun was deafening and could be heard throughout the dockyard from one end to the other all day long. The riveters were on bonuses and worked hard to get an extra-fat pay packet.

I moved on to the four graving docks at the far end of the works the largest one was the Alexandria, originally the world's largest, with dimensions of 800 feet long by eighty feet wide and twenty-five feet depth. On the bottom lay several small ships which had been damaged by explosions. I climbed down to take a look at the damage. One had had its bows blown off and required some twisted frames and jagged plating to be removed along with a section of bent keel. By drilling out sets of rivets on the first pieces of unbent metal a new part of keel could be attached with frames and stempost, then plated over to form a new bow section. Another ship had suffered from an explosion in the boiler room, requiring a new boiler. Also, much work needed to be done on the hull, including a midsection of the bent keel to be removed along with a number of frames which wanted renewing before the section could be replated. Another ship had run over a magnetic mine which blew off her stern and rudder. It was fortunately beached on a sandbank in a river estuary before she could sink. Her prop shaft was badly bent; which called for a new stern with sternpost, rudder, prop shaft and propeller, along with a new after section of the ship. It needed the bent shaft, plates, frame and keel removing before the work could start.

Finally I had a look in another dock where they were busy with a plumb line, lining up two separate surviving halves of different merchant ships. It was a tricky job as both halves had to be lowered onto the keel blocks together so the damaged ends could be straightened out and lined up to be joined together with a new section of keel, frames and plating.

After an interesting afternoon I packed up then went home for tea.

The *Black Prince*

The *Black Prince,* a light cruiser with eight 5.25-inch dual-purpose surface and anti-aircraft guns was on a slipway being prepared for launching. She was nearly ready. Her four prop shafts were protruding (thrust or pushed out) from their glands and bearings, with the outer pair being supported by A brackets with bearings of an extremely hard Australian wood called lignum vitae.

Several sections of the upper-deck plating had been left off and the supporting beams that held it were bolted across in a temporary manner so as to be removed to allow easy access for the large cranes to drop the heavy boilers, engines and other machinery into place once the vessel reached the fitting-out basin.

There was much to be done on the slipway. Bilge blocks had to be inserted in between the keel blocks which carried the weight of the ship; and the shores were added as the ship grew in shape and the building progressed.

A wooden cradle had been built around the base of the hull to take the weight of the ship, which was supported by sliding ways built on top of the groundways. The cradle was built high up around the bows of the ship to take the extra pressure as the hull lifted aft on entering the water.

As the launching was in a restricted width of waterway in the river, several piles of rusty old chains of a known length were attached to both sides of the vessel. They were secured by strops to eye plates which were welded on temporarily. They made a cloud of brown dust as they were dragged over the ground during the launch. They suddenly left the ground and went taut as they finished paying out, bringing the ship to a sudden halt as she was fully afloat.

The groundways had been heavily coated with tallow worked in hot, then afterwards received a coat of tallow and train oil with some soft soap or equivalent lubricant. They were coated right down to the water's edge. (A good example of just how much lubrication was required for the groundways: in the launching of the Hamburg-American liner *Imperator* 8¼ tons of tallow, 5½ tons of soft soap, 2½ tons of waggon grease and 2½ tons of paraffin wax were used.)

At last the day for launching had arrived. There was little fuss made during wartime launching; a small knot of naval officers, ratings and some wives had assembled from different ships around the yard.

First a team of shipwrights started to remove the keel blocks and the wooden shores that had been added as the weight of the ship grew heavier. They started aft near to the water's edge, knocking them all out except for the last few blocks and shores, which were kept in position until the ceremony was due to take place (it had been known for a ship to launch herself without one).

When it was high tide a local vicar's wife performed the ceremony by breaking a bottle of plonk over the ship's bows with the customary words, "God bless this ship and all those who sail in her." The final shores were knocked out and hydraulic pressure was exerted on the vessel, giving her a final shove that started her sliding slowly down the slipway, gathering speed as she went. The small group of naval spectators cheered her on her way. They were soon joined by everyone in the yard, who downed tools to cheer her along with the hoots of odd ships anchored around the harbour.

Soon the stern had entered the water, making a large white wave. The cradle dropped away. She was fully afloat and upright when suddenly her speed was checked by the drag chains which straightened out bringing her to a sudden halt. Three small tugs pushed her to one side whilst the chains were disconnected. Then they pushed and towed her into the fitting-out basin where she was secured to be worked on.

The slipway was cleared up ready for the keel blocks to be replaced so a fresh ship could be laid down on them.

The launch had gone without a hitch. A rough launch or a fatal accident on the ship in building or launching, especially on Friday the 13th, was regarded as an evil omen to sailors.

Soon after the launch an ex-messmate, Chief ERA Henry Tregembo, came to stand by the *Black Prince* along with a commander 'E' as an advance party to keep an eye of the engines, boilers and fitments being installed.

Several weeks later another ex-messmate, Jimmy Ball, who had survived the return Arctic run from Murmansk, had turned up to take charge of a small minesweeper that had just been launched.

One morning I watched a medium-sized single-screw cargo ship being launched. It refused to budge and had to have some extra hydraulic-jack power applied to it. This was an occurrence which usually happened in winter when the thick oil and tallow froze. Suddenly she started moving until she was checked by the rattling chains in midstream where two tugs took over.

The Ship Enters Dry Dock

She was manoeuvred in by two tugs along with the dockside capstans. The linesmen in charge skilfully swopped over the steel ropes to and from the tugs along with the various capstans and inched the ship to the far end of the dock, dead in the centre. When the gates were shut the water could be drained out to lower the keel onto the blocks to take her weight so she could be propped up all round. Once the dock was empty, work commenced on scraping rust from her plates overall so that painting with battleship grey could commence. Starting from the water line extending the whole way up past the gallery decks to the flight deck, then working on upward over the island, the funnel, the mainmast and the wireless masts the ship was painted until until completed.

Then below the water line was painted with a red antifouling paint. This was used to deter marine growth from attaching itself to the bottom plates, which would affect the ship's speed and cause oil-fuel consumption to increase.

Figures were painted on both sides of the bows up to thirty feet to indicate the ship's displacement, which was usually around twenty-six feet when fully loaded.

The port and starboard electric paravane winches had been installed and wired up on the lower gallery deck, with the two paravanes mounted on cradles alongside them. They were attached to long 150-foot steel cables which ran down both sides for'ard to a guard around the keel. The paravanes were set to stream outward, well away from the ship's sides (opening out like opposing spokes on an umbrella). They were lowered into the sea when the ship steamed out of harbour to operate in a simple manner, so when a mine was washed to one side with the bow wave its anchor cable would run outward along one of the cables as far away from the ship's side as possible until it reached the sharp steel jaws on the paravane which cut the mine free. Then a marksman posted on deck could take aim with his rifle to sink or explode it if the bullet accidentally hit one of the horns.

Both anchors and chains were lowered to the bottom of the dock, then painted black before being threaded through the hawse pipes around the capstans then lowered into the freshly cleaned out and red-lead painted cable lockers in the hold of the ship.

The instrument panels were installed in all machinery spaces to be easily observed with round gauges calibrated in pounds (per square inch) beyond the normal working pressure, which was usually indicated by a thin red line; or if it was a temperature gauge it was calibrated in degrees Fahrenheit.

The main panels in both of the boiler rooms had two main steam pressure gauges with the red line at 300 pounds working pressure for each boiler. Also, there was a saturated-steam gauge for the oil-fuel heaters; a pressure gauge for the oil-fuel discharge to sprayers; a pressure gauge for the auxiliary feed-pump discharge to boilers; and a glass U tube graduated in inches to indicate the boiler-room pressures from the forced-draught fans.

The panels in each engine room were fitted with main steam pressure gauges and also auxiliary superheated and saturated ones. In the turbines progressive drops of pressure until the steam had passed through to the turbines into the condensers, where the steam pressure was reduced to 29.8 inches of vacuum, were shown on another type of gauge. The temperature of the superheated steam had a red mark at 700°F, which was the maximum heat of the steam.

There were other gauges for the extraction-pump discharges (which registered up to 45 pounds), the main feed pump (which registered 400 pounds or over) and the lubricating-oil pump (which registered up to 45 pounds). Also, the saturated steam for the turbine glands (which varied from 5 to 10 pounds), the condenser circulating pump's discharge water pressure (which varied from 5 to 10 pounds), the exhaust steam pressure (which swung about from 5 to 15 pounds) and the fire-main pressure (which registered up to 80 pounds to lift the water up to the flight deck).

All the other self-contained auxiliary machinery had their own small instrument panels.

The telegraph shafting was completed from the wheelhouse under the bridge to both engine rooms at eye level above the working platforms. It could be seen from the throttles with a bell for ringing down the changes (and an electric reply bell). Below the bell was a large round-faced dial with an indicating finger pivoted in the centre. It was generally positioned at STOP in the bottom centre of the dial, and was turned upward to the right for the ahead movements of SLOW, HALF and FULL; then to the left for the astern movements of SLOW, HALF and FULL. The number of revs was shown in a slot in the top centre of the dial, with three sets of revolving figures which showed up to 240 revs.

The port and starboard cranes were mounted on their sponsons on a level with the upper hangar deck. The main 4-inch guns were mounted on their sponsons so their shields on top were level with the flight deck in order to allow them a large angle to train in. They could swing over the flight deck to train on any hostile aircraft which was attacking the ship once the wireless masts had been lowered.

All the guns had been mounted around the ship and island, along with ammunition lockers for instant use. Some of the guns were fairly ancient, being scraped from the bottom of the barrel, whilst other small ones were quite up-to-date with hydraulic training gear and radar directed to follow the target.

The pipes of the fire main were installed from all the various fire and bilge pumps to most compartments throughout the ship with fire hydrants with valves, hoses and nozzles which could cover all adjoining compartments as well as spaces over or below.

Work had started on all the secondary wiring from the switchboard to the junction and fuse boxes. About twenty of the smaller sizes of electric cables were threaded through the bulkhead glands on both sides of each compartment hanging down like large festoons in long sweeping curves. They were tied together waiting to be neatly clipped and bolted up to the carriers for small electric starters and motors, as well as the electric light switches and bulb holders throughout the ship.

All bilges were cleaned out thoroughly in the engine-room departments, including the auxiliary machinery compartments. All electric motors and starters had been wired up from the completed switchboards to the auxiliary machinery (namely, the steering gear, capstans, refrigerating compressors, high- and low-pressure air compressors, auxiliary lift pump, evaporator pumps, the electric fire and bilge pumps), along with all starters and motors for the ventilation systems. Also the first of the numerous light fittings and switches began to appear in the working spaces before any other parts of ship.

All compartments were cleaned out then the bilges were painted out in red lead with the rest done in white.

The insulating of steam and hot-water piping was started by lagging with bullmuck, as it was called. It was applied to the pipes several inches thick, then carefully finished off with spatulas to a smooth white finish, which looked somewhat similar to the finish on an iced cake. Most of the joints and valves had loose covers laced around them.

A white broken line had been painted running down the whole length of the flight deck in the centre. Then about 150 feet down from the for'ard end was a small brass knob containing the steam jet, which replaced a windsock to indicate which way the wind was blowing. Four white lines, radiating from it at different angles on both the port and starboard sides, indicated the direction of the wind. A steady wisp of steam blew over one of the lines until the ship had altered course. When the wisp passed over the centre line, this indicated that the ship was steaming into the wind in order that the flying programme could commence.

There were also two rows of landing lights, with heavy rounded watertight covers and thick toughened glass facing aft to take the weight of several tons of aircraft when a tyre would occasionally run over one whilst being manhandled. They were evenly spaced out along the deck to be lit up in fog or darkness to illuminate the flight path so all the kites could land safely.

As the ship neared completion the cluster of air pipes for windy drills, riveting guns, chiselling and caulking gear, and the large drums of assorted electric cables began to disappear. The decks, passages and various spaces were cleared out and began to look a little more shipshape.

Work started on all the plumbing through the ship, with hot and cold water being gradually laid on to all sinks, basins, showers and baths, etc.

Seawater was piped from the fire main for flushing out the heads along with taps in the bathrooms for swabbing the decks. Also work started on installing all the necessary large and small drainpipes overboard.

The aviation-spirit system along with filling valves was installed in the waists on the upper deck, with the system running through both hangars with discharge valves spaced about them, and with a few valves on the flight deck. The aviation spirit was contained in six tall tanks, standing upright in an isolated compartment based on the hold deck with the control cabin directly above. Both of these had been sandblasted, then thoroughly cleaned out along with the tanks. The tanks were then coated with thick bitumen along with the rest of the compartment to prevent rust (as it was to be filled with water to surround the tanks of highly inflammable spirit to prevent fire or explosion as an extra precaution).

The pipes to the tanks for filling, venting and discharging, and for the depth gauges, which indicated the amount of spirit in the tanks, had all been fitted. They were grouped together as they passed through the deckhead into the control compartment above, where they were joined up to a cluster of brass valves and handwheels (operated by a brass wheel spanner to prevent sparks). These connected each tank to the filling system and also to a low-pressure air supply, which applied air pressure to the top of each tank so that the spirit could be forced out into the system until the tank was empty. Also, there was a rubber mat laid on the deck as an extra fire precaution.

All the various tanks — the double-bottom oil-fuel, freshwater, main and auxiliaries, overflow and drain tanks, and also the ship's freshwater tanks — had been cleaned out and tested for leaks ready for use. The water tanks had been painted out with a special solution to prevent rust.

Some of the smaller tanks for diesel oil supply — for the E.E.C. diesel generators (for emergency lighting and the motor boat), and for the Perkins diesel engines — and a much smaller tank for petrol for Ford V8 engines (used to power the aircraft lighter, the forklift and the motor crane), were all cleaned out and tested for leaks ready to be filled.

The rudder, with four massive rams of the Hasties steering gear, were lined up to operate two short tiller bars which turned the rudder with two electric-driven hydraulic pumps. Pipes were coupled up to the opposing rams so that when the hydraulic fluid acted on the two rams to move the rudder to port the fluid was sucked from the two opposing rams. Then, to move the rams back to midships or to starboard, pressure was removed from them and applied onto the other two opposing rams. These movements were controlled from the wheelhouse under the bridge. The wheel was normally kept at midships and was spun to the number of degrees port or starboard required by the quartermaster to steer the ship.

There was also an emergency wheel installed in the steering-gear compartment in case of hydraulic failure from the wheel above to the pumps.

The special six port and starboard flooding tanks had been installed and painted out with red lead. Their flooding valves and seacocks had extended spindles to the deck above, where there was a simple brass indicator which had been installed to show when the ship was sitting upright, or the number of degrees she listed to port or starboard. In the event of a collision or explosion the ship's side could be torn open, taking in thousands of tons of water, which would cause her to list one way or the other. The levels in the various oil-fuel and water tanks would drop and would be liable to uncover the various suction outlet pipes. The various pumps would then suck in air, speed up and trip out and stop, causing the boilers and engines to grind to a halt. Also, the generators would stop, causing a blackout down below. In this case the tanks on the opposing side to the damage would be flooded to counteract the list so the ship could complete her voyage on one unit. The *Ark Royal,* which was sunk by a solitary torpedo in her starboard boiler room, lost all her steam and water. With all three engines grinding to a halt, she wallowed in the water like a sitting duck, losing valuable time and taking in tons of water by the hour. Unable to pump it out, her weak bulkheads began to bulge and leak. The engine-room staff, with the help of a destroyer which came alongside, managed to raise steam in the port boilers and get the port engine running at 5 knots. Unfortunately the fumes from the boilers were causing the stokers to faint, so their effort failed and next day the water started lapping over the upper deck into the boiler-room air intakes, causing her to turn turtle and sink along with her sixty aircraft, which she could not fly off.

In the event of the *Unicorn* being damaged, little time would be wasted getting under way and there would be one generator on board to allow damage control to start up the fire and bilge pumps to keep the rising water down. The damage could be contained by shoring up the bulkheads, which had been strengthened.

The doors, passages and hatches were completed and marked with X-Y-Z stencils, to indicate the order of importance of being shut. X doors were always kept shut and fully dogged. Y doors were clipped with two dogs at sea and could be passed through then re-clipped. Z doors were mostly above the upper deck to keep the high seas and stormy weather out.

The chief engineer of the ship was Commander 'E' Tony Oliver, who had been the senior engineer aboard the *Ark Royal* when she sank. He was determined that if the *Unicorn* was damaged she would not be lost so easily, and made sure she had all the latest improvements, such as an armoured flight deck, two lifts with keeps underneath, to hold them level with the flight deck so as to withstand a 500-pound bomb, and also a catapult. In the two hangars there were four foam-making plants to smother any aviation-spirit fires and put them out. The hangar curtains had been installed with some inflammable material to replace the hinged slatted steel ones, which were found to be a terrific hazard on HMS *Illustrious* when a 500-pound bomb had burst down the lift shaft into the hangar causing the steel curtains to splinter into thin slivers of metal. They burst and sprayed all over the hangar cutting into everything they touched. Ammunition boxes started popping off and firing all over the place, ripping into the fabric of the fuselages and cutting them to ribbons; and bursting tyres exploded with a terrific bang, giving any bod that happened to be standing in their way some nasty deep gashes.

Also, he had two electrical fire and bilge pumps installed along with two emergency diesel generators for extra power and lighting.

Other alterations and improvements completed were as follows:

1 The boiler-room air intakes had been raised from the upper-deck level to the flight-deck level to prevent tons of water flooding in in the event of any damage causing the ship to list heavily to starboard.

2 Additional oil-fuel cross-connection valves were added to the suction valves so in case of damage to the ship the list on one side could be partly balanced by pumping any surplus oil to the other side. As the ship carried 2,000 tons of oil when fully bunkered there would always be a few hundred tons left in the numerous tanks.

3 The same idea was applied to the feed-water tanks for the boilers, and the auxiliary superheated-steam ring main which ran around the ship to supply the two turbogenerators.

4 The hydraulic pump for the lifts and the hydraulic pump for the catapult had several cross-connection valves inserted to provide them with steam from any one boiler.

5 All fire and bilge pumps were connected to the bilge suctions and the fire main, which ran to the hydrants through the ship, was also used for spraying the magazines if they became overheated. The pressure had to be increased to 80 pounds to reach the hangars, hydrants and foam-making plant before reaching the hydrants on the flight deck.

6 An electrical ring main was installed which consisted of terminals mounted high up on the bulkheads so the cable could be run across to the next one to connect up any breakage in the system.

The aviation fuelling system was completed to run from the upper deck to the six tanks below, and from there on up to the hangars and flight deck. The high- and low-pressure air systems had been installed from the compressors around the engine-room department, the smithy, the coppersmiths, the hangars and the aircraft-engine test-bed compartment.

The ship had taken on enough oil fuel and feed water to steam out all the boilers and steam lines in the ship, before running up and testing all the machinery. First of all the four boilers had to be filled with water then flashed up with a small pressure of steam with the air cocks open and the two blowdown cocks on each leg of the boilers being blown down constantly, to remove any foreign matter or sediment collecting at the bottom of the legs, every half hour. Then after twenty-four hours' steaming the boilers were shut down with all three manhole covers removed.

It was in this period, when we were trooping up the gangway, that Taff noticed a thin wisp of black smoke rising from the funnel and a wisp of steam from the waste pipe. He remarked, "It won't be long now, lads," meaning the ship was nearing completion. It dawned on us we would soon be leaving our cushy billets to be back under naval discipline.

All the internal gear was taken out and all the numerous water tubes were brushed out. Then the boilers were cleaned out. The internal gear was blackleaded and replaced. All three manhole covers were replaced and filled up with water to be tested at 300-

pound pressure.

Now came the big job of opening up all the steam lines, inserting grease filters at the ends to arrest the swarf or any other foreign matter lodged in nooks and crannies along the lines, and steaming them out with all the drains opened up to the bilges. These precautions were taken so that no foreign matter was left in the pipes to work through and damage the turbine machinery, whose rotors spun around at terrific speeds up to as much as 6,500 rpm.

With very fine clearances between their blades, even droplets of hot water could damage their blading, causing them to shear off and damage the rotor so it became unbalanced and liable to burst. One such incident occurred on the liner, *Queen Elizabeth*, on her maiden voyage, when one of her turbines was damaged and put out of action, causing her to limp back to port on one engine. Now No. 1 Port and No. 1 Starboard boilers were flashed up to steam out all the pipes, starting with the main steam pipes from the boilers to both of the turbine ahead and astern throttle valves. As each pipe was steamed out the grease filter was removed, the joints were remade and bolted up all ready for testing the machinery. Then all the pipes in both boiler rooms and engine rooms were steamed out. The machinery was the same in both boiler and engine rooms. The boiler rooms had four turbofans, an oil-fuel heater, an auxiliary feed pump, oil-fuel heater and pump, and a fire and bilge pump, and each engine room had a main feed pump, a circulating pump; a lubricating-oil pump, an extraction pump, a fire and bilge pump and an air ejector. Once this lot had been dealt with the machinery on ring-main lines was dealt with. There were two turbogenerators, one for'ard and one aft, the high-pressure air compressor, the hydraulic pump for the lifts and wireless aerials, and saturated steam to supply the evaporators for the fresh water. Once all this lot of pipes had been steamed out it was time to start testing all the auxiliary machinery.

Chief ERA Rodgers, Joe Anning and myself were required for an early start to arrive at 07.00 to take notes on all four boilers being flashed up and where all the control valves to the oil-fuel heaters, the oil-fuel pumps, the auxiliary feed pumps and the controls for the eight forced-draught fans were. This meant visiting the port and starboard boiler rooms from time to time after the pressure in all four boilers reached 50 pounds, and all the various pumps and oil-fuel heaters were brought into use. Then when the boiler pressure had reached 300 pounds we went up into the forced-draught fan flat where four fans for the port boilers, and four fans for the starboard boilers were started up to reduce the black smoke from the funnel.

After dinner we split up, with the chief looking after the two boiler rooms, Joe looking after the starboard engine room, and me, the port engine room.

All the main stop valves were opened on all the boilers and main steam bulkhead valves in the engine rooms. The auxiliary superheated and saturated steam had been opened up to the engine rooms, so that the condenser cooling pumps could be started up. Also, the condenser extraction pumps, which removed the condensate back into the water feed tanks, and the forced-lubrication pumps which oiled the turbine bearings and the reducing gearing and bearings, were started up.

Now was the time to open up the ahead and astern throttle valve so both sets of turbines could be warmed up to 160°F. Then the valves were shut and the air ejectors were started up. The gland steam was opened up to seal the bearings on both sets of port and starboard turbines so a 15-inch vacuum could be maintained in the condensers. Now came the tricky bit: to open each throttle valve slightly to turn the prop shafts one turn ahead and one turn astern every two minutes for fifteen minutes, to heat up the turbines without moving the ship. Then the full vacuum was raised to 29.8 inches, and we were ready to obey telegraphs. After this we watched the engine rooms being shut down.

The next week, Walt told me he and his mate were preparing to start the for'ard turbogenerator up. He had just completed topping up the oil sump, and was bleeding the air trapped in the top of the condenser. All the steam drains were opened up to drain out the superheated and saturated ring mains so the rest of the machinery could be tested — namely the hydraulic lift pump, the high-pressure air compressor, the two turbogenerators and the evaporators.

Having opened all the steam drains on his turbo, Walt then opened up the gland steam and the air ejector until the vacuum gauge showed 20 inches. This indicated it was time to set the emergency vacuum trip valve so the steam would pass through the throttle valve, which was cracked open. Then he operated the hand oil pump quickly to lubricate the turbine bearings as the rotor began to spin with a slight hum. Then the gear-driven mechanical pump took over, increasing the oil pressure to around 45 pounds. The throttle valve was opened wide with adjustments made to the air ejector and gland steam to raise the full vacuum to 29.8 inches, so that the machine was ready to be put on the switchboard. We could watch how the machine performed on load; and the EAs could start work testing all the electrical circuits for power to the degaussing gear, all starter boxes, motors for steering gear, paravane winches, capstan winches, air compressors, refrigerating compressors, auxiliary hydraulic pump for lifts, evaporator pumps, two electric fire and bilge pumps, galley equipment (including dough mixer, spud peeler and ovens), power and lighting for the guns where needed, power for workshops, lathes, milling machine and electric welding gear, and many more places and machines.

I went through all the starting-up routine, which stood me in good stead for future use — especially in several blackouts, where I had to grope my way in the darkness from any part of ship, and grope around the valves to start up the generator in the dark.

When all these tests were completed, the steam drainpipes, which had been blowing into the bilges, were bent back to be grouped together in the various pig's ears where the water ran off into the drain system. This was connected to the overflow tank (so it was not wasted), and was pumped back into the boiler's water main feed tank and was used again. Once all the machine tests were completed the bilges were cleaned out and painted with red lead.

By this time we were all feeling hungry so Walt's mate made his way ashore to the works canteen. He brought back three meat and potato pies along with chips and a brew-up which we all had with relish. Then, as the turbo and gearing was performing well without fault or teething troubles, or the bearing getting hot, I decided to wander down to my other part of ship, the CO_2 compressors, where Norman, along with Jock (his mate) and Sandy the draughtsman, were preparing the refrigerating plant for starting up. They had already filled up the ice pan tank with brine, and were starting to charge up the system with about 800 pounds of CO_2 gas from twenty heavy bottles to test out all the high-pressure-pipe joints with a soap and water solution. Any leaks around the joints were shown up by a line of bubbles blowing out. Each leak was immediately stopped by retightening the bolts. On my return to the turbogenerator it was still running well without fault. At 18.00 it was shut down.

I did not arrive back to my billet until late, as the rush hour was over and the transport was few and far between.

Next morning another boiler had been warmed up then connected to the auxiliary lines, with the first one being shut down. They were all to be tested alternately during the week.

Also, it was the turn for the after turbogenerator to be started up on load alternately with the other one during the week. Walt and myself arrived early each day to start one up using a different boiler. Both machines completed their trials with flying colours without a moment's anxiety, which was a good start.

The next Monday No. 1 Starboard boiler was flashed up with the auxiliary stop valves open to supply its own pumps and forced-draught fan along with one of the turbogenerators which was charged daily to supply lighting and power to test all the machinery driven by large electric motors.

We also tested all secondary wiring which had been installed in the machinery spaces and hangars for ventilation and lighting. When complete, each of these compartments could be lit up by a flick of a switch. In this way he gradually replaced the string of lamps hanging around the ship as work continued installing the circuits in the living space, offices, stores and magazines.

The saturated-steam lines were thoroughly tested along with the evaporators, the oil-tank heating coils (for use in Arctic conditions), the bug binder (for sterilising foul linen or dirty hammocks), calorifiers (for heating up the cold water), and the sirens (for making sure that all other vessels kept clear of our ship's course).

The auxiliary superheated ring main, including bulkhead and cross-connection valves, were fully opened out to test out the remaining pipes and machinery in the boiler rooms, which so far had not been used. They were the spare oil-fuel pumps, the auxiliary feed pumps, turbo-driven fans, all the fire and bilge pumps (which were tested on the bilge suctions) and fire mains to supply water.

The rest of the outlying machinery was then tested out. It consisted of two steam-driven hydraulic pumps for the lifts and catapult, along with the suction and discharge hydraulic pipes systems, which extended to the wireless masts, the windbreak barriers and arrester wires.

Ted, Taff and myself visited the various compartments to get genned up on the various machinery as it was being tested. We started off by visiting one of the two Peter Brotherhood high-pressure air compressors, which were Taff's part of ship. They were being tested by the firm's rep. He opened up the line to one of the six large reservoirs, which were each filled in turn up to the pressure of 4,000 pounds per square inch. The compressed air was for use with the catapult, the starting motor for the emergency diesel generating sets, for blowing out the gun barrels after firing, and for powering the small motor which drove the torpedoes. The air pressure was reduced where necessary.

The rep opened up all the drains, then turned the starting handle in stages, pausing to allow the compressor to gather speed before turning it to the next notch. Soon it was running at full speed, filling the room with a terrific din as it grunted, then sucked in great gulps of air. The first stage of the compressor changing note as the other three stages gradually built up their pressure. Milky-white water flowed from the drains as the damp air was compressed. They were shut down to a steady trickle so as to build up the air pressure. The compressed air was then cooled before entering the reservoir.

Once several reservoirs were full, we left to watch one of the two Revell low-pressure air compressors being tested. Much the same procedure was used to start up, but the machine was higher revving, making much more of a clatter. The small reservoir was soon topped up to the working pressure of 150 pounds when the relief valves lifted, then started to blow, changing into a hissing sound until the pressure dropped.

The air was piped around the boiler and engine rooms to blow through blocked pipes or to test condensers, etc.; also for the forge in the coppersmith's shop; and last, but not least, for blowing aviation spirit up from the tanks, then blowing back through the lines to keep them empty, otherwise a leak or a burst pipe would soon become a huge fireball.

During the next few days we visited numerous tests being carried out around the ship. Ted's compartment consisted of the main hydraulic lift and catapult turbo steam pumps below deck. They had been started up then left ticking over ready for use, at which time they would suddenly speed up and scream into action. Meanwhile all the upper-deck machinery was tested out. Then we went on the flight deck for a ride down on one of the lifts. A starting handle was inserted into the deck then turned a quarter of a turn causing the lift to move steadily downward (accompanied by the ringing of a warning bell to alert anyone standing near the edge of the lift that a sudden sheer drop of up to thirty-three feet had opened up). It passed through the upper hangar to the lower hangar, then the handle on the lower part of the extended shaft was turned the other way causing the lift to move steadily up to the top where it formed part of the flight deck.

At the end of the month I joined Chief ERAs Rodgers and Williams to wander around the four engine- and boiler-room compartments We took notes of all the various valves' positions and details as the Harland men prepared all four boilers and both sets of engines to be tested together. No. 1 Starboard boiler was used as auxiliary to supply all the superheated and saturated steam by opening up all the necessary cross-connection and bulkhead valves and lines to supply all four compartments with steam.

The main stops on the other three cold boilers were opened wide along with the steam lines' bulkhead valves and throttle valves in each of the engine rooms. The boilers were then flashed up from cold taking four and a half hours to raise a full head of steam, warming up the pipelines and engines at the same time. All the air cocks and steam cocks opened along the pipelines until they began to blow hot water and steam violently, then they were eased down gradually until they were shut off.

Meanwhile we watched the auxiliary machinery being warmed through with exhaust valves open, then started up in both engine rooms. Then we split up, with Chief ERA Rodgers returning to the boiler rooms, and Chief Bungy Williams descending to the starboard engine whilst I stayed down the port one.

The Drysdale main condenser circulating pumps were the first to be started to keep the condenser cool. Then the extraction pumps were started along with the contraflow valves to maintain the water level in the bottom of the condensers. The turbine drains were left open. The lubricating-oil pumps were also started to supply both sets of port and starboard engines and gearing with lubricating oil at 45 pounds pressure around the system reduced to 12 to 15 pounds pressure on each bearing. The lubricating system had recently been cleaned out, with about 2,000 gallons of lubricating oil added to each of the bilge tanks from 50-gallon oil drums. It had been circulated round each of the systems by pumps around the ahead and astern turbine bearings, the single reduction helical gear bearings, then on around the Michelle thrust blocks with kidney pieces which took the whole thrust from the propellers to move the ship. The oil was then returned via the oil filters. Special filters were added to ensure no metal flakes or grit still lurked in the system, which could have damaged the soft white-metal bearings causing the journals to score and overheat. In that case the turbine would have to be shut down to prevent the white metal from melting and running out. The oil then continued to be pumped around the coolers back into the tanks. The special filters were then removed along with all the foreign matter. The usual filters were cleaned out so the systems were ready for use.

After a long wait the turbine temperatures reached 160°F so that the throttles were shut down with the gland steam turned on to seal the turbine labyrinth glands as the air ejectors were started to raise the vacuum to 20 inches in both condensers. Then each engine prop shaft was turned two revs ahead, then two revs astern alternately, then to stop for three minutes spread over one hour (this was done in order that the ship did not strain at her moorings and break away).

Whilst this was going on the main feed pump was started up on the extraction-pump discharge to feed the boilers. Also, when required, in the port boiler room the oil-fuel heater and pump were started up along with the auxiliary feed pump. All four forced-draught fans had been run up for testing with their louvres open and airlock doors shut.

One day I joined Taff down below to watch the test on the Weirs evaporators, which consisted of three large drums in each of the two high sets. Each drum contained twelve double 2-inch copper heating coils, whose function was to boil up the seawater. The seawater changed into steam vapour, which filled each drum before passing through a set of baffles and a regulating valve opened about two turns to adjust the flow of the steam so as not to carry any solids up with it into the condenser. A pressure of about 15 pounds of steam was admitted into the coils to boil up the seawater, which was kept at half a glass. It covered the first few bottom coils to create the steam, which then passed through the upper coils.

Each set had its own condenser to cool the steam back into fresh water. There was a set of three combined pumps, one of which pumped the water, or condensate, discharging it into the boiler feed tanks to make up any losses of water through the numerous steam and water gland leaks around the various systems; also to the ship's tanks for domestic purposes of cooking, washing and cleaning.

The second pump supplied the seawater into the drums for the coils to boil up, as well as the cooling water for the condenser.

The third pump was connected to the brine valves near the bottom of each drum, which were finely adjusted a crack from an eighth to a half turn open, so as to maintain a regular density. The water was tested at intervals by the killick or stoker of the watch who drew a potful of brine from each drum to test it with a hydrometer. He also tested the condensate by filling up a test tube with water, then adding several drops of silver nitrate which would turn milky if contaminated (in which case the water was switched to the bilge until he had adjusted the set and the test tube showed it was clear).

A gradual build up of brine around the coils caused a loss of output, which occurred periodically. This loss of water was restored at regular intervals by emptying the brine pan, then allowing the coils to get boiling hot before suddenly letting the seawater flood in. This caused the coils to contract so the thick coating of brine cracked off. It could be collected then scraped out of the pan through a small door at the bottom and the supply of fresh water would be brought back to its normal output.

We moved off to watch the catapult being tested by compressed air, which hurled a pile of sandbags over the bows. We also watched the wireless masts being extended outward, then raised again by hydraulics. The windbreak and the two barriers were raised and lowered the same way. The arrester wires were pulled out by a tractor then allowed to slither back into position across the deck.

Next we climbed up to Hookey Walker's part of the ship to the wheelhouse directly under the bridge, where we heard the sirens being blown for the first time. Also, we watched the engine-room telegraphs being tested to ring down from stop to full ahead and astern, then up to 240 rpm on both port and starboard indicators. The wheel was spun around to work the telemotor system, which operated a set of valves on each of the hydraulic pumps via two long small-bore copper pipes filled with hydraulic oil. When the pumps were running these valves would respond by opening to supply rams with enough oil to turn the rudder the amount of degrees shown on the wheel indicator to port. When the wheel was brought back to midships or so many degrees starboard the flow of the pumps was reversed by opening another set of valves which sucked the oil from the rams in use to discharge it into two opposing rams that had received the last order.

The island structure was positioned on the starboard side of the flight deck. The main armaments for protection were two multiple pom-poms, one for'ard and one aft. All the main compartments had been painted out and completed with power and electric lighting. The bridge was situated on the top deck, facing for'ard. A small swing bridge alongside could be drawn out over the deck so that the captain could see over the port side when manoeuvring the ship in harbour or confined spaces.

The captain's sea quarters lay aft of the bridge (so he could be called immediately when his expert judgement was required). The wheelhouse was directly below the bridge. The wheelhouse was completed with the port and starboard engine-room telegraphs coupled up. The steering wheel had been installed to transmit its orders in degrees port or starboard to the steering gear that controlled the rudder via the telemotor system, which transmitted them via two small-bore copper pipes. A box compass was installed in front of the wheel for the quartermaster to steer a course given him from the bridge through a speaking tube. He would be given orders of how many degrees to turn the wheel port or starboard, and the orders for the engine rooms — slow, half and full ahead or astern with number of revs per minute.

There was also the wireless cabin for broadcasting and receiving equipment and a radar cabin, complete with a scanner, wired up to a pick-up at the top of a long mast. (The mast operated like a long eye, with a vision of thirty miles beyond the horizon, and was able to detect an enemy surface ship or aircraft in a dense fog.)

The funnel jutted out of the island complete with sirens and waste pipe to release steam from the safety valves. Higher up from the bridge was the base of the mainmast, which had a crow's-nest near the top for the lookout; also the yardarm where several halyards hung for the bunting tosser to fly his flags to send out messages to the fleet. He kept the flags in pigeonholes when not in use. Also, there was a hand Aldis lamp for flashing out Morse messages along with the searchlights and the red and green navigation lights.

Below the wheelhouse was Fly Co's controlling office and platform for directing the flying operations as he could see exactly what was going on down below on the flight deck. Also, he was in a handy spot to confer with the captain and keep in touch with the pilots whose waiting room was aft on the flight deck below. This was handy for them to nip out and man their aircraft when required.

When everything had been completed, including the guns, the heavy weight of the island was counterbalanced by ingots of pig iron which were piled into specially constructed bunkers down below on the port side of the ship. A tilt test was then applied to the ship to ensure it was well found and balanced in perfect trim. Also the propeller shafts were realigned with their bearings bolted down.

Both hangars were completed with groups of lighting, sprinkler system, twin hoppers for making foam to smother any fires, and the fire hydrants with their usual valves, nozzles and hoses. Several small sumps were let into the deck to drain any spillage overboard through long scupper pipes with flap valves at the ends to prevent the seawater flooding back if the ship listed too far over for any reason. Each hangar was divided into three sections by two fire curtains. There were several battery chargers fitted around the hangar sides to charge up the batteries which were contained in boxes on wheels for starting up some makes of aircraft.

There was a number of aviation-spirit filling valves along with some high- and low-pressure air valves around the sides. The deck had numerous flat securing rings welded to it to fasten strops when striking down the aircraft (securing).

The galleys had been completed then painted out. Their ventilation systems were installed, along with white tiled decks with all the necessary working tables, sinks, boilers, steam and electric ovens, benches and stools, dough mixers and spud peelers, etc. The offices were equipped with desks, chairs, cupboards and racks, bins and pigeonholes, etc. The magazines were equipped with shell and bomb racks and cradles for the 18-inch torpedoes. The keyboard flat was fitted out with a small desk for the marine who was responsible for issuing keys for all the ship and the rifle rack.

The last of the messes had been completed with the last of the sandblasting to remove all the rust from the top, bottom and sides. The cleaning had been carried out and all the portholes cut out along the sides where possible. All the ventilation trunking with louvres, starters and electric fans, along with all the electrical fittings, switches and bulbs, had been installed throughout the ship.

All hammock bars and hooks had been welded up, spaced at 18 inches apart, alternately facing opposite ways to accommodate the next row from for'ard to aft so they all moved together at each roll of the ship. They were welded up in all messes, locker flats and passages high up out of the way, and then they were painted black. Also, hammock bins (or netting) were installed nearby and then painted with aluminium paint. All messes, cabins, offices, etc. were painted out (mostly in white) after cork granules had been stuck on the deckheads and ship sides to prevent sweating and painted mostly in white. All the corticene had been laid in the living spaces fore and aft. In the captain's quarters and keyboard flat, the wardroom, pantries and cabins and offices, with a wide strip of corticene running down the passages, also in the for'ard mess decks, locker flats, in between the rows of lockers and messes. All deck spaces with obstructions or fittings such as hammock, bins or lockers secured to them were first painted with red lead to prevent them rusting.

The island's cabin compartments and passages were also fitted out in a similar manner. The furniture for the captain's quarters and officers' wardroom had been installed with a large table and chairs, with a large sideboard for serving up from. The cabins were fitted out with bunks, wardrobes, drawers and small wash bowls with mirrors.

Our mess was situated for'ard on the port side on a level with the upper deck. From the door entrance, along the ship's side, lay the hammock bin painted with aluminium along with two dozen aluminium lockers in pairs on top of one another, secured to the deck, which had already been red leaded beneath them. Thick corticene had been laid and stuck down on the deck in the pantry, as well as the mess right up to the locker fronts to form a gangway. We had two tables secured to the deck. The long one had a loose bench running alongside it to form the inner side of the gangway, with cushioned seats along the inner wall. A short table lay thwartships at the end of the mess, with a cushioned seat backing on to the pantry wall and a loose bench on the opposite side of it for the chief ERAs.

All the hammock hooks and bars had been welded up into place, also the fan trunking and its louvres along with the lights and fittings had been completed. All the chiefs' and petty officers' messes were fitted out in a similar manner, with a pantry (for use by two seamen or stoker messmen), a serving hatch, a sink with hot- and cold-water taps, a draining board, a worktop for dishing up the meals, an electric oven (to keep them hot), a multi-sliced toaster, several drawers and racks for cutlery and crockery, and a small cupboard for brushes and cleaning gear.

The chiefs' and petty officers' messes had the option of being painted out in several light pastel colours so we had ours painted out in a light green.

All the plumbing was completed from the freshwater tanks to the calorifiers where the cold water was pumped to. It was heated up from there on and was split up into two systems, namely the hot and cold. They ran around the ship for wash bowls and baths, etc. in the captain's and officers' quarters aft; a sink for the photographic darkroom; washbasins and showers for the crew's bathrooms; wash bowls for the dentist; wash bowls and a bath for the sickbay; and sinks, etc. for the for'ard and aft galleys' and the chiefs' and petty officers' mess pantries.

There were also seawater pipes for flushing out various heads and urinals from the fire main, along with taps for flushing down the decks (including the bathrooms). All large and small drainpipes had been completed to discharge overboard. Some of the bathrooms (including ours) were positioned below water level. They had all the waste water draining into sumps so they could be emptied overboard by weird and wonderful ejectors. They were operated by the pressure from the fire-main water, which rushed through venturis sucking up the water in the sumps then discharging it overboard through seacocks.

All the various bathrooms were completed then painted out, with white tiled decks, lighting and ventilation trunking. Our bathroom had four small air louvres, twelve wash basins and six showers, along with duckboards. There were also two large round tin baths for dhobiing hammock covers, blankets or overalls, and sometimes were used for having a good warm bath in. There was an adjoining changing room, through an arched doorway, with corticene laid on the deck. It had a long wooden bench and two dozen small long narrow lockers mounted in pairs above one another (for our towels, washing and shaving gear, shoes and overalls), where we could change before going on watch.

All the magazines were completed, cleaned and painted out with their seacock and flooding valves, along with the sprinkler-system valves (for cooling the atmosphere) having extension rods to a small locked flooding cabinet on the deck above containing handwheels with cotter pins inserted. Only ERAs or other responsible people could draw the keys from the marine sentry in the keyboard flat.

The Carley floats had been hung on the starboard side beneath the island. All the motor boats (powered by Perkins diesels) had been hoisted up by the port crane then lowered onto their cradles on the platform decks. The aircraft-lighter lifting gear had been installed aft, under the sloping deck, which was rounded off for aircraft landings-on. The lighter had been winched up in position after the power had been switched on.

The Advance Parties Arrive

One Monday Taff, Ted and myself reluctantly bade farewell to our landlady, settling up the score of 35/- a week for the last time, and collecting our ration books. Then we waited for the transport, which was touring around the area picking up all the lads who had been standing by the ship, with our kitbags and hammocks, etc. before arriving at the dockside where the ship was moored. She looked much more inviting with her freshly painted hull than she did when we first arrived.

We unloaded our gear, then clambered up the long steep gangway with it, dumping our baggage in the mess and our toolboxes in the fitting shop. We mustered outside the jaunty's office to have our names entered in the ship's log, along with our rank, mess and part of ship. We also had our names added to the rum list for the daily tot. Then we went back to the mess for the chief to allocate our lockers and slinging billets, then stowed our gear in our lockers. The messes had been thoroughly cleaned out and were fully illuminated, so we stowed our hammocks in the bin, then waited for everyone to turn up.

Only two more ERAs arrived with the first contingent of about 200 men from Guzz (Devonport), bringing the number in our mess up to ten.

Once they had all settled in we all went ashore for the first of our meals. This was organised by the pay bob as a stop gap until he had arranged for all the necessary provisions and utensils to be shipped aboard so that the cooks could get organised to produce the meals in their galleys.

As the ship was still the responsibility of the builders, they provided the men for the auxiliary boiler for the turbogenerator to supply the power and lighting, the steam for the hot water, as well as the cold water and the fire main around the ship — especially for flushing the heads and swabbing the decks or washing mud off the anchor. Also there were many small jobs to be tidied up and completed around the ship. So, during working hours, there were no sentries posted on the gangways. Also, from then on, everything was chaotic as the naval routine clashed with the work routine.

From 16.00 to 08.00 the gangways were manned; also, daily leave was granted with chiefs and petty officers ticking off in the jaunty's office to go ashore, then cross ticking when coming aboard.

On Friday we paid our final visit to HMS *Caroline* at Donegal Quay to surrender our ration books, then collected our pay from the usual Jenny Wren killick writer.

During the next few weeks vast quantities of stores and boxes of spares kept arriving. They were hoisted up by the dock crane, which lifted them right onto the lift so they could be lowered down the lower hangar, where they were piled up ready to be manhandled by parties of seamen and stokers.

Unlike a merchant ship, with large open hatches which gave direct access to the cargo holds where goods could be easily lifted in or out to be discharged on the jetty, loading an aircraft carrier or any warship, with all its bulkheads plus subdivisions and decks, was a nightmare. After leaving the lower hangar on a level with the upper deck cargo (provisions and armaments) had to be distributed around various nooks and crannies to be stowed away below the main deck in storerooms on the lower platform or hold deck (where all the magazines were situated). To reach their final destination, light to heavy packing cases, packages, cardboard cartons and sacks had to be manhandled onto small hand trucks. They passed through passages, over ramps (to get over the high bulkhead door coamings) and down hatches (sometimes with the ladders removed to get large boxes lowered down by block and tackle), then across mess decks until they reached a labyrinth of stores. Here the supply staff opened up the containers to check their contents against their lists before stowing the goods in the various racks and bins provided.

Most departments had their own ready-use stores. The bosun's store required coils of rope and steel hawsers, drums of paint of the various basic colours, and paintbrushes and cans, etc. The EAs store required bulbs, switches, fuse wire and carbon brushes for the DC motors and generators. The OAs required spare parts for their guns, hydraulic oil and greases. The shipwrights (chippies) required a large assortment of nails, screws and fittings and also various sorts of wooden planks of different thicknesses and lengths. The engineers' department required a vast range of equipment with various oils and greases, acetylene and oxygen bottles for welding, CO_2 bottles for refrigeration, various other bottles, permanent and consumable tools like 14-pound hammers, hammers, chisels, hacksaw blades, packing tools, taps, stocks and dies, nuts and bolts, chain blocks, lifting tackle with strops, gags for boiler pilot valves, spare sight glasses for boilers and condensers, etc., tube expanders, reamers, drills, lathe tools, milling cutters, steel and brass bars for turning, rods for electric welding, hollow punches, steam and water packing for glands, rubber insertion and Permanite for pipe joints, as well as a host of other items.

Spare parts for each piece of machinery in the ship were distributed to their own or adjacent compartment as well as the workshop, fitting shop, and engine and boiler rooms. They were all dealt with by Harland's. Heavy machinery was secured to walls or decks with steel bands to prevent them moving.

The paymaster was responsible for victualling the ship, aided by his staff of writers who made up the ledgers for our weekly pay. They also ordered up the huge amounts of provisions to keep the ship's company fed for a month. The supply staff under the chief or PO (Jack Dusty) were responsible for keeping stock of the goods as well as issuing out the daily provisions for the galley, and such items as tea, sugar, tinned milk, margarine, jam and marmalade for the messes.

Once the daily menu had been made out, Jack Dusty's staff would move goods from the main store to his ready-use store (such as tea chests, bags of brown sugar and cartons of milk, etc. for the messes). Then items for the galley, such as sacks of flour and yeast for the bread, meat, eggs or dried egg, sides of bacon, tins of corned beef, pilchards, tomatoes, and a host of other items such as salt, etc. were moved. Vegetables, such as sacks of potatoes and crates of cabbage, were kept separately, conveniently near the galley.

Each forenoon Jack Dusty and the jaunty, who were equally responsible for the issue of the daily tot of rum or grog, opened up the store to draw out the required number of bottles, taking great care to lock it again. They measured out so many tots for each mess according to the number of men. Any grog left over was ditched overboard from the barrel. No one was allowed to bottle it as it was powerful stuff and made one drowsy.

When empty, the earthenware brown jars, with their strong basketwork around them, were returned to the store along with all the copper measuring devices, jugs and funnels. Special precautions were taken when a consignment of rum jars were delivered to the ship. They were carefully counted and guarded before being locked away with an extra-strong lock and key in a store of their own. The reason was that it was duty-free, like tobacco, cigarettes, Ticklers and wine for the wardroom. They were all treated with equal care, having come from bonded warehouses untaxed.

Other stores contained slops (ratings' clothing from caps to boots or shoes could be purchased by filling in a slop chit and signing it), and cleaning gear such as scrubbing brushes, brushes, dishcloths, Pussers Hard yellow or soft soap, cleaning cloths, bundles of cotton waste for cleaning up oily messes down below, and even mundane squares of brown toilet paper. The duty-free tobacco included leaf (which could be made up into a brick of tobacco), as well as tinned shredded pipe tobacco and Tickler tobacco in tins for rolling fags.

Also in the stores were the various pots and pans for the galley, large deep serving dishes used to distribute the grub for each mess, combined tea and sugar boxes, plates and other crockery, cutlery, mess kettles (for washing up the dirty plates, etc.), tea infusers and teapots for each mess.

After the first few weeks these articles were issues to the various messes as required, along with cleaning cloths and brushes, soap and dishcloths. Our one messman went down to the store with the chief to draw all the items for the full mess of twenty-two hands (another messman was added when the ship was fully commissioned on 12 March 1943).

We had to wait until the two cold and cool rooms had been washed out all ready for the sides of meat to be hung up; and also the racks cleaned to take bags of offal and boxes of cooking fat, etc.

Meanwhile, Cyril and Charlie, my main watchkeepers, started to prepare the refrigerating plant ready for running.

The first job was to locate the forty spare CO_2 bottles for two complete charges of gas in the system, as well as several others to top up the plant, then find the regulating chief stoker to organise a working party to move them from the lower hangar. This was no easy job as they weighed 180 pounds and had to be lowered down two hatches to the adjacent compartment where all the bottles were stored and clipped upright around the room.

Then we acquired a drum of non-freezing oil for the compressor glands, a candle for securing on the deck in an out-of-the-way corner so it would not get knocked over. It was secured by lighting it, then allowing the hot grease to drip on the deck, then sticking the lighted candle on top of it where it stayed lit until their was a bad CO_2 leak which would snuff it out through lack of oxygen. Also we acquired a taper which was lit to be used around the compressor glands. The flame would be snuffed out if there was a leak. Also we acquired two empty cans and two paintbrushes, one for a solution of soapy water to be brushed around pipe joints when searching for leaks (which were shown up by a stream of bubbles); and the other can to be filled with non-freezing oil to brush around the piston-rod glands when they started to heat up.

Now we were ready to prepare the system for starting up. The first step was to start up the exhaust and supply fans, then open up the sea inlet and sea discharge valves overboard, and finally start up the circulating pump to the condenser to keep it cool.

The next job was to prepare the compressor for starting by checking the level of oil in the sump, then filling up the non-freezing oil pump by pumping back the piston until the cylinder was full. The gas would exert a pressure on it, so that it kept the gland seals flooded to retain the gas. The next job was to open up the regulating valve two and a half turns, along with the inlet manifold valves, one turn open, with the return valves fully open so that the gas could pass through the strainer back to the suction side of the compressor. Now the only thing left to do was to open up the suction and discharge valves on the compressor and start it up. As the gas completed each cycle it was discharged into the condenser at a high temperature to be cooled and liquefied, then passed on through the regulating valve where it was allowed to expand and change its state from liquid to gas in the evaporator or grids of piping hung up in the cold and cool rooms. It then made its way back through the scale trap to the suction side of the compressor where it was discharged to begin another cycle. After half an hour's running the temperature began to settle down a little with the gas pressure in the evaporator beginning to drop from 200 to 300 pounds to about 20 pounds with the grids beginning to freeze, gradually dropping to 18°F in the cold rooms, and 38° to 40°F in the cool room. From time to time the regulator had to be shut down a crack to maintain a pressure of about 800 pounds in the condenser in home waters (or about 1,200 pounds in the tropics), to ensure the gas temperature in the condenser remained higher than the cooling seawater temperature to transfer some of its heat so that the gas liquefied. After several hours' running the regulator had been closed to one and a half turns open and the cold rooms' manifold inlet valves had to be shut down to a quarter of a turn as they were starving the cool rooms of all the gas. Once down to temperature the plant was shut down.

Every hour the room temperatures were checked on a remote-control recorder dial by turning a handle to connect up to the different rooms, which swung the needle around to indicate the correct temperature. The rooms also had thermometers on the end of a long rod, which could be withdrawn from a long sealed tube to read them. We also tested the pipe joints, which were made of copper diamond-shaped rings, for leaks by applying a good strong mixture of soapy water around each joint with a paintbrush. Several had a slight leak causing a stream of bubbles to be blown out. The two bolts which held the flanges together were tightened up to squeeze the copper ring until the bubbles stopped. They were all tightened up with a large special chrome-vanadium ring spanner which was extra-strong so it could be made in a thin hexagon to fit around the nuts (a normal spanner of that size had thick jaws which prevented it from fitting on the nut). Sometimes a bolted pipe joint would spring a leak which was hard to detect as there were a hundred or more joints made around the system. Each one had to have soapy water applied until the bubbles appeared, which was a long job.

Then we turned our attention to the daily logbook:

No. of compressors in use: 1 or 2.
Time started/time stopped.
Times rooms were opened and shut for daily supplies and restocking.
Total hours run per day.
No. of circulating pumps in use: 1, 2 or 3.
Condenser cooling water, in/out temp.
Condenser or compressor discharge:
    Pressure up to 1,800 pounds.
    Temperature up to 180°F.
Evaporator or compressor suction:

Pressure up to 200 to 300 pounds.

Temperature up to 180°F.

Adjust regulator: from 2 or 2½ turns down to 1 or 1½ turns.

Adjust manifold discharge valves: from 1 turn down to ½ or ⅛ of a turn.

Temperatures in:

No. 1 cold room and No. 2 cold room: 12° to 18°F.

Cool room: 38° to 40°F.

Ice tank: 15°F.

Cool-water tank: 40° to 45°F.

In tropics, pre-cooler in use:

No. of ice blocks issued out of 24 blocks.

Signed: *Stoker E. Brown*.

After taking the hourly readings, careful adjustments had to be made to the various valves to ensure that the rooms were kept down to the right temperatures, especially the cold rooms after they had been opened up for the daily supplies of meat.

The ambient ship temperature and seawater temperature around the UK coastline affected the running hours of the compressor, which was stopped and started several times a day when the rooms reached their correct temperatures.

The warm currents of the Gulf Stream can be detected in the English Channel. The effects of the extra warmth can be seen in various places around the coast of Cornwall, where palm trees grow. The currents curve around into the Irish Sea, passing by the Isle of Man, then to Rothesay and up the Firth of Clyde where more palm trees grow. Then the Gulf Stream carries on northward, melting the ice floes into pack ice between Greenland and Iceland, as well as around the Kola Peninsula to Murmansk (making it the only ice-free port along that part of the Russian coastline).

Hourly checks: Check piston-rod gland-seal pump, keeping it topped up with non-freezing oil and pumped up; check both piston rods for leaks by applying a lighted taper to the glands, which would be snuffed out by any escaping gas; then immediately check the compressor discharge temperature to ascertain that it's not overheating at 180°F or above (if so it is a sure sign of gas shortage, in which case add one bottle of gas to the system); make sure the piston rods are not overheating, as they would change colour to blue, then dull red, and start smoking, making long score marks down each rod (if so apply extra lubrication with a paintbrush). Then, in all cases of malfunction and sudden alterations in pressure or temperature ring the chief stoker or the engineer's office to have me or the duty ERA piped over the tannoy.

On the day before the cold rooms were loaded up, ready to take over a hundred tons of meat, the rooms were cleaned out with the doors shut tight, and dogged on completion so as to contain the cold. The refrigerating plant was then prepared for starting. A small 5-gallon drum of special non-freezing oil, with as high a viscosity as possible (thick and sticky), was opened to supply a small container for the gland-seal pump. This consisted of a small handpump which discharged its oil through a non-return valve into the front of a long cylinder. The oil acted on the front of a piston, with a rod indicator sticking out from the front to indicate the position of the piston, and was pumped to the back of the cylinder when full. Then the piston was gradually pushed forward by gas to the other end of the cylinder where it was empty and had to be filled up again by pumping it back into the full position. This oil was fed to both piston-rod lantern rings to flood the packings to lubricate the rods which retained the gas pressure in the system. This could rise to 1,800 pounds pressure on occasions before the safety discs burst.

Failure to keep the cylinder full of oil at all times could result in scored piston rods and packings, causing a bad leakage of gas and causing the compressor to become U.S. (useless for service).

The compressor was then barred around. Then, with all the necessary valves being opened around the system, along with the condenser circulating pump and the fans, and with the candle lit in the corner, all was ready to turn the starting handle notch by notch in the starter box. The motor gradually worked up the compressor to a speed of 500 rpm to circulate the gas from hot to cold in this cycle around the system continuously through the night to be ready for storing the meat next day. The temperatures of the rooms were taken hourly, and adjustments were made to the valves so that all the various grids in the rooms were freezing.

Next day after breakfast the first refrigerated lorry arrived on the jetty for unloading. A party of seamen, who had been detailed off, were piped to assemble on the jetty under the charge of the PO supply rating, Jack Dusty, who was under the pay bob's command. He kept a tally of the number of sides of beef, pig and sheep carcasses, and square sacks of offal. His assistant killick attended to the opening and closing of the cold rooms and ensured that the meat was hung properly with an air gap between each piece. The cold rooms had been positioned under the stokers' mess on the lower deck, which was the shortest distance from the jetty — up the gangway on the upper deck, then down two decks. The party were clad in protective clothing and gloves as it was a cold job handling slabs of icy-cold meat. They were split up into relays: some were in the lorry, some handled the meat up the gangway to the first hatch on the upper deck, some took it down the ladder then across the mess deck to the next hatch, then finally some took it down the ladder to hang in the rooms.

Once the first lorry was unloaded the party stopped for stand easy, a brew-up and a warm-up before the next lorry arrived. Eventually, with pauses for a thaw-out by a glowing brazier, a smoke and a cup of tea they carried on until the job was completed.

Finally, after three hours or more the last of the carcasses had been hung and the loading party was fallen out as it was dinner time.

PO (Jack Dusty) and myself then went down below to check that the meat had been properly hung, and the sacks of offal had been stored separately with air space around each item, as the time spent manhandling the meat had caused it to thaw out a little, or a lot, depending on the season of the year or what part of the world the ship was tied up in.

The area of contact between any two pieces of meat touching together would remain several degrees above freezing, being insulated from the icy-cold air circulating around the room, causing the centre to go rotten (also tending to keep the room temperature up slightly). Eventually, when the rotten meat was discovered, it had to be ditched as it was unfit for human consumption. Once we were satisfied, the cold room door was shut tightly, dogged and securely locked up.

Then I returned to the compressor room to check the temperatures of the rooms on the extended temperature recorder. It read above 32°F as the meat had thawed out slightly and had taken some heat in whilst being manhandled aboard. Before pipe down I paid a quick visit to ensure the plant was working properly and the room temperatures were beginning to drop, before slinging my hammock and turning in.

Next forenoon the temperature of the rooms had begun to fall;

also the plant was showing signs of requiring more gas, as the lack of it caused the system to heat up so that the freezing evaporator grids began to thaw out. The first thing the watchkeeper and myself had to locate was the clip to fasten onto each bottle so it could be slung up with a strop from the scales. We had to draw this from the engineers' stores, then sign for it, before we could hang it on the ring attached to the deckhead in the bottle room. Then we slung up the bottle, which weighed 180 pounds, and connected the small-bore copper pipe which was connected from the bottle to the evaporator side of the system. Then the two valves were opened for the gas to flow into the system until a third of the gas was left in the bottle at the bottom. This began to freeze and liquefy and had to be forced out by a bucket of boiling water (which the bottle bottom was immersed in), until all the liquid had been changed into gas and the weight of the bottle had dropped to 140 pounds. Then the valves were shut and the bottle was removed back into the rack, then chalked up to indicate it was empty. Then the next bottle was lifted on and exactly the same routine was carried out until the system was fully charged.

Meanwhile, another small lorry arrived on the jetty with small boxes of yeast for the bread, margarine, lard, suet, dripping and a meagre supply of butter (which was severely rationed). These boxes were carted away on a small hand truck on the same route to the cool room where they were stowed away under lock and key.

For the next few days I paid numerous visits to the compressor room to make sure the regulator and manifold valves were set right. Once the room temperatures were down we were able to stop the machine for two or three hours at a time.

Orders were given to me to start up the second turbogenerator, so I went down to the for'ard one which was stopped, then switched on the lights along with the inlet and exhaust ventilation fans. I then checked the two inlet and outlet seacocks were open for the circulating water and then proceeded to crack open the auxiliary superheated bulkhead steam valve to allow the pipeline to warm up thoroughly until all the cold water had been expelled before opening the valve wide. Too much steam would cause a massive steam hammer which violently hammered in the pipes as if trying to break its way out as it caused the pipes to jump and vibrate in a terrifying manner as if about to fall apart. As the pipes got hot the drains were eased down to a whisper of steam, then shut off.

The condenser air cocks were then vented to allow any trapped air to escape. Then the gland steam was opened up on the labyrinth gland seals on the shaft to prevent any air being sucked into the condenser where a vacuum was being created by turning on the air ejector. Once the vacuum had risen to 20 inches the vacuum trip steam valve was set to allow steam to pass through it from the throttle valve which was cracked open. Immediately after, I started to crank a small oil pump to flood the turbine and gearing bearing with oil until the mechanical pump started to show over 30 pounds on the pressure gauge.

The pump was geared to the turbine along with two other pumps: the circulating pump for cooling the condenser and the extraction pump which took its suction from the condensate in the bottom of the condenser where it was maintained at half a glass of water by adjusting the discharge valve. The rest of the condensate was pumped to the overflow tank where it was automatically pumped back into the boiler feed system.

By now the set had started to hum pleasantly with the throttle valve wide open and the vacuum increased to 29.8 inches, with the gland steam set to show a wisp of steam escaping from each of the glands.

The pilot lights began to glow, and the finger on the voltmeter swung up to 230 volts, which indicated the set was ready for the board. I made sure the salinometer was showing a white light to indicate the condensate (water) was pure and made a final check before ringing the EA on the switchboard to report the turbogenerator was ready for load. I then watched the load building up on the ammeter as the board was made up, breaker after breaker, until the load had been shared out, showing at least 800 amps for both machines; then the governor and the gland steam were reset.

Then the generator was turned over into the care of one of Harland's men until the regulating chief stoker had organised his men for the various duties.

Next day I had to instruct the senior or killick stokers on their watchkeeping duties: to keep the compartment clean and tidy and pump out the bilges when necessary. Then, when preparing for a start up, switch on the lighting and the ventilation inlet and exhaust fans. Then check the seawater strainer to ensure it was not blocked up with any bits of paper, wood, seaweed or jellyfish, then open up the seawater suction and discharge seacocks for the condenser and oil cooling. Then check the air vents on the condenser to ensure there were no pockets of trapped air and then check the oil in the sump to ensure it was at the correct working level.

Once the set and board had been started up the gland steam and governor were adjusted when the load had been increased to anything up to full power of 1,600 amps at 230 volts or 400 kW DC. This was the maximum output of the generator, or at any time when the load was decreased. The extraction-pump discharge valve was adjusted to maintain half a glass of condensate in the bottom of the condenser, at the same time keeping an eye on the salinometer. If the white light changed to red it was a warning that the condensate was contaminated and to switch the extraction-pump discharge valve to bilge so as not to contaminate the boiler feed water. (In event of the water not clearing the load would have to be reduced so that the other generator could be loaded up to take it all. Then the turbo could be shut down so that a Canterbury test could be applied to find the faulty tubes in the condenser and the oil filter handle should be turned two or three times each watch to ensure no blockage occurred.)

Then the daily logbook had to be made up with hourly readings:

Time set was started, hours run per day and week, time when set
    was shut down.
Load in volts (230) and amps (850).
Steam pressure: 300 pounds.
Vacuum (in condenser): 29.8 inches max.
Condenser cooling water: in 50°F: out 65°F.
Oil temperature: 110° to 120°F.
Oil pressure: about 45 pounds.
Six bearing temperatures (up to 135°F): all defects noted.

Signed: *Two-Badge Stoker Smith*

All defects such as contaminated water, loss of vacuum, loss of oil pressure, hot-oil or bearing temperatures, or hot condenser, would be reported to the chief stoker or the engineer's office. The condition of sparking brushes on the dynamo would be reported to EAs on switchboard.

Finally, on 12 March 1943, the remainder of the ship's company arrived, so now we had a full mess (give or take one or two) along with the extra stoker messman. Our messmates consisted of the three chief ERAs who were all from the West Country. Rodgers was the senior chief (a boilermaker from Torpoint), Bungy Williams (a fitter from Brixham) and Fred Crate (a diver and fitter from Cornwall). Ex boys were: Hookey Walker and Ginger A. B. Evans (fitters and turners), and Jack Frost (a coppersmith). Direct Entries were: Taff Gunney (a fitter and turner from Cardiff), Ted Perkins (a boilermaker from Cornwall), Ed Hibbert (myself, a fitter from Cheshire), and Alf Seldon (a fitter and turner from Devonport). HOs (hostilities only) were: Jonno Johnson (a boilermaker from Cumbria), Taff Drinkwater (a fitter from Swansea), Tommo Thompson (a Scouse fitter from Liverpool), Jock Baxter (a Glaswegian fitter), Willie Franks (a Lancastrian coppersmith), Syd Chaffey (a coppersmith from Sheffield), and Hill and Drinnan (fitters from Bolton). Special Entries were: Syd Parkinson and Buck Taylor.

Our regulating chief was responsible for making out the lists for everyone's part of ship. Three watches for steaming were kept once the ship was being prepared for sea until she had returned to harbour then shut down. There were three watches for duty and leave, which meant, when leave was piped, anyone not on duty was free to go ashore providing the work he had been doing was boxed up ready for use. There was also a list for action stations made out to fit with one's watch below, which was worked normally through the whole shift, then, when relieved, we would muster at one of the magazine-flooding cabinets or one of the counter-flooding tanks.

The regulating chief stoker made out similar lists for his chiefs, POs, killicks and stokers, starting off with the cooks of the mess for each day, and permanent watchkeepers for the auxiliary boiler and auxiliary machinery — including motor-boat drivers, flight-deck party, and oiling party (which included freshwater and aviation spirit). Working parties were organised for various requirements which cropped up daily, such as boiler cleaning, duty and leave watches and steaming watches. Chiefs of the various other departments worked out similar lists.

When we were in harbour we were in three watches for duty for all emergencies. One was free to go ashore if not on duty when leave was piped. The chief ERAs, Rodgers, Williams and Crate, were in charge of the watches. I was in Chief ERA Williams' watch. Each ERA had a separate duty to perform. One was for the boiler room to take a pot of water from the steaming boiler to test it with a hydrometer for excess solids, and with silver nitrate for purity free from salts; also for changing dirty sprayers, broken gauge glasses or tightening up gland steam leaks. Another ERA looked after the motor boats and was called out any time of day or night (often having to climb onto the perilous boom and its swinging rope ladder with a bag of tools on a dark and stormy night with the boat pitching and tossing at its moorings in a terrifying manner). My job was to look after all the auxiliary machinery with repairs to the turbogenerators, refrigerating plant or evaporators, or start up the high- or low-pressure air compressors if necessary, or stow the lifts when required.

One of the young ERAs would attend the daily fire party, firstly to learn where all the different compartments in the ship were situated, so that everyone could muster on the right spot quickly in the event of a fire; secondly to know where all the fire hydrants were situated. Occasionally he would have hose drill to practise connecting up the hose, unrolling it rapidly, connecting the nozzle and switching on. He became accustomed to handling a hosepipe, which would snake about unless handled firmly, so the jet could be adjusted into a spray and directed overboard at the double. He also had to learn about the minor appliances and where they were stowed, such as small hand extinguishers, buckets of water (for putting out small fires) or buckets of sand (to smother small oil fires) as well as foam extinguishers. On no account was a water extinguisher to be used on electric fires. They had their own type of extinguisher. A water extinguisher on electricity was liable to give the operator a tremendous shock or a nasty burn.

I showed several young ERAs around where the four steam-driven fire and bilge pumps were situated in each of the engine and boiler rooms and told them which steam cross-connection and bulkhead valves to open so that they could be started, and also where the two electric ones were situated for'ard and aft. These electric ones were much easier to start, and speed was a vital factor in fighting a fire. Unlike on a battleship, where the pressure was 50 pounds on the upper-deck level (or the lower hangar level on a carrier), the pressure had to be increased to 80 pounds to reach the flight deck. For sea or anchor watchkeeping if a storm should suddenly blow up with the ship liable to drag anchor and be driven on the rocks, the duty watch would go down below to open up with steam on both engines for slow speed.

All hands were piped to clear the lower deck and fall in on the flight deck where the master-at-arms brought us all to attention. The captain suddenly appeared on the flight deck from the lift. We were stood at ease whilst the captain made the usual type of speech, with the usual guff about having a clean and happy ship to be kept shipshape and Bristol fashion, also that she had been built as a treble-purpose ship.

Firstly, she was built to serve the fleet carriers across the oceans in any part of the world as a floating repair ship, for which she was to carry a large Fleet Air Arm repair staff and a vast selection of spare parts for the various makes of aircraft in her extra-large stores, to keep them serviced and in good working order.

Secondly, as an aircraft carrier she was built to accommodate three squadrons of aircraft with pilots, crews and maintenance staff for warming them up and ranging them aft on the flight deck ready to take off or be catapulted off with the ship steaming into the winds with speeds up to 24 knots.

Thirdly, she was to be used as a fast ferry, being able to transport fifty or more aircraft up to the speed of 18 knots.

He also told us that our first job was to work the ship up to full efficiency, with every man having a good working knowledge of his part of ship. Also, that the ship would start off by training several Fleet Air Arm squadrons in the art of taking off and landing on the small confined area of the flight deck.

His final words were that he would grant as much leave as possible, but would deal with anyone adrift or defaulting severely. The jaunty then called us to attention whilst the captain disappeared down on the lift, then he turned us for'ard to dismiss.

The seaman's branch covered many jobs on the upper deck and above. There were specialist branches of seamen: the gunners, under the gunners' mate, who were already trained in gun drill but needed to know the different types of anti-aircraft guns they had to operate and their positions around the ship; torpedomen, who usually dealt with torpedoes but were needed as electrical artificers (EAs) mates to assist on the switchboard, electrical equipment, or operating the cranes, etc., the signalmen (bunting tossers), who needed to draw out all their various flags and pennants to store in the correct order in the pigeonholes provided on the signal platform, along with a portable Aldis lamp from the store for flashing out Morse code messages around the fleet; wireless, radar and telegraph operators, who needed to familiarise themselves with the layout of their equipment.

The seamen were split up into various parties along the upper deck and above under a chief or petty officer. They were responsible for keeping the deck clean and tidy, so they easily got into their daily routine of swabbing the quarterdeck and waist first thing.

The bosun (a chief PO) was in charge of a ready-use store where all the paintbrushes, chipping hammers, and paint was stored for the non-ceasing job of removing rusty patches on the hull, then repainting them. His party looked after these small patches, but if the hull or superstructure needed painting all seamen hands turned to the job. The bosun's party was responsible for slinging out the motor boats and the cutter, or hoisting them back into their cradles as required. Also, they were responsible for running out the gangways and the booms (for securing the motor boats to), for lowering the fenders as required, then stowing them all safely away again out of the way when the ship was preparing to go to sea, and keeping the upper deck shipshape and Bristol fashion.

Cable parties were piped to close up fore and aft when securing and berthing the ship alongside the jetty, or when tying up or casting a tanker off alongside, or when the cables required casting off for the ship to return to sea. The cable party was also piped to fall in on the fo'c's'le when required to weigh or drop the anchor.

The quartermaster (a PO seaman) was stationed on the quarterdeck near the after gangway to control the sentries; and near the various pipes for visiting high-ranking officers and also for the various pipes around the ship when in harbour. When special-duty men were piped to close up, he occupied the wheelhouse with his assistants to steer the ship on course. Two of his assistants operated the port and starboard engine-room telegraphs, whilst the third man made all the pipe calls for the daily orders over the tannoy system throughout the ship.

Other special-duty men were the port and starboard and crow's-nest lookouts, as well as the bridge messenger. Other parties were detailed off for the motor-boat crews, including the stoker for driving the engines.

There was a cutter's crew required as oarsmen to row around the ship and secure the anchor chain to the buoy, or for the diving party or other emergency.

All seamen when not on duty were required for lining the flight deck on entering or leaving harbour. There was a cleaner for the toilets (sometimes referred to as 'the captain of the heads' when someone was being sarcastic), as well as cleaners required for passages, flats or bathrooms down below.

The Cooks were already fairly well organised, but had to get used to producing large quantities of daily bread and food for the large influx of men.

The writers had to include many new names on their ledgers for the weekly payments.

Storekeepers were kept busy doling out all the equipment in stock, then reordering everything else that was required.

Sickbay attendants had to draw out bedding for the cots, ointments and medicines for the doctors and operating tools for the surgeons and dentists.

Stewards had to get used to serving in the captain's quarters and the officers' wardroom.

A solitary blacksmith drew out his tools and metal for his forge for repairing storm damage, such as bent guard rails or stoved-in doors or portholes, also for opening or closing the split anchor-chain link when tying up to the buoy.

The shipwrights drew out their stock of planks, nails, screws and fittings for repairing woodwork around the ship and the motor boats.

The electrical artificers (EAs) had plenty of equipment to locate all around the ship (from the switchboards to the electric lighting, electric motors and fuse boxes). They also needed plenty of spare bulbs, fuses and carbon brushes.

Ordinance artificers (OAs) had an assortment of anti-aircraft guns to look after around the ship and drew out from the stores the necessary greases, oils and spare parts to maintain them.

The damage-control headquarters was the nerve centre of the ship. Operated from one compartment down below, with all the emergency telephones (or blowers, as we called them) connected up to it from the mess decks, workshops, stores and offices around the ship. It was manned by officers from all the various departments, as well as some ratings. Also there was a permanent switchboard operator always on watch at sea, so that all calls were answered immediately.

If the ship's company was already at action stations the damage-control parties would already be at their stations, with the gun crews and control parties piped to close up at the double as there was always a bottleneck of men waiting at the bottom of the ladders from the mess decks.

One of the worst places for a fire would be the paint shop next door to the torpedo parting shop. There was a host of other places where a fire could start, especially if one of us was careless in throwing away a lighted stub. (We would normally throw our cigarette stubs into a spittoon.

There were plenty of fire hoses around the ship, especially on the upper-deck and mess-deck levels, where there were also sand and water buckets, and portable fire extinguishers (not to be used on electrical equipment, but could be used by any bod in the area to put out a small fire before it became a raging inferno). Once a fire had been tackled it was essential to use the blower and inform damage-control headquarters that it was put out so one of their staff could make sure it was thoroughly extinguished.

There were three damage-control substations with groups of all the various departments to tackle all kinds of jobs. Their tasks included reducing the list by shifting boxed equipment to the other side of the ship, or pumping out tanks to the other side where possible; pumping out flooded compartments; battening down hatches to starve a fire of oxygen; removing inflammable goods from one area to prevent them catching fire; coupling up the electrical supply or fire main; or any other job to make the ship safe on an even keel.

In event of any damage occurring at any other times the damage-control parties were piped to close up at the double.

Also damage control had a party to go around the fire-main system to check the hoses and valves to ensure there were no gland leaks and that there were no valves seized up, and to see that the fire and water buckets were kept full and there was nothing missing. They also ensured that the fire hoses were stretched out properly and kept thoroughly dried out.

The Admiralty always used CO_2 gas for its refrigerating plant. Although it is slightly toxic, it is not unpleasant to work with as it is odourless. It has no noticeable ill effects except in large quantities, when it can snuff out life as well as putting out fires. Its main disadvantage was that it worked at high pressure with direct expansion in the cold-room evaporator grids and also had gland leaks at regular intervals.

The merchant navy refrigerating plants, which were highly efficient, worked at low pressures with the evaporator cooling a brine tank, which pumped the brine in below freezing temperature around the large storage compartments. The big difference in ours was that the ammonia gas has a highly pungent smell and is corrosive, so it instantly affected one's eyes and nose if there was a leak. Consequently it would play havoc if it ever happened to escape into a mess deck.

My first call out was to tighten up a leaking gland seal on the CO_2 compressor. It consisted of four diamond-shaped rings of soft white metal above the lantern ring, which was kept flooded with non-freezing oil, with another four white-metal rings below it. These two sets of packing gripped onto both piston rods lightly to seal the gas as they moved up and down alternately, so eventually slight wear took place causing them to leak.

It was vital that any leak or defect should be dealt with immediately, or it would have a knock-on effect of having a room full of rotten meat on one's slop chit.

I tested the glands with a lighted taper to see which one was leaking, then searched around for the special C spanner, which was shaped to fit in the slots around the gland nut, and carefully tightened it up a fraction of a turn making sure not to be heavy-handed — which would instantly result in the rod heating up, then changing colour to blue, then a dull red along with a small cloud of smoke with long score marks appearing on the rod. However, being quite conversant with this type of gland I slacked it off immediately before any damage was done. Then gradually tightened it up again, making sure the gland-seal pump cylinder was kept full of oil with its piston back to its fullest extent, as well as coating the rod with oil which was slapped on in liberal quantities with the paintbrush. Within an hour the watchkeeper had charged the system with another bottle of gas until the compressor was running cool again and the plant was freezing properly. The gland cooled down with the leak sealed once again so I could depart without further worry.

The Day of Departure

Alas, the day of departure had arrived, which was a sad moment for a number of us who had become natives. I had an early shake at 04.00 for the morning watch to learn the layout and flashing-up routine down the port engine room. There were about thirty assorted valves or more to open, and numerous drains to open, then gradually we shut them as the steam dried out and the steam lines were free of water. Several lubricating-oil valves needed adjustment once the various pumps had been started up.

At 08.00, Jack Frost, the coppersmith, relieved me for a leisurely breakfast. After this the cables were cast off, and two tugs were tied up ahead and astern to tow the ship out into midstream. Suddenly the ships' sirens blasted out their mighty farewell hoots, so I joined a crowd of foremen, draughtsmen, fitters and dockyard mates, who had just come aboard to help with conducting the speed trials, logging and recording the various readings to obtain the speed and efficiency of the engines and boilers at various speeds. Some of the ships in the harbour joined in the hooting and all the dockyard workers downed tools to let out a massive cheer.

Soon one could feel the gentle vibration as the ship's engines started to turn, taking us past a series of buoys either side of the narrow channel down the River Lagan. Then I watched the ship progress through the narrow channel and noticed the gantries and cranes of the dockyard fade out of sight before making my way down below to make sure that my two turbogenerators and refrigerating machinery was working correctly. They were already manned by watches of stokers with the works representatives standing by in case of emergency,

My next visit was down the port boiler room, passing through the noisy fan flat where all four turbofans were screaming away. Then I passed on through the two airlock doors which always had to be left shut so the inner door could be opened against the forced draught in the boiler room of about 7 or 8 inches, which was required for the combustion of the oil fuel sprayed into the furnaces. The air had to be equalised on each side of the door before it would budge.

Once through onto the grating I shut the door then climbed down two short ladders onto the working platform. It was terrifically hot with a mighty roar from the boiler furnaces. Flickering red-hot balls of flames formed from a mist of fine oil spray showing out of the various chinks in the boiler facings. There were several Harland's men operating the controls sweating cobs along with several chiefs, POs and stokers watching the proceedings. Several draughtsmen were recording all the various hourly readings, such as steam pressure, temperature of superheated steam, oil pressure, temperature and consumption, number of sprayers lit up on each boiler, forced-draught air pressure, feed-water temperature, and funnel flues and room temperature to make charts to ascertain that the efficiency of the boilers was up to scratch.

My next visit was to the starboard engine room with all the senior officers who controlled the department when at a sea. But found it was full up with Harland's top-brass men and Admiralty inspectors. There was little room to move, let alone observe what was taking place, so I scampered back up the ladder.

Meanwhile the ship passed on through Belfast Lough with Holywood to starboard, then Carrickfergus with its small castle to port and the seaside of Bangor several miles ahead on the opposite side. She was soon passing over the North Channel up into the Firth of Clyde, heading for the measured distance between Paddy's Milestone and the tip of the Isle of Arran.

So far so good, everything was running well. I made my way back down to the port engine room which was nice and roomy, and quite comfortable to work in. This suited me because most of my working hours would be spent taking charge of a watch down there during the next two years.

The Harland men were in control, but I took over the throttle whilst they adjusted the auxiliaries. The foreman floated around the different compartments ensuring that none of the bearings became overheated, whilst the draughtsman logged all the hourly readings, then made efficiency graphs of the engines. He noted the revs per minute recorded on the tachometer; the steam pressure and temperature; condensate temperature; steam pressure and temperature of different stages in turbine, which showed a drop at each stage finishing up as a vacuum in the condenser (29.8 inches); expansion of turbine feet measured in fractions of an inch; the pressure and temperature of the closed exhaust steam to condenser and feed heater; the condenser and oil-cooler sea inlet and outlet temperatures; and the lubricating-oil pressures and temperatures for the turbines, gear case bearings, thrust block and plumber block.

An oil party dipped the double-bottom oil tanks in use for the hourly readings. To work out the oil consumption of the ship in tons they were armed with long steel tapes, marked off in inches and feet, starting from the 3 inches marked off from the bottom of a small brass weight. The tapes were unwound and lowered to the bottom of the tank via the sounding tube, then withdrawn so the depth of the oil was indicated by its level on the tape. This was recorded, then the tape was wiped clean ready for the next dip.

On approaching the measured mile the revs of the shaft were reduced to fifty for the first run then gradually increased for the following runs until full speed was reached. A countdown of ten seconds was relayed over the tannoy to give the draughtsmen time to set their stopwatches then record the revs shown on the tachometer. The oil-fuel tanks were also dipped.

At the end of the run, which was broadcast, the watches were stopped, the revs were taken and the oil tanks were re-dipped on the port and starboard sides to work out how much oil had been consumed by converting feet and inches into tons. Then the exact speed of the ship was worked out from how long the ship took to travel over the nautical mile (1 nautical mile per hour = 1 knot) at 50 rpm, which was increased at each run over the mile. It was essential to have a set of figures to refer to as different revs greatly affected the range of the ship, especially above speeds of 13½ knots, which was found to be the most economical speed. Every knot beyond this speed caused the oil consumption of the ship to rocket in leaps and bounds owing to the outside pressures greatly increasing on the hull at high speeds; e.g. a destroyer or smaller ship was liable to run out of oil fuel in mid-ocean if high speeds were maintained for long periods.

With all this activity the forenoon slipped by, so at eight bells I departed for my dinner, after which I climbed up to the flight deck for half an hour's breather and watched the coastline passing by and the purple heather on the hilltops, which was glistening in the sun, and several merchant ships with their dirty red dusters fluttering from the flagstaff as they passed in the distance.

At 13.30 I descended several flights of stairs into the engine room to take over the port throttles. The ship was still plodding up and down the measured mile, increasing speed by a few revs at every turn about. Then eventually the final order was rung down on both the port and starboard engines. It was 'full ahead'. It was answered with three rings on the bell, then '240 revs' which was answered with two rings on the bell. I opened up the throttle wide, then soon after the ship crossed the starting line for the last time. The circulator was run up to full speed, then started to whine. Steam began to pour out of the turbine glands and had to be adjusted so as not to heat the bearings; also, the cooling water to the oil cooler was opened wide. The note of the main turbines changed from a pleasant hum to a harsh whine as we passed the finishing line at full speed, which worked out at 23½ knots. But instead of slowing down steadily, out of the blue came the order 'full astern' on both engines (usually an emergency order), which was answered with three rings on the bell. I began to obey the order by shutting the ahead throttle. A feeling of exhilaration passed through my body as I swung on the valve. Commander E. Oliver told me to shut it as quickly as possible whilst he threw the astern throttle wide open to apply the most excruciating punishment that we could mete out to boilers, turbines and safety valves that they would ever have to suffer (like the reverse thrust on an aircraft as it is about to land but about tenfold more harsh).

Suddenly all hell broke loose as a cacophony ensued. The main feed pump roared away, the air ejector sucked away in gulps, the circulating pump whined, the main shaft rumbled, then the hissing steam screamed through the astern turbine blading, whining as it fought to stop the main prop shaft. The hull creaked and groaned at most of the rib joints in the ship, along with a terrific vibration.

Meanwhile down each stokehold every sprayer had been crammed on to keep the steam up to the red mark. The turbofans screamed overhead at full speed, trying to suck in extra inches of air to prevent the black smoke pouring out of the funnel. The glow from the flames lit up the beads of sweat rolling off the brows of the men as they flickered around the room. Then, shutting my throttle tight, the steam pressure shot up to 320 pounds momentarily, until the two full-bore safety valves suddenly lifted in unison with a terrific swooshing roar, bellowing forth literally tons of scalding water per minute up the waste pipe into the atmosphere. When the astern throttle was open wide they suddenly snapped shut as the steam had dropped to 280 pounds.

The ship seemed to drift ahead for ages before responding to the astern turbine pressure as the weigh kept her travelling ahead for several minutes, driving the propeller in a clockwise direction. Eventually the astern turbine stopped the prop with a short pause before beginning to turn anticlockwise. This was indicated on my tachometer by a small red dial, which stopped then reversed its direction. It gradually built up speed to 180 revs, indicated by a large black finger on the dial.

A further five minutes elapsed, then both engines reverted to half speed ahead at 120 revs, which was rung down on the telegraphs. The whole procedure was reversed until the ship came to a casual halt from astern. Then the little red finger started turning in a clockwise direction and the black finger slowly rose up to 120 revs on the tachometer. The noise abated as the speed of the auxiliary machinery had been slowed down, leaving the pleasant hum of the turbines in its place.

The engine trials were completed, the draughtsmen had finished working out their various sets of figures for the engines and boilers, and all the other parts of ship had been fully tested — i.e. the guns, lifts, cranes and flight-deck equipment.

The ship changed course, leaving the sheltered waters of the Firth of Clyde, steaming some fifty miles back over the North Channel to anchor for the night in Bangor Bay along with the derelict merchant liner *Georgic*. It had been gutted by fire and looked like an old rusty hulk from stem to stern, but was still afloat and swinging at anchor.

Having left the engine room after all the excitement of the day I went up for my tea, then returned there in readiness for entering harbour and shutting down (so as to know the routine for future reference after the ship was securely anchored).

The Admiralty had accepted the ship although there were several things to be finished off, such as the radar. Also there were several defects in the fan flat where the two starboard fans were taking more than their fair share of air, leaving the two port fans gasping for air. As a result the port boiler room got extra-hot and the burners were producing black smoke up the funnel (which was considered to be more or less a crime as it could be seen by an enemy for miles away on the horizon). Also, it became unbearably hot for the watchkeepers, so ducts had to be made to direct more air into the port boiler room.

Harland's flag was hauled down and the white ensign replaced it until sunset. A lighter, drawn by a tug, came alongside to take off most of Harland's men (the bigwigs, foremen, draughtsmen and any others not required on board to sort some minor problems), who quickly scrambled aboard to be taken up the river.

After shutting down and making notes of the various valves, I climbed the ladder and left the room to change out of my overalls. Then made my way to the flight deck for a breather and to collect my scattered thoughts whilst pacing fore and aft.

We had anchored in the small harbour of Bangor, a small holiday resort at the mouth of the Lagan. I watched a small Kelly's coal boat, which tied up alongside the jetty and soon started discharging its coal for household use. On the other side was the shipping lane which was quite busy with the comings and goings of several small coasters, all belching out different shades of black smoke. Then came the Burns Line ferry to Glasgow, heavily laden with troops who were singing as if going on leave, passed down the lough.

It was supper time, so I returned to the mess where the latest buzz had just been announced. The ship was returning upriver for some modifications and items, especially in the fan flat where it would take ten days to modify the air flow so that the port boiler room would get its fair share of air. (It turned out to be only partially successful, especially later on when the ship was steaming in the tropics).

Being in harbour I slung my hammock at 22.00, which was promptly after pipe down, then hopped in to get a good sleep before being shaken to go on watch below at 05.30 by the office messenger. After stowing my hammock I went down to the bathroom for a quick swill and then changed into my overalls in the adjacent locker room. Then climbed down the steep metal ladder to take over the watch in the port engine room, and was joined by my throttle watchkeeper, Fourth-Class Mechanician Tom Smith, along with Stoker Bob Black. His job was to check up the oil level and temperatures in the auxiliary machinery bearings, especially the main-shaft plumber-block bearing, to make sure the main-shaft gland did not leak, and to keep the bilges pumped dry and the checker plates and catwalks clean and shipshape.

As we were unfamiliar with the layout of all the different main steam auxiliary, ring-main and cross-connection valves, also feed-water valves in the engine room we had to proceed with great care. Starting up the necessary auxiliaries, we gingerly 'groped' our way around the numerous valves which were still hot along with the turbines, so eventually we had everything warmed up ready for my relief, Jack Frost, who came down at 08.00 to keep the forenoon watch. I carefully explained to him exactly what we had done and the few minor points that still remained to be completed.

The pilot boarded the ship to navigate it up the narrow channel of the River Lagan, and two tugboats were tied up for'ard and aft as the anchor was being weighed. The ship began to move slow ahead on both engines.

Within the hour the ship was being safely berthed alongside the wharf at Queens Island where the tugs were cast off to nudge the ship into position alongside. Heavy hawsers were run out ahead and astern to secure the ship to some large bollards. Then a gangway was lifted up into position to allow the workmen to climb aboard to start work on the modifications.

This was an unexpected return to Belfast, which was an added joy for the natives and courting couples who had left their parties behind. Also, there was plenty of leave from 16.00 to 08.00 next morning, which was used to the greatest advantage. But like all good things our free time rapidly ran out once the modifications had been completed.

Tankers arrived alongside for embarking oil fuel and aviation spirit, with no smoking throughout the ship being piped over the tannoy system. This also applied when an ammunition lighter tied up alongside (with a red flag fluttering from the stern). The feed and freshwater tanks were fully topped up from the shore supply, along with a large supply of victuals and other goods for the NAAFI canteen.

On Tuesday morning Taff had an early shake to lash up his hammock then stow it in the netting. He had to start flashing up down below at 04.00 to warm up all the necessary cold boilers and machinery so as to have everything ready for the forenoon watch.

Flashing up with one boiler auxiliary, with the other three cold, took four hours. The boiler-room ERA was responsible for the hard job of opening up all six main stop valves on the three cold boilers in both the port and starboard rooms, as well as opening up and shutting the air cocks on top of the boilers and steam drain valves as required. The two chief stokers, one in each of the boiler rooms, lit up one sprayer on each of the cold boilers. Down the port and starboard engine rooms the main steam bulkhead valves were opened wide, along with the ahead and astern throttle valves (with the turbine drains always being left open in harbour until completing manoeuvring on the next trip out).

All cold steam lines had their drain cocks fully opened until thoroughly warmed through. (One could get a nasty burn from their unlagged drainpipes if a bare arm or hand happened to brush up against one.)

Meanwhile the auxiliary superheated steam was admitted through the bulkhead or cross-connection lines, depending which auxiliary boiler was lit up (as they took it in turns about to be auxiliary).

The port and starboard main circulators were prepared for starting with the large suction and discharge sluice valves being opened up. The exhaust valves and lines, steam chests and steam lines were thoroughly drained of water before the turbo circulating pumps could be started by cracking the steam valve enough to allow them to tick over. At the same time the handpump was used to flood the bearings and reduction gearing with oil at 15 pounds pressure, until the mechanical pump took over with a wisp of steam escaping from the carbon packings.

The turbo-driven extraction pumps were started in a like manner. The contraflow valves were opened up to the main feed tanks to maintain half a glass of water in the condensers, aided by the pumps, also to discharge to the main feed-pump suction valve. The lubrication pumps were also started up in a similar manner. The inlet and outlet valves were opened up so the oil could circulate around the system through the strainers, on which handles were turned to prevent them choking, then on through the oil coolers back into the tanks holding several hundred gallons of oil. The turbine sliding feet were logged when cold, then afterwards every hour.

After one and a half hours, hot water began to dribble through the steam lines into the drain cocks and pipes, which changed within half an hour into an angry raging torrent. It spluttered out at the pipe's ends into the pig's ears causing them to overflow like waterfalls. This soon developed into a mighty roar as the steam mixed with the water forming a terrific cloud of steam which cast a large white shroud over the immediate areas. It was at this stage the aircocks and drains were eased down to a steady flow, but they were not shut off completely until the steam was perfectly dry. (Otherwise any water trapped in the lines would set up a terrific hammering as if trying to escape, causing the lines to dance and jump around their mountings in an alarming manner each time the water caused a large bang.)

Once there was a full head of steam in the three boilers the auxiliary boiler was married into the system by carefully opening up its two main stop valves. The remaining auxiliary superheated- and saturated-steam valves were opened on all three boilers as necessary, along with all four forced-draught fans being brought into use. The port and starboard main to auxiliary stop valves were opened along with the necessary bulkhead valves. The cross-connection valves were shut so that the two port and starboard boiler rooms supplied each engine room separately in units.

The port and starboard main feed pumps were started up to supply their own boilers through the feed heaters, the robot valves and the main feed checks. The closed exhaust system was opened up to the feed heaters and the condenser pilot valves.

The gland steam was opened up a crack to seal off the turbine glands to prevent air being drawn into the condensers. Steam to the port and starboard air ejectors was opened up to maintain a vacuum of 20 inches, whilst the engines were turned two revs ahead and two revs astern every three minutes for half an hour to warm up the turbines evenly.

At this stage I was always sent for to start up the second turbogenerator. If I was on watch a relief was sent down to allow me to drain the steam line, warm up the set, raise the vacuum, pump around the oil, and crack the steam valve to start the turbo spinning, then open it up to maximum revs, at the same time as pumping up the oil pressure for the bearings. I then gave the EA a tinkle on the blower to let him know all was ready for him to put the generator on load by making up the breakers on the switchboard to supply the port or starboard side of the electrical ring main.

By now the outside machinery ERA had tested the sirens by giving them a few hoots. Then he tested the engine-room telegraphs by ringing down: 'slow', 'half speed' and 'full speed ahead, 240 revs', then up to 'full speed astern', then back to 'stop'. He also tested the reply bell. Then he started up the hydraulic system for the massive steering rams, whose pump could reverse the flow of oil from one set of rams to the other set, according to which way the rudder had to be turned.

The rudder was controlled from the wheelhouse through the telemotor system. When the wheel was turned it forced oil down a long small-bore pipe, which operated the pump to turn the rudder so many degrees to port. Then, when the wheel was turned back again in the other direction, oil was forced down in the other pipe which brought the rudder back to midships or further on so many degrees starboard as required. This system was always checked as a slight leak into it would cause a variation of the rudder movement in degrees to that of the wheel indicator, which would cause an error in the navigation. The two readings had to correspond. The system had to be bled to get rid of the airlock before the ship put to sea. (The same trouble sometimes occurs in the braking system of a car when the brakes fail.)

The time for my first watch had arrived and I was feeling a little apprehensive as I stepped down the long ladder onto the checker plates on the control platform below (they were made to prevent skidding on them). I had to relieve Taff Gunney in charge of the forenoon watch down in the spacious port engine room, with a 20,000-h.p. turbine and auxiliaries to look after.

It had been painted out in white, with the bilges in red, and had a large inlet fan positioned over the controls with an exhaust fan back aft to draw out any fumes or hot air. The high- and low-pressure astern turbines were mounted around the centre and were lagged with insulation, then covered with dark-blue planish steel; so was the auxiliary turbine machinery. The ahead and astern throttle valves were mounted close to the bulkhead. The pressure gauges, with a Leeds-built, Harding Rhodes tachometer and engine telegraph from the wheelhouse were mounted nearby, along with the telephone and emergency telephone. The main feed pump and air ejector were mounted on top of the main feed tank by the ship's side. The condenser circulating-pump controls were extended through the plates for easy adjustment. The turbine nozzle valves were mounted in front of the turbine along with the pressure gauges for the various turbine stages, and the oil-pressure gauges. The thickly lagged steam pipes and exhaust pipes were suspended high up well out of the way. The exhaust system had a pilot valve which led into the condenser. The rest of the machinery was down a short ladder, which was easily reached from the catwalk which ran around it.

We were in three watches for steaming (Taff, myself, and Jack Frost). My throttle watchkeeper was Mechanician Tom Smith, who kept the logbook on a small desk situated conveniently nearby, as well as controlling the throttles and logging all movements. Bob Black was my stoker for most watches (except when he was required to be cook of the mess, when another stoker was sent down in his place).

Both sets of engines and boilers were isolated from one another to steam (in units), which meant the auxiliary superheated ring main was split in half by closing the necessary bulkhead and cross-connection valves in order that the port boilers supplied the port engines and auxiliary machinery. They also supplied steam to the for'ard turbogenerator and the catapult hydraulic pump. The starboard boilers supplied the starboard main engines and auxiliary machinery, the aft turbogenerator plus the turbo hydraulic lift pump. The saturated steam for the evaporators, etc. could be supplied by any one of the four boilers. In the event of an explosion, a bad leakage of steam, lack of water or water in the oil fuel, it was contained to one unit so as the ship could carry on her voyage uninterrupted steaming on one engine and one propeller at a reduced speed. The load on the remaining turbogenerator would be distributed to the bare essentials, such as the steering gear, refrigeration motors, and lighting for working spaces to control the ship, etc. The electric supply from both turbogenerators and switchboards was split up to supply the port and starboard sides of the ring main.

As the engines were warmed up we were all set to go. The order 'stand by main engines' was received from the bridge, then all that was required to be done was to open the steam to the air ejector fully, then open the gland steam a crack (a fraction of a turn) to increase the vacuum in the condenser from 20 inches to 29.8 inches. This ensured that the last ounce of efficiency was wrung out of the steam when passing through the turbines. I made sure that all the turbine drains were fully open, as any hot water trapped in the steam pipes would protest violently and bang in the pipes as if trying to escape, causing them to vibrate in a most alarming manner, as if they would break up at any minute and drop down on the deck.

Eventually two tugs, one for'ard and one aft, drew the ship away into the midstream of the River Lagan. We received the first order on the engine-room telegraph from the wheelhouse: 'slow ahead 50 revs', to which Tom replied by one ring on the answering bell. Then he opened the throttle accordingly, noting each movement in the logbook.

After half an hour we reached the end of the river, which opened up into Belfast Lough. The speed was rung down: 'half ahead 120 revs', to which Tom replied by two rings on the bell. Then he increased speed, noting the change of revs in the logbook. I adjusted the gland steam pressure to seal the vacuum in so that only a wisp of steam leaked past the carbon packings, then slightly speeded up the circulating pump to keep the condenser cool. I then shut off the turbine drains as the steam was dry, then adjusted the oil cooler, which was kept at 120°F or more.

At the end of each hour Tom filled in the logbook taking various readings, such as the main steam pressure (300 pounds); temperature of superheated steam (around 700°F); pressure of several of the stages of the high-pressure and low-pressure turbines; vacuum in the condenser (about 29.8 inches); the turbine sliding feet (which moved a fraction of an inch either way according to the amount of steam entering the turbines); the condenser cooling water in and out; the lubricating-oil-pump pressure (45 pounds and about 15 pounds pressure on the bearings); temperatures of various other bearings (thrust, turbine and gearing bearings, and the plumber-block bearing that held up the main shaft); the total revs per hour and the average revs per minute.

Whilst Tom took his readings, I looked after the throttles. Bob Black, the stoker, visited the plumber block hourly, which was nearly halfway down a long shaft passage to check the temperature and the oil level, which had to be kept at half a glass. (If it was overfilled the bearing would overheat caused by the drag rings fetching up too much oil with them as they turned around in the sump.) He also checked the stern gland to make sure that no seawater was pouring in, otherwise I would have to go down the passage and nip up the gland whilst he pumped the water out of the passage. Bob was also responsible for keeping the engine room clean and the checker plates dry as they could easily get slippery.

Meanwhile, the ship plodded on across the North Channel, heading for the Firth of Clyde. As she passed Ailsa Craig we proceeded to carry out a full speed trial over the measured mile to test the modification of the fan flat, which had proved to be disappointing as it turned out to be only partially successful in improving the combustion in the port boiler room.

Whilst the trial was in progress constant checks were made on the machinery and the bearing temperatures. When working my way around, everything seemed to be running normally until I reached the after end of the gear case where an amazing sight struck my eye. Where the propeller shaft entered the case it was rising and falling half an inch out of true (like a small eccentric on a model steam engine). It was bound to create excessive wear on the helical teeth of the gearwheels. It was an amazing sight and the shoddiest piece of work that I have ever seen. Chief Mechanician Bradley was informed over the blower so that he could contact the office for the engineers to come and examine it; also we made a note of it in the port logbook.

Strange to say, after the engineers had examined it, nothing was ever done about it as it turned out that the starboard shaft suffered from the same complaint, which was caused by wartime lack of material. Each prop shaft should have had another plumber-block bearing to support its extra-long length. (So the job was spoilt for a ha'p'orth of tar, as the saying goes!) Needless to say, the gearing and plumber blocks had to be nursed, and top speed was used sparingly. Surprising to say, they outlasted her commission in the Pacific and far beyond that!

It occurred to me to take a look at the other end of the shaft, which ran through the stern gland, only to find that there was a steady trickle of seawater flowing through it. It was gradually filling up the shaft passage and required a large spanner to nip up the four gland nuts just enough to stem the flow.

Bob and I started up the steam-driven fire and bilge pump on the shaft-passage bilge suction until the space was pumped dry. Then we switched it over to the engine-room bilge suction, watching the water run into a round large sump with the suction pipe in the centre and a filter around it to stop any foreign matter being sucked in. When the bilge was nearly empty, large gulps of air were sucked in causing the valves to rattle on their seats, so we shut the pump down.

The ship had passed by Ailsa Craig and was approaching the Isle of Arran, well out of the way of the shipping lane in a quiet spot. She slowed down then hove to, waiting for a hired ferry boat to transfer a large party of Fleet Air Arm bods under the command of Fly Co, who controlled the flight-deck officers and flying arrangements, as well as the deck party under the POs and killicks. the deck party was responsible for all the movements of the aircraft in the hangars and on deck, as well as driving the jumbo (motorised crane) and the Clark Cat forklift. Also they were in charge of the aircraft lighter, powered by two Ford V8 petrol engines, which was used for ferrying new, repaired and damaged kites around the fleet (one at a time) or ferrying spare parts to or from the ship.

There was a large repair staff, which consisted of several engineer officers, air artificers for the engine, fuselage, electrical and ordinance repairs, along with mechanics and airframe fitters to carry out repairs or servicing for the whole of the fleet carriers. They were all under the charge of Commander E. Oliver, who was the ship's chief engineer. There were also storekeepers, who dealt with a massive supply of spares for the Fleet Air Arm. There was the maintenance staff of the three self-contained squadrons, which were all numbered above 800, who prepared the kites ready for take-off. They included several armourers for loading the gun belts into the machine guns and also securing the bombs, torpedoes, depth charges or rockets under the wings. The crews of the Swordfish bomber squadron included navigators, air gunners-cum-wireless operators, and a photographic PO, who had a small caboose back aft which he used for storing his films and equipment, and as a darkroom for developing his films.

Eventually the ferry tied up alongside the port crane, then ran a gangway across to the upper deck. All the officers trooped over, followed by the bods carrying their kitbags and hammocks, which were dumped in the for'ard section of the lower hangar.

The bods then returned to unload the ferry of officers' tin trunks, Fleet Air Arm toolboxes, battery boxes, chocks and all manner of gear to operate the various squadrons. They filled up large rope nets attached to the hook of the port crane. They hauled up the various loads, which were dumped in a large pile on the flight deck by the ship's-company working party.

Meanwhile, the POs and leading hands (or killicks as they were often called) mustered at the jaunty's office with all the draft chits containing all the different names, ranks, occupations and numbers to be entered into the ship's log. They were allocated messes and billets, added to the ship's rum list, and put into a watch for leave and duty.

Once the ferry was unloaded the gangway was removed and the ropes were cast off, allowing both vessels to head back to their anchorage. The *Unicorn* anchored off Lamlash, a small coastal village on the Isle of Arran (nestling behind Holy Island), a few miles from the main town of Brodick, which lies nearly opposite Ardrossan and Saltcoats in Ayrshire on the other side of the firth.

The bods then went on the flight deck to remove their gear and toolboxes, etc. down below on the lift to be sorted out later. They were then mustered in the lower hangar for the roll call to make sure everyone was there, also to hand in any cigarette lighters (which were a fire hazard). By now the mess lists were drawn up, along with locker numbers, hammock sleeping billets and hammock nettings (some of which were on the mess decks, whilst others were in the locker flats or passages).

Finally everyone was sorted out into groups under a senior rating or leading hand. Then they were all dismissed to be shown where their messes, lockers, sleeping billets and hammock nettings were situated.

Each killick was in charge of the day-to-day running of his mess, which consisted of a long table with stools either sides to seat up to twenty men in all. The tables were secured to the deck in rows (port and starboard sides of the mess deck) lying thwartships across the compartment.

As it was rapidly approaching dinner time the first thing to be done was to draw all the mess traps from the stores. They consisted of knives, forks, spoons, cups, plates and dishes, a large tin box for tea and sugar, a slop pail for scraping the gash (leftovers) from the plates and emptying the tea leaves from the cups, a large tea kettle with an infuser in the centre for filling with tea, a large oblong mess kettle with a lid for washing up, a bar of soap, a round fanny and a dishcloth.

As the messes were not organised it was a case of everyone mucking in until next day when a daily roster for cooks of messes was worked out.

At 11.00 'up spirits' was piped for one hand from each mess to muster in the locker flat to queue up and draw the daily issue of grog (watered-down rum). Each man sung out his mess number which was checked by the master-at-arms who told Jack Dusty, the stores PO, the number of tots to measure out. He poured the tots in the man's fanny to be taken back to the mess and carefully divided up (otherwise the last man to draw his grog would be short). Also, the watch below was relieved one by one by his opposite number so each man could go up to his mess to draw his tot.

At 11.30 'cooks to the galley' was piped, so two hands mustered at the galley where the chief cook and party had been suddenly overwhelmed, having to cater for the influx of several hundred extra hands. They were given two or three large metal dishes with the meat, vegetables and sweet, which they had to carry carefully down the ladder onto the mess deck. Each killick had to ensure it was doled out evenly, then after dinner all the plates were scraped into the gash bucket to be emptied overboard down the gash chute. (This was a far better idea than on the old sailing ships where a sudden gust of veering wind was liable to blow the whole contents back into one's face when ditching gash overboard.)

Everything was washed-up in the large mess kettle and the large metal dishes were returned to the galley, with everything being left neat and tidy for the next meal. The weekly rations of tea, sugar and Nestlé's tinned milk were drawn from Jack Dusty's ready-use store, along with a ration of daily bread, margarine and jam (sometimes a cake of Pussers Hard soap was issued).

Meantime, the hands collected their bags and hammocks. They stowed their gear in their lockers and their hammocks in the bins, then went into the hangars to stow their toolboxes and tackle around the sides.

Tea and supper had passed by when the next pipe came over the tannoy: 'clear up mess decks and flats for rounds'. When the commander came around the messes with the jaunty and his entourage at 21.00, the senior killick on the mess decks reported, "All correct for rounds," and saluted. (This nightly routine was carried out to ensure nothing was amiss.) Then pipe down was sounded off at 22.00, which meant all hammocks had to be slung and lights put out.

For the next two days the Fleet Air Arm hands settled in familiarising themselves with the innards of the ship, including the labyrinth of passages, stores, compartments and magazines.

The Squadrons Arrive

On Friday, at 01.30, the three cold boilers were flashed up so the watch below was shaken at 01.00, had a quick swill and changed into their overalls for the middle watch (which took four hours) to raise steam. When I relieved Jack Frost for the morning watch everything had been started and was ready for use. When the order 'stand by main engines' was rung down on the telegraph from the wheelhouse, all that remained to be done was to raise the vacuum from 20 to 29.8 inches, then stand by the throttle valves. At 05.00 special seamen were piped to fall in along with the cable party on the fo'c's'le. All men out of the rig of the day were piped to clear off the upper deck.

Soon the anchor chain began to rumble as the capstan turned to bring it in and haul the anchor up from the murky depths. It was safely lodged and secured in the hawse pipe with the rest of the chain disappearing down a hole in the deck into the cable locker. The capstan was then stopped with a large brake band applied to prevent any movement. Also, the chain was secured by a wire strop. By this time the engine-room telegraph had rung down '50 revs slow ahead', whilst special sea-duty men lined the port and starboard of the flight deck for leaving harbour. On passing an HM ship at anchor or entering harbour they were called to attention by the PO in charge, who saluted when the shrill pipe was sounded and were stood at ease when 'carry on' was sounded. Once clear of the harbour the hands were fallen out as the pipe 'hands to flying stations' was sounded. The flight deck was then prepared with the wireless masts lowered and the lifts raised to flight-deck level; also the arrester wires and crash barriers were slung across.

We had left Lamlash for the vast space of the Firth of Clyde, where we were able to turn into the wind to start our flying programme. This caused a great deal of excitement around the ship. There were three squadrons to be flown aboard, consisting of twelve Swordfish (stringbags) torpedo bombers, twelve chunky Martlets and twelve flimsy Seafires.

Fortunately the weather was calm as the ship speeded up to 16 knots, which helped the kites to land or take off.

Most of the pilots were fully trained with forty hours' experience of landing and taking off on a large airfield, but they had no experience of landing on a tiny 300 feet of flight deck. The routine was to fly down the port side of the ship, and observe the signals from Fly Co's platform for permission to land. If not, they flew another circuit until the deck was clear. If clear, they carried on to the stern of the ship, then reduced engine speed and turned left so as to straddle the centre line of the deck. They obeyed the instructions given by the position of the batsman's bats, which indicated the right height of ten to fifteen feet above the deck, and when to cut the engine and drop on the deck. Hopefully, his hook would catch on one of the arrester wires, which gradually pulled out and stopped the kite.

The first kites to be flown-on were the stringbags without their crew of two. Being slow and manoeuvrable they all managed to land without mishap, with the ship's company not on watch observing how they landed and giving them a cheer. As each one landed it was taxied to the lift, had its wings folded, then it was struck down in one of the hangars. The second squadron of chunky American Martlets arrived and landed-on with a few near shaves. After dinner the flimsy Seafire fighters arrived, but with their high speed of landing they had a few minor accidents.

The ship then reduced speed to 12 knots, whilst the engine-room staff on the flight deck lowered the arrester wires, unshackled them on the port side and rolled them up neatly over the deck to stow them away on the starboard side so the deck was clear with the wireless masts raised.

The ship then wended her way up the firth, passing the Great Cumbrae Isles, Largs and Wemyss Bay, rounding the bend to Gourock and Greenock on the starboard side and passing by the Isle of Bute with its chief town of Rothesay separated from the mainland by the Kyles of Bute. We then passed Innellan, Dunoon and Kilcreggan on the port side, finally dropping anchor towards the tail of the bank.

Next morning the mess decks and flats, bathrooms and heads were cleared up for captain's rounds. Anything left sculling about was put in the scran bag to be reclaimed later. The mess decks were swabbed, tables were scrubbed, lockers were cleaned (especially on the tops), hammocks were straightened up in their netting and any bits of brass or copper were polished until everything was shipshape and Bristol fashion. Meanwhile our branch carried out minor repairs down below.

At 11.00 the senior hand of each mess stood by to report, "All correct for rounds, sir," as the captain came around with his retinue of several officers and the master-at-arms. If he was dead pusser (strict) he would search the compartment with a fine-toothed comb until he found some dirty spot that had been overlooked. Then he would order a re-scrub. The mess would be recleaned then reinspected. Once the rounds were completed, 'up spirits' was piped, then shortly afterwards was followed by 'cooks to the galley', followed by 'afternoon watchmen to dinner'.

After dinner all night leave was piped for the port watch from 13.30 until 07.00, and an extra half hour for chiefs and POs next morning. I took the first liberty boat, then caught a train up to Glasgow for big eats and a cinema show.

On Sunday the rig of the day was No.1 suits and we were piped to fall in on the flight deck for divisons into two files facing one another.

Chief ERA Rodgers lined up our group, calling us to attention when the captain inspected each division. Once completed the jaunty stood us at ease with caps off for a short church service, which was held with the captain reading the lesson. The jaunty then ordered on caps, calling us to attention whilst the officers fell out. Then he gave us the order, "Turn for'ard. Dismiss."

By this time the Sunday papers had arrived so everyone was reading until dinner time. Then it was the turn of the starboard watch for shore leave (not so many went as there was not much happening on a Sunday afternoon with no pubs open).

Next morning the duty watch flashed up from cold boilers and engines down below and prepared the ship for flying. Any man who had stayed ashore and had the forenoon watch below had to hurry over his breakfast, then change into his overalls to relieve his opposite number. At 08.30 the anchor was weighed to leave harbour.

132

All the kites in the hangars were checked over and tanked up by the chief stoker's fuelling party, which consisted of six stokers, a killick and a PO, who were also responsible for fuelling the ship. Six Fleet Air Arm bods assisted them to fill up the tanks with aviation spirit. This was highly volatile, so everyone wore plimsolls so as not to make any sparks with their soft soles; also not to damage the paintwork as they had to scramble up on top of the wing to fill up the tanks.

The kites were always checked up and tanked up as soon as they were struck down securely, so as to be ready for immediate use. It took a long time owing to the fact that the spirit was blown up by compressed air and contained globule of water and sediment so had to be filtered into a large funnel through a large shammy leather.

The engineers' flight party came under Commander E. Oliver. They were Lieutenant E. Archer, Chief ERA Fred Crate, ERA Ted Perkins and six stokers.

The first job in preparing the flight deck for use was to remove the eight keeps from under the lifts. Being the duty ERA I had shut down the main hydraulic pump and started the auxiliary pump to raise the lifts above the deck, to insert the eight keeps onto which the lifts were lowered in the evening after all the work was done. They were then safe for a marine corporal to exercise his defaulters on, or for a game of deck hockey, an evening stroll, or divisions on a Sunday.

I then started up the main hydraulic pump to bring the lifts back into use by the ERA or chief, who were responsible for preparing the flight-deck machinery for action. The next job was to remove the safety pins from the wireless masts and stow them in clips in a small control box on the port side of the ship next to the control box of the crash barrier. The crash barrier consisted of four wire ropes held together loosely by a few wire strops between two raised metal posts. (They were raised off the deck by a killick stoker when required to stop a kite.) He would raise the barrier enough to stop the kite on its legs so as to do as little damage as possible (most likely the wooden propellers would break off, or if aluminium they would curl up at the ends). The next job, to be carried out by the ERA and two stokers, was to uncoil the eight arrester wires and run them across the deck to the port side where they were secured. They lay flat on the deck usually, but were raised several inches above it when kites were about to land so that the arrester hook at the tail end of the kite would catch onto it. The wire was gradually drawn out to cushion its sudden stop. They were held up by two springs which were usually held down tightly against the deck and had controls in the wireless control box.

A steam jet was used instead of a windsock because it trailed directly over the deck and did not cause any obstruction. A windbreak could be used to shelter the flight-deck party when ranging the kites, or when the repair party was working on an aircraft.

When flying was taking place there was always an accident party standing by at the side of the island. There were operators for Jumbo (the motor crane), a Clark Cat forklift, a CO_2 bottle with a large spray nozzle (which soon put out a single aviation-fuel fire), a foam-making machine with a long hose to smother a large fire, and the usual fireman's hoses from the water main.

A small lighter was carried aft beneath the deck at the stern so a damaged kite or a new one could be removed from another fleet carrier. Also there were deck lights running up the deck in two columns for a kite to land in the dark or fog.

If the catapult was going to be used the chief ERA would start up a large hydraulic pump and open up the 4,000-pound bottles of compressed air.

The flight deck had been prepared for action and the flight-deck party had been piped to close up and brought up the first six kites of the Swordfish squadron.

They were torpedo bomber biplanes of a bygone age with two wings and two open cockpits (for the pilot, navigator and machine gunner). They were death traps when making their long slow 18-inch-torpedo attacks (they could not penetrate armour plating) out of the sun or had fighter protection.

They only had a small radial engine and had a slow stalling speed of 67 knots. Their wings were folded backwards to fit in the hangars. They were tough, and the only kites that could operate in rough weather, but nevertheless they were successful in sinking several Italian ships in Taranto Harbour and crippling the German battleship *Bismarck* with a torpedo hit in her steering gear, which forced her to turn in circles instead of steering ahead. Also they were successful in convoy work, dropping depth charges on German U-boats, which occasionally sank them, or at least prevented them from surfacing to sink our convoys.

As the ship approached the flying area the wireless masts were lowered and the steam jet was opened for her to sail into the wind. The first six kites of the Swordfish squadron (nicknamed stringbags) were brought up from the hangars, had their wings unfolded, then they were ranged aft in two rows from port to starboard. The mechanic then connected up the leads from the battery boxes to start up the engines and warm them up, and also checked up all the controls ready for the pilots who were all assembled in the waiting room at the foot of the island structure. They had just been genned up on the landing techniques by the senior officer, who took notes on each pilot — how he took off and landed on the small piece of deck (about 300 feet long, which in proportion to their usual landing ground was the size of a stamp on an envelope). He noted the kite's speed (the fuselage should be in the centre of the deck when turning), its height (which should be ten to fifteen feet above the flight deck), and, thirdly, whether the kite had its wings parallel with the flight deck so that the kite did not land on one wheel and probably burst a tyre. If the kite was not in the right position it would be waved off. An extra hazard was the island — when taking off it would suddenly loom up into the view of the pilots, giving them an inward fear. It could easily be avoided by closing the right eye for a couple of seconds whilst they passed it (a similar idea to a horse's blinkers).

The pilots were all seated in the restroom ready to go, kitted up in their flying suits, helmets, goggles, gauntlets, boots and Mae West life jackets. They were suddenly alerted and rushed out scrambling for their kites and climbed into their open cockpits where they were fastened in their seats by a safety harness with their heads against the rest. Each pilot restarted his engine as required with the front centre one being the first. The pilot revved up the engine from a hesitant flutter to a full-throated roar, then tested the magnetos by cutting one out to ensure the other would maintain full power on its own, and checked the flaps by moving the joystick and kicking the rudder bar to waddle the rudder. Then the starter leads from the battery box were removed as the kite was ready to fly. Two bods from the flight-deck party, who were all dressed in overalls with yellow waistcoats and white plastic caps, which were strapped under their chins, scrambled under the kite to wedge their chocks firmly against the wheels.

Bats waited for the affirmative signal from Fly Co's control platform, then stood in front of the leading kite with his right arm fully extended above his head with the bat. He then swung it around faster and faster for the pilot to respond and rev up his engine flat out. It roared at full speed, shaking the kite violently as if it would fall apart at any minute. The slipstream from the propeller tore at the chockmen's clothing so it rippled in the breeze. Then suddenly Bats dropped his arms with the bats below his knees, which was an order: 'away chocks'. The chockmen scrambled sideways, dragging the chocks behind them, and the pilot released his brakes. The kite began to taxi forward and gather speed as it trundled down the flight deck, becoming airborne just before reaching the end. Its undercarriage wheels lifted above the deck. It rapidly gained height, and carried on straight ahead until it was soon out of sight.

Then the port kite had to be centred into position by Bats, who stood in front of it. He directed the pilot to apply his right-hand brake to pivot the fuselage round on the right wheel. The pilot then revved up his engine a little so the propeller turned it 90° to face the centre line. He then released the brake to taxi forward within about 3 feet of the line. Then, by using the left brake on the wheel and revving up his engine, he turned the fuselage 90° to straddle the centre line ready to take off. This was soon carried out. Then the starboard kite was dealt with in a similar manner, but starting with the left-hand brake on the wheel to reverse the process — so the starboard kite was centred and flown off. The rest of the kites were dealt with in a similar manner until they were all airborne, circling in a large circle waiting to land.

Bats had a great deal of experience of landing kites in stormy weather on the *Ark Royal* and had been perched on the port aft corner of the flight deck with the wing of a Swordfish dangerously over his head, the deck below him rising and falling several feet. This was constantly altering the landing space of ten to fifteen feet, making it difficult to judge the exact moment for the pilot to cut off his engine. Also, on approaching his vision was somewhat obscured by the red-hot glow from the top of the engine cylinder, which shone before his eyes. However, he managed to make a safe landing. If he had misjudged his speed the kite was liable to stall and drop into the water. These were the reasons for the pilots having thirty lessons, so that they could judge speed, height and the turn in all kinds of weather.

When flying was taking place there was always a crash boat handy to pick up any pilot who had the misfortune to drop into the water. Also at the side of the island the flight party waited around with a mechanical crane and a forklift. The crash barrier was manned by a killick stoker. Also there were two bods in fireproof headgear and clothing who manned a large bottle of CO_2 gas with a large nozzle to extinguish a sudden aviation-spirit fire, which could develop into a huge fireball in seconds. Also there were several bods manning a foam extinguisher to smother a fire, as well as the hoses from the fire main. If a kite crashed on the deck, and pancaked with its under carriage collapsed, and if it was considered U.S. (useless), it was quickly removed by Jumbo lifting it up and, assisted by the forklift, dumping it over the stern out of the way.

To continue with the flying, the second six Swordfish were brought up from the hangars with their wings unfolded by the flight-deck party. They were secured, then ranged aft to be started up and warmed, ready to be manned by the pilots. By using exactly the same routine Bats soon had them all ready and flown off, which cleared the deck ready for the landings to take place.

By this time a large party of spectators had gathered, never having seen anything so spectacular taking place. Everyone waited a few minutes with bated breath as the first one adjusted his speed and flew down the port side. He got the all-clear flag from Fly Co's platform and lowered his arrester hook. He then slowed down to make his sharp turn inward so that the fuselage lay over the centre line and the pilot could obey Bat's signals to raise the starboard wing so it was parallel with the flight deck. He adjusted his height to ten to fifteen feet above deck. Then finally Bats signalled to cut out his engine by his bats being brought down and crossed over his knees. Ideally the arrester hook would catch on the third arrester wire, with the spectators gasping a sigh of relief. They were also intrigued by the way the wire pulled out, gradually stopping the kite. When it was disconnected it slowly slithered back across the deck like a snake until it was taut. The landing-on was dependent on the split-second timing of Bats' order to land and the pilot's reaction in stopping his engine and dropping his kite so it caught on the first arrester wire, if possible, or ended up on the sixth wire or the crash barrier. This was operated by a killick stoker who raised the barrier halfway up to catch on the legs to minimise the damage. They usually broke off the laminated wooden propeller blades (if they were Yankee kites the blades were metal and would curl up at the ends).

The flight-deck party gathered round the kite and guided it onto the after lift where the pilot applied his brakes and climbed out of the cockpit with a sigh of relief showing on his face. He then went to report to his instructor for a pep talk and to discuss anything he had misjudged on his final approach and landing. He was instantly replaced by a mechanic to control the brakes off and on. The wings were unlocked then unfolded backward, depending on the make of the kite. It was then swiftly taken down below and struck down by cables attached to the deck fittings. Once out of the way the landings continued.

The second pilot was making his approach down the port side of the ship in exactly the same manner, but unfortunately he had not got the fuselage lined up accurately and was violently waved off by Bats. He suddenly revved up his engine flat out, with it screaming at full power. The tip of the wing dipped dangerously near to Bats' head, nearly knocking him off his perch. He side-slipped away from the island to make another circuit around the ship. He was more successful this time and hooked onto the fourth arrester wire and was struck down in the hangar without any more ado. The rest of the squadron landed-on with varying degrees of success, and within half an hour they had all been struck down in the hangar out of the way. By this time the ship was rapidly approaching the shoreline and was running out of wind space, so she slewed around, turning out of the wind on a reverse course.

Then preparations were made for the Seafire squadron to be brought up six at a time. As they emerged on the lift their wings were unfolded from above and locked manually into position. Then they were ranged back aft.

They were cast-off Spitfires from the RAF, who had new better versions which were more powerful. They still had their original powerful 1,470-h.p. Merlin Rolls-Royce engines, with a range of 465 miles at 352 mph, an operational ceiling of 33,800 feet, armaments of eight .303 Browning guns or one 250-pound bomb under each wing. They were the fastest aircraft the Fleet Air Arm possessed and played a useful part in protecting the fleet and landing craft at Salerno, Italy. When the army landed ashore they attacked any German bombers which came over to attack the operation, until our troops had a strong foothold ashore. They shot down several attacking Stuka bombers.

The arrester wires were always pulled down on the deck so that the flight-deck party would not trip over them when ranging the aircraft. Also, it made the wheels easy to pass over when manoeuvring the aircraft into position. They were always raised to stop the aircraft when landing-on.

The ship turned into the wind and the battery boxes were dragged into position so the cables could be attached to the starters and the mechanics could start up the engines and check the controls all ready for the pilots to man their aircraft.

They scrambled out, climbed into their cockpits, fastened themselves in and pulled over the perspex shield (which all the latest aircraft had to protect them from the weather). They then ran up their engines, the starter leads were disconnected and they checked their controls all ready to go. Bats soon had them lined up one at a time ready for take-off. Soon they were all airborne, circling around leaving room for the other six to be brought up and dealt with in the same way. Soon all twelve kites were circling around waiting to land.

They all landed safely with various errors of judgement. A couple were waved off and most of them missed the first four arrester wires. One flew into the crash barrier as the faster-revving engines did not answer the controls quite as quickly, and one landed heavily on the tail wheel and ruptured the tail end which had to be strengthened by the repair party.

That concluded the first day of flying and the ship raised its wireless masts, shut off the steam jet and headed back to harbour. The flight deck was cleared, with the arrester wires coiled up on the starboard side.

Next forenoon the ship weighed anchor and the flight deck was prepared for action. The wireless mast was dropped and the steam jet was opened for the ship to turn into the wind. As usual, the crash boat followed close behind.

This time it was for the Martlets (renamed Wild Cats), which were sturdy purpose-built American fighters, with 10,200-h.p. Wright Cyclone radial engines and a maximum speed of 310 mph. They were surplus to the Americans, having been replaced by Grumman Hellcats with 2,000-h.p. radial engines with a top speed of 395 mph. They were good fast fighters, easy to land, and could take some punishment.

The Martlets had squared-off wing tips with hydraulic wings, which folded backward with a twisting motion, and a sturdy-looking rounded-off fuselage, which was better for landing.

The first six Martlets were ranged and manned ready for take-off. They flew off in the normal manner. The second six were soon brought up from the hangars, ranged and flown off. Soon they were all circling around awaiting to land and put up a better performance than the Seafires, catching on to the third and fourth arrester wires.

The catapult was a useful addition to the aircraft carriers, especially when with the fleet or convoys. It could launch its aircraft without preparing the flight deck, lowering the wireless masts, or using the steam jet to alter course and fly into the wind — which was the normal way to take off. This meant the carrier would have to waste time, especially when an attack of German Stuka dive-bombers was imminent. Its fighter aircraft were part of the ship's protection and it was quite vulnerable without them (Hitler sent 100 Stukas to annihilate all our carriers in the Mediterranean). The whole squadron of twelve fighters had to be brought up at once. Six were ranged on the port side. The leading one was positioned against the two chocks, which were worked in conjunction with the launching lever and the trolley-return lever which controlled a large hydraulic pump. This was started and left ticking over. The levers were housed in a small control box hung over the port side. The launching lever gave a 4,000-pound blast to a piston which was attached to the trolley. The other lever controlled a large pressure of water from the hydraulic pump, which screamed into action to put pressure on the other side of the piston to shove the trolley back into the starting position. The trolley had a strong steel strop attached. This was fastened to the fuselage by two strong hooks which dropped off at the end of the 150-foot run when the aircraft became airborne.

When the aircraft was ready to take off the pilot revved up his engine and released his brakes. The launching lever was pulled and the chocks dropped down to allow the wheels to pass over them. This allowed the trolley to hurl over with the aircraft to the end of the track where the aircraft overtook the trolley and became airborne. Then the return lever was pulled, which brought the trolley back and at the same time raised the chocks again ready for the next aircraft to be brought forward and positioned against them so that the strop could be hooked on. As soon as the aircraft had been catapulted off and the trolley returned, another aircraft was brought forward to be catapulted off and the next one moved down the line for the same treatment. As each one moved the others moved to take their place and the other six began to join the line, manned by the pilots and with their engines running so that when the first six were airborne, the other six were lined up ready for take-off.

All three sets of squadron pilots were to have experience of being catapulted off, so Chief ERA Crate or ERA Perkins would start up the large hydraulic pump and leave it ticking over. They would open the air bottles to provide the blast of air. One of them would man the control levers in the control box. As usual the Swordfish were the first to use it. The flight-deck party brought up all twelve of them, and spread out their wings. They ranged the first six in line on the port side with the leading one against the chocks so it could be attached with the steel wire strop on the trolley with its brakes on. They were all tested and left running by the mechanics. The pilots were all firmly strapped in. Fly Co watched the operation from his platform above and gave the order to Bats to proceed with his little red flag, which he waved around his head for the pilot to rev up his engine flat out. Then he lowered it to the deck for Ted Perkins to pull the control lever and the pilot to release his brakes with the chocks dropping down allowing the wheels to run over them as the trolley shot forward hurling the aircraft into the air. Then Ted pulled the other lever to bring the trolley back to the starting point, with the chocks rising ready to position the next aircraft to be fastened to the trolley with the strop. It was soon waved off, with another aircraft taking its place. As each aircraft was catapulted off the next one was taxied forward and each of the next ones moved up one place. The other six were prepared, with their engines running and manned by their pilots, and joined the line so they were all ready when the first ones had been catapulted off. Once they had been catapulted off the ship turned into the wind with the steam jet blowing, the wireless masts down, and the arrester wires across the deck so they could all land-on.

They all landed-on without any major incidents taking place. The flight-deck party manhandled them onto the lift, folded their wings backwards and struck them down into the hangars out of the way. Then the ship raised its masts and shut off the steam jet. The deck was cleared, and she made for harbour.

Next day it was the turn of the Seafire squadron and then the Martlet squadron. They went through exactly the same procedure without any major mishaps.

Next day the Swordfish started off on the normal training routine. The ship headed down the Clyde making for the confined waters of the firth to continue the training programme which was to last for the next three months (April, May and June). Fortunately it took place in rare glorious mild spring weather without the usual Scottish mist shrouding the hills of purple heather in the background. This helped to make our odd hours off watch more interesting, as we could see the take-offs and landings-on the flight deck from the vantage point aft of the island.

The flying programme ran from Monday until Friday, then the ship headed upriver to anchor near Greenock, so we were able to have leave at weekends and travel up to Glasgow.

When the ship reached the broad expanse of water of the firth, a search was made for the longest possible course which enabled her to sail into the wind for about an hour. The shortest course was at the mouth of the firth, from Girvan, passing Ailsa Craig to the Mull of Kintyre — about a twenty-mile run. Another course was on the far side of the Isle of Arran down Kilbrannon Sound as far as the Mull of Kintyre, having navigable water for about forty miles. The longest run of all was from Loch Fyne past the Isle of Bute, through the Sound of Bute then down the coastline for about fifty miles passing by Farland Head, Ardrossan, Saltcoats, Troon, Prestwick, Ayr to Girvan. The course depended on which quarter the prevailing wind was blowing from. This was because when the kites were flying on and off, the ship steamed into the wind at full speed to give them extra lift to take off on the short runway of about 600 feet, and just over half that amount to land-on again. So at 22 knots the ship covered about twenty-five miles within the hour and could easily run out of wind and navigable water in less than an hour, or two hours at the most depending on which course she was running on.

She was joined by the ancient nippy little crash boat, a 40-knot destroyer (such as the *Velox*) in attendance. This was stationed astern, ready to speed to the scene of an accident when a kite was ditched or careered over the side and plunged into the sea sinking like a stone. It would pick the pilot up, who had fought to release his safety harness, opened the perspex canopy (if there was one fitted) then floated up to the surface in his Mae West life jacket.

As we headed for our first run we passed by the old coal-burning ship SS *Pegasus*, which had been the *Ark Royal*. She was employed as a training ship for the old amphibian aircraft Walrus, which was used on the big ships for reconnaissance or target practice, reporting the fall of the shells if they were short, straddled or over. We passed by her several times during our stay in the area and sometimes we caught a glimpse of her firing off a Walrus from her catapult. This made an interesting spectacle as it suddenly shot across the deck, then glided into the air. When it landed on the water its sturdy little bows cleaved the water making a large bow wave until it soon slowed down.

At about 16.00 the ship returned to harbour. At 16.30 the engine-room telegraphs rang down 'finished with main engines'. The boiler-room ERA promptly started to shut down three boilers completely, leaving the remaining one starboard boiler on auxiliary. This meant shutting the two main stop valves and leaving the auxiliary superheated- and saturated-steam valves open to supply the turbogenerator running for lights and power, the hydraulic machinery for lifts, etc., and the evaporators with steam to produce. Feed water for the boilers or the ship's tanks was sometimes supplied by a water boat coming alongside.

By this time the boiler-room ERA was knackered and drained of all his energy. All the eight main stop valves he had shut were hard to turn, with the handwheels being red-hot because the three fans were shut down except one for the auxiliary steaming boiler. He would often sit down near the fan-flat intakes in sopping-wet sweaty overalls for about half an hour to recover before making for a shower in the bathroom.

On the other hand our engine rooms were large and spacious, being quite comfortable to work in except in the tropics. I was in charge of the port 20,000-h.p. engine room, assisted by a throttle watchkeeper (who manoeuvred the engines and kept the engine logbook) and a stoker (who kept the room tidy, oiled up the plumber block and auxiliary pumps and assisted generally).

Meanwhile, we had started to shut down the port engine room. First we opened the auxiliary superheated cross-connection valve and the main steam to the auxiliaries. We then shut off the gland steam and the air ejectors and the main steam bulkhead valve. We opened all drains, shut off the closed exhaust valve to the condenser and shut down the extraction pump and the contraflow valve on the M.F.T., which controlled the level of water in the condenser. We also eased down the speed of the main circulator to cool the condenser for half an hour. Finally we shut it down along with the lubricating-oil pump, which had been left running to cool down the turbine bearings. We then packed up the watch and climbed up the long metal ladder before going to change out of our overalls and have a good wash.

Meantime leave had been piped from 17.30 to 22.30, but being such a small town with few facilities it was hardly worth getting ready for.

There were always several sacks of mail awaiting collection ashore by one of the motor boats, but they had to be sorted out in the mail office before the pipe 'hands muster at the office for mail' was sounded.

As most evenings were warm and pleasant, Alf Seldon, Willie Franks and myself would often spend an hour pacing up and down the flight deck before supper or sunset. After this we would sometimes have a dhobi session down in the bathroom, then hang the laundry up in one of the boiler rooms where it dried before pipe down was sounded.

Some nights there was a film show in the for'ard end of the lower hangar in front of the first fire screen, which was lowered to isolate the section from any inflammable material left sculling about as well as the kites.

Next morning (Tuesday), as the engines and boilers had retained their heat overnight, the watch below was shaken to lash up and stow their hammocks by 05.30 to start flashing up and preparing the engines to be ready for sea at 08.00.

As soon as the anchor was weighed the ship steamed out into the Firth of Clyde to continue our training programme.

Everything was going well until the turn of the dumpy Yankee Martlet fighter squadron, with their high-powered radial Wright Cyclone engines (they were procured on the Lend-Lease system). Unfortunately there was some carelessness in the construction for the tanking-up of aviation spirit as a particle of grit or rag caused a total blockage in the pipeline of the last kite to take off. It roared off down the flight deck in fine style, but, as it approached the end, the engine suddenly spluttered then faded away, then stalled, cutting out dead. Instead of lifting off gracefully it simply ran for'ard over the edge of the deck and plunged down like a stone into the path of the ship (much to everybody's horror and amazement).

The captain on the bridge ordered 'full speed astern' on both engines, but to no avail as the ship was travelling too fast to stop dead in her tracks. The weigh kept her ploughing forward for several minutes. Everyone who saw the accident turned their eyes aft hoping that the wake of the ship would have swept the pilot out of harm's way but we realised he must be dead as the bows must have mowed into the kite, tearing it asunder, leaving the pilot with no chance of survival.

The crash boat searched the area for some time but found no trace of the pilot. There was much talk about the terrible tragedy and there was an air of sadness around the ship.

The ship then gained full speed, then swung back into the wind to collect the remaining kites before returning to harbour with the flag flying at half mast.

The flying programme continued next day and for the rest of the week. After flying was completed on Friday the ship ran upriver past Greenock to anchor for stores, supplies and weekend leave.

It was doubly galling for the pilot's family as he was due for a long leave, which he lost as well as his life. On Sunday after divisions there was a memorial service for him on the flight deck.

During the following months at Lamlash, whilst the ship was busily engaged in her training programme, the ship's company were busily engaged in the working-up period to become fully conversant with the layout of the ship and her workings (especially with their own parts of ship), so she could be run efficiently.

The seamen's branch covered a vast range of jobs. The quartermaster's two assistants helped with the steering and controlling the speed of the ship. The cable party dealt with the anchor and the securing of the ship when tying up alongside the jetty. The anti-aircraft gun crews and control parties operated and supplied the guns with ammunition. The paravane party streamed paravanes from the bows when leaving harbour to ward off floating mines. The seaman's branch also supplied lookouts in the crow's nest and port and starboard quarters; telegraphists to man the switchboard; messengers for the bridge; hands for swinging the lead to sound the depth of shallow waters or channels; deckhands for keeping the deck shipshape and the waists and quarterdeck scrubbed; painting parties; motor-boat crews; hands for storing magazines; store parties for provisioning the ship; parties for cleaning bathrooms and messes; captains of the heads for keeping the toilets clean; and men for many other small jobs required to keep the ship in tip-top sailing order.

There were torpedo ratings for assisting the EAs with the electrical gear. Signal men (known as bunting tossers) became familiar with the platforms and pigeonholes. They had pennants and flags to hoist up to the yardarm with the halyards; and also used Aldis lamps to send Morse messages around the fleet. There was a wireless operator for transmitting and receiving Morse messages; and a radar operator to scan the oceans and heavens for thirty miles around in search of hostile ships and aircraft, on his screen. The master-at-arms (the jaunty) with his POs (crushers) were responsible for discipline, joining and leaving ship, leave, mail and the rum ration.

The sickbay attendants (sometimes called tiffies along with the artisans) familiarised themselves with the sickbay, making up the cots and dispensing mercuric oxide (known as crab fat), jallop, ointment and condoms; also they set out the operating tools, and the tables and tools for the dentist's equipment.

The writers took notes for the officers, and also prepared the ledgers for Friday payment. They were on the pay bob's (or paymaster's) staff along with the storekeepers, who consisted of Jack Dusty's supply staff. The storekeepers issued the daily victuals for the cooks in the galley (such as flour, meat, vegetables, eggs and bacon, and anything else required to bake bread and cook meals for the crew). Also they were responsible for the daily rations of tea, milk, sugar, jam and marmalade, margarine (or occasional butter) and rum ration drawn from the store by cooks of messes. Another part of the supply staff issued slops (or clothing) at their store, along with Pussers Hard soap and duty-free tins of tobacco (known as Ticklers) for cigarettes and tins of shredded leaf tobacco or a bundle of leaves to be processed into making a prick of pipe tobacco. Another part of the supply staff dealt with spare parts, especially for the engine-room department; consumable goods and tools, such as files, hacksaw blades and emery paper; packing for steam glands and joints; nuts and bolts; and gauge glasses for boilers, etc. They also issued permanent tools which were part of the ship, such as sledgehammers, large ring spanners, drills, reamers, special tools for lathes, tube expanders, 100 bright steel balls used for rolling down the boiler tubes to make sure they were clear, surgical and dental tools for the sickbay. The EAs required hundreds of spare bulbs, fuses, carbon brushes for the motors, and many other different fittings. The OAs needed various spare parts for their guns, as well as hydraulic oil. The bosun's store required much paint and brushes, along with ropes and wire ropes.

The cooks, stewards and messmen looked after the officers'

needs back aft.

The Royal Marines in their barracks, complete with the band, were responsible for numerous duties, including gun crews and control parties as well as keyboard sentries, officers' batmen and store parties.

The engine-room department was responsible for a vast range of equipment around the ship. The chief stoker's oiling party was responsible for oil fuel, water and aviation spirit, connecting up the various hoses from the different tankers to standpipes screwed into the port and starboard waists decks. ('No smoking' was piped around the ship when taking on oil fuel, aviation spirit or ammunition, and a red flag was flown.)

Taking on oil fuel was one of the trickiest of operations, as there were numerous filling valves spaced out in various compartments on the port and starboard sides of the ship. A stoker would be in charge of filling several tanks one at a time and dipping them with a long steel weighted tape measure (similar to the function of a sump dipstick in a car). If he didn't pay strict attention to his job the oil fuel would suddenly spill over from the air vent on the top of the tank, creating a large overpowering smelly mess around it whilst he struggled to shut off the supply valve before opening the next one. Then he was left to clean off a horrible dark sticky brown stain of thick oil on the surrounding bulkhead and deck. Subsequently all surplus oil and spirit was drained safely away before any hoses were disconnected or removed.

Taking on water caused no such spillage problems, as it was easily dealt with by mopping up. Aviation spirit was a deadly fire hazard and handling it was an exacting job, calling for much greater care to be taken, as one small spark could easily cause a huge fireball.

The chief stoker was responsible for operating the aviation fuelling system from a control room directly above the six large upright tanks containing about 50,000 gallons of aviation spirit when full. The tanks were evenly spaced out, like islands in a compartment full of water, to insulate them from sparks, heat or fire. They each had two inlets at the top, which were connected to a large cluster of brass valves grouped together then mounted on the bulkhead with a brass wheel spanner to open them up. Each valve for the tank had a dual purpose: it acted as an air vent or allowed low-pressure air to be admitted to the top of the tank to drive the spirit up a long tube.

147

The spirit passed through the other valve into the system and was discharged into a long copper line which had numerous branches with valves on throughout the hangers and flight deck. Also, it could be connected up to the filling valves on the upper deck from the tanker. All valves had brass caps to prevent any foreign matter from entering the system. Also, there were several sets of brass tools available for removing the brass caps, coupling up the hoses and opening up the valves; all were made of the same material to prevent sparks. Also, the hoses were earthed for the same reason.

The control room also contained two mercury tubes with handpumps which supplied air to operate the gauges. These gauges were used on each tank separately to indicate the level of the spirit when filling up. Also, there were heavy rubber mats on the deck, a sealed light fitting with a switch outside the compartment, and a special phone encased in rubber as extra fire precautions.

When taking on aviation spirit the chief stoker with his party consisting of a killick and several stokers, would muster on the upper deck wearing plimsolls. As soon as the tanker was secured alongside, 'no smoking throughout the ship' was piped and a red flag was run up to indicate danger.

Hosepipes were then passed over from the tanker, and a set of brass spanners was used to remove all the dust caps from the hoses and valves. The hoses were coupled to the valves and they were earthed before the valves were opened (to prevent any static electricity causing sparks and starting off a fire).

When all was ready the chief went down below, switching the light on, then he grabbed the brass wheel spanner to open up the necessary valves to fill up the first tank. He also pumped air up into the gauge to operate on the tank. He then phoned through to tell those on top to start pumping. Once the level of aviation fuel approached the full mark, he opened the second tank in exactly the same manner, then shut down to isolate the first tank when full. He carried out the same procedure until every tank was full, then he got on the blower to order then to stop pumping. He then shut the remaining valves to isolate the last tank. The discharge valves on the tanker were left open so that the chief could blow the surplus spirit back into the tanker to clear the filling lines. The hoses could then be disconnected without spilling a drop. Then he left the control room in darkness with all the valves shut down, returning to the upper deck to make sure the valves were shut, the dust caps had been replaced and the tools collected. He then returned them to his caboose to be safely stored for future use. Then the hoses were retrieved by the tanker so she could be cast off. Then 'carry on smoking' was sounded off over the tannoy.

When tanking up the chief stoker's party turned up in plimsolls as worn by the flight-deck party when scrambling over the decks and kites. The chief went below to open up a tank on the system whilst the killick stoker went down to the low-pressure air-compressor room to start up the machine, then open up the line to supply the air to drive the spirit out of a tank into the system. The stokers used their sets of brass spanners to remove the dust caps, then coupled up their hoses, earthing them to the deck, then opened up their valves with the wheel spanner. Then a Fleet Air Arm bod opened up a tank on each kite ready to be tanked up with the hose (through a nozzle similar to that of a petrol pump).

A large oblong funnel was then inserted with a very fine mesh wire soldered around the base; also with a large shammy leather spread out over the top piece of the funnel to ensure no grit or drops of water from the compressed air passed through into the tank. It was a lengthy process as the spirit took its time passing through the shammy, causing the nozzle to be opened and shut cautiously to prevent spilling. Once full the tank was shut when the funnel had been removed. Then the team climbed down, and shook the funnel and shammy to ensure no sediment or drops of water remained before taking the hose up to the next kite.

It was rumoured that several kites had been forced to ditch owing to engine failure, and the most likely causes were a modicum of carelessness in fuelling up or empty fuel tanks. When all the kites had been tanked up in the squadron, the chief released the air pressure in the tank then vented it to allow the remaining spirit in the pipeline to be blown back and drained into the tank so the system was completely empty. Then he would shut the two valves on the tank so it was isolated. The low-pressure air compressor was then stopped and the stokers removed their hoses without spillage by unscrewing them with C-shaped spanners. Then they screwed on the dust caps, and collected their tools and hoses to stow away for further use.

This method of emptying the pipelines back into the comparative safety of the tanks was far superior to that of the Yanks or Japs, who left their pipelines full of inflammable spirit. This meant that in the case of even a small gland leak it only needed one spark to set off a roaring fire. Also if the pipeline was ruptured or broken in action the whole system would spill out many gallons of aviation spirit, which was liable to become a massive uncontrollable conflagration within a matter of seconds.

As one kite landed heavily its undercarriage collapsed from underneath it. It then pancaked flat on the deck, sliding to a grinding halt with the metal fuselage causing a rasping screech. This caused a delay in the flying programme, forcing the other kites to circle around, waiting to land-on when the deck had been cleared. Fortunately such badly damaged kites were a rare occurrence and generally had all their laminated wooden prop blades broken off. (If it was a Yankee kite it would have its blades curled up at their tips as they were metal blades.) Often such kites were pronounced U.S. (useless for further service), in which case Jumbo, the petrol-engine crane, assisted by the Clark Cat forklift, lifted it to be ditched over the stern. The fire party put out the fire which sometimes occurred as the fuselage scraped along the deck causing a spark and fireball. No smoking was allowed on deck or in the hangars. Also all cigarette lighters were banned on board ship and anyone possessing one had to hand it in at the master-at-arms' office.

One day as I was passing through the lower hangar to get to the port side of the upper deck a blinding flash suddenly occurred. Apparently a Fleet Air Arm sprog (or erk) had been holding his cigarette lighter out to collect the drips from the top wing of a stringbag which was being tanked up by a fuelling party. Suddenly he let the lighter drop on the steel deck, which caused a spark which caused a few drops of aviation spirit to produce a large ball of fire. Fortunately it did not reach the kite to do any damage. But it caught the erk, who stood there aghast riveted to the deck with fear. His hair was singed and his face was ghostly pale except where it was scorched with the sudden heat. It was a nasty experience but it could have been worse had there been a bigger spillage. However, it was fortunate that the erk was standing on the edge of the fireball which suddenly went out in a flash.

The fuelling party hopped down to confiscate the lighter which they threw overboard to prevent his getting involved with a court of inquiry. They then gave him a good dressing down so he would remember not to do such a foolish act again as it could have caused a big fire with much damage. He was then taken to the sickbay for treatment of shock and a slight searing of hands and face.

It suddenly occurred to me that I would be roped in as a witness, being the most senior rating present, so hurried to my work, spending the next ten minutes thinking what one would have to do in the event of a fire in that part of the hangar to prevent it spreading. The first thing to do would be to shut both the port and starboard for'ard hangar doors then drop the fire curtain to limit the supply of oxygen in the air. Then there was a choice of three systems to use: the sprinkler system, which was the quickest as it could be operated by one man; the fire main with its hoses and nozzles; or the foam-making hoppers to build up a blanket of foam to smother a fire.

I witnessed a pranged kite being lifted off the deck with the highly volatile aviation spirit suddenly bursting into a huge ball of flames. This was instantly brought under control by the firefighters using their large bottle of CO_2 gas. They directed their large flat fantail nozzle into the heart of the flames so they instantly died down.

In most cases there was no time to salvage any useful spare parts from the wreck, especially if there had been a squadron out on patrol and the remainder of the kites were eager to land. If their fuel gauges were hovering dangerously low above the empty mark, it meant that at any minute their engines would begin to splutter. If not landed instantly they would all be lost, having to ditch in the sea, which would have been a costly business besides leaving the squadron short of aircraft.

The kite was unceremoniously dragged aft then nudged over the rounded overhang into the sea, so the deck was clear for action allowing all the other kites to land quickly one after another. Each one was taxied for'ard beyond the two barriers, which were both raised to protect any kite in front of them, until they had all landed-on safely.

When a kite returned to the ship from an attack carrying any bombs, torpedoes or depth charges they had to be ditched before landing as they were liable to blow up in the case of the kite crash-landing. If a pilot had to ditch his kite in the sea it was prudent to jettison them first, especially if they were depth charges. Otherwise he would be blown to smithereens when they reached a depth of about thirty fathoms.

If any kite was damaged whilst landing it was quickly manhandled beyond the for'ard end of the island to be dealt with when the rest of the squadron had landed-on.

One day, when I was watching the flying, one kite came to a

sudden halt then burst into a massive ball of flame which shook all the onlookers. As usual the two firefighters, who were always stationed near the barrier, stepped out clad from head to foot in special helmets and asbestos suits with a large bottle of CO_2 gas mounted on wheels. This supplied a large fan-shaped spray, which was directed right into the centre of the fire, putting it out instantly. No apparent damage was done to the kite or the pilot, who stepped out of his cockpit as if nothing had happened, much to everybody's amazement. It certainly worked well, depriving the fire of oxygen so it had to go out.

Occasionally when a kite bounced off the deck, missing all the arrester wires, the pilot would tend to flap instead of letting the barrier stop the kite. Then he would rev up to take off again at full throttle with the nose down. This unfortunately happened in the case of a kite which charged into the barrier. The top wire broke off the laminated wooden propeller blades then it slid over the fuselage, shattering the perspex canopy, catching the pilot across the throat and killing him instantly — a tragic error of judgement.

Training Completed

The training had been completed and the ship left harbour, travelling at 10 knots, with its attendant crash boat trailing behind for the last operation on a sunny forenoon. It made for a long strip of water to catapult all three squadrons off with their thirty-six aircraft. The first twelve were brought up from the hangars fully fuelled and prepared. There were two mechanics whose job it was to hop into the cockpits to apply the brakes off and on (they were always parked with them on to prevent any movement). Also they were responsible for securing the folding wings and locking them when they were spread out again. They started up the engines to warm them up and checked all the controls before the pilots took over. The flight-deck party swarmed around the first of the six kites to range them along the port side so they would straddle the catapult track. They were steered by a killick steersman. He connected his long tiller handle to two short stubs at the sides of the rear wheel to steer all the kites across the deck into line with the leading kite's wheels resting against the dropping chocks. Their brakes were on so that the steel strop from the trolley could be connected to the port and starboard sides of the fuselage hooks to be adjusted.

The flight-deck party, with the aid of the steersman and his tiller handle, soon ranged the other six kites in line on the starboard side aft to keep the ship on an even keel.

The mechanics prepared the first six kites ready for take-off, warming them up and checking the controls for the pilots, who scrambled into their cockpits and were fastened tightly into their seats with their heads erect, all ready for take-off.

Meanwhile the ship was now on course for the operation to start and the captain gave the order for flying to begin. Fly Co had been

153

watching the proceedings on the deck from his control perch several decks up in the island structure. A red flag was fluttering to indicate he was watching the proceedings on the deck below, and he changed the flag to a green one to indicate the catapulting could start. The deck officer raised his green flag to indicate to the pilot to start revving up his engine. He swung it around faster and faster till the engine was screaming at full power, blotting out the noise of the waiting aircraft engines, which were spluttering unevenly as they ticked over. It gave a terrific roar, with the fuselage vibrating like a jelly. The officer lowered his green flag, which was an order for the catapult operator in his control box to pull the launching lever. This automatically lowered the chocks for the wheels to pass over. The pilot released his brakes, allowing the kite to shoot forward with a terrific whoosh.

Suddenly the clumsy deck-bound object had gained a speed of about 70 knots as the trolley reached the end of its short run, which was cushioned at the end. The wire strop dropped off and the kite to flew off, transformed into a more graceful-looking object as it took to the air.

The catapult operator then pulled the return lever to start up the idling hydraulic pump. It suddenly screamed into action, pumping the hydraulic fluid to form a pressure at the back of the piston which rapidly removed the trolley back to its starting point, also raising the chocks ready to take the next kite. It was taxied forward to have the steel strop connected and adjusted ready for take-off. It went through exactly the same procedure as before and was soon catapulted off the ship.

The remaining kites were lined up on the port side behind the catapult track and were dealt with in exactly the same manner. Then the other two squadrons were brought up from the hangars and were dealt with in exactly the same manner. Within three hours they had all left the ship and flown back to their base. The ship turned around and headed back to harbour where the squadron crews started to pack up all their gear and dump it in the upper hangar or on the flight deck ready to be loaded on to a transport which tied up alongside next day. Then the various personnel attached to the squadrons, including the air gunners, bomb loaders and mechanics, under several officers, brought up their bags and hammocks along with the pilots' tin trunks, etc., and various aircraft equipment. They loaded it onto the flight deck. The crane lifted it onto the ferry boat, which had berthed alongside to take them ashore. Then they loaded up a few trucks to take them back to base.

Various officers and men were left behind to operate the flight deck as kites from the fleet carriers would be flown-on for servicing, light repairs or modifications by the repair staff. Also, the aircraft lighter would be used to ferry damaged kites over from the carriers for repairs. Then, once the working-up period was over, the ship steamed upriver, anchoring beyond Greenock towards the tail of the bank to take on oil, water, aviation spirit and NAAFI supplies (cigarettes, tobacco, pens and ink, bars of Nutty, shoe polish, soap, and numerous other items).

Next day it was Friday and the hands were piped to fall in on the quarterdeck for payment.

On Saturday all the messes were cleaned for captain's rounds. After dinner leave was piped for the port watch until 08.00 on Sunday, then it was the turn of the starboard watch until 08.00 on Monday (most of the crew ending up in Glasgow).

On Tuesday the ship slipped her moorings and proceeded down the Firth of Clyde with half a dozen aircraft landing-on for slight repairs or modifications. A ferry boat waited down the loch to pick up the pilots before rounding the Mull of Galloway, and passing through the North Channel and the Minch, up the coast of Scotland. We rounded Cape Wrath then on through the ruffled waters of the Pentland Firth, passing by the boom defence vessel into the dark-green stormy waters and grey skies of Scapa Flow to join the home fleet. We anchored to the allotted buoy which was the ship's for a fortnight or so. The Fleet Air Arm lighter kept busy transporting aircraft from the fleet carriers (needing servicing or wanting slight repairs) and returning them to the carriers or to base, and bringing more back for repairs.

The ship's company carried out the usual routine of cleaning and touching up the paintwork, whilst down below maintenance work was carried out on steam and water valve glands which were blowing or leaking. Machinery was dismantled for periodical inspection as laid down in the engineering manual. The boilers required opening for cleaning every twenty-eight days for main steaming, which was a big dirty job for the stokers and boiler-room ERA. All the internal gear had to be removed for cleaning with wire brushes, then blackleaded along with the boiler drums, with several hundred water tubes being brushed inside and outside for cleaning. When all was finished the internal gear was reassembled and with new jointing for the manhole doors which were bolted on then they were filled up with water and pressure tested to ensure there were no leaks.

On the flight deck the arrester wires were coiled up and left on the starboard side. The springs that held them up were pulled down flat by hydraulics to aid the deck party as they wheeled the kites over them. The repair parties carried on with their maintenance and repair work.

The chiefs and PO stokers along with the chief and ERAs became familiar with their numerous parts of ship (from on the wheelhouse, on the funnel and flight deck — then from the anchor chains for'ard to the steering gear aft — along with all the auxiliary machinery, boiler rooms and engine rooms).

Last but not least was the most important part of ship, the Fleet Air Arm repair party, which consisted of a supply staff. It looked after a huge range of spare parts, consisting of Merlin engines for Seafires and Barracuda engines, engine spares, pieces of fuselage, wings, rudders, wheels, tyres, propeller blades, various types of engine and hydraulic oil and greases in drums, a variety of machine-gun belts and bullets, bombs, 18-inch torpedoes, depth charges and flares. All the warheads and ammunition were stowed in the magazine for various types of aircraft.

The repair party consisted of various artificers for engines, airframe fitters and electrical and ordinance bods. The fitters worked along with the mechanics, consulting the engine manuals for engine changes or adjustments to tappets, carburettors and magnetos; they also tested out a new engine ready for replacement; worked on the hydraulic legs when they got airlocked and refused to fold up; or renewed burst tyres or damaged wheels.

The airframe fitters carried out repairs on the old stringbag's fuselage by applying a serrated linen patch cut out with pinking shears to stick over a torn hole in the wing or fuselage, then they stuck it on with highly potent-smelling dope. Also the flimsy tails of Seafires, which often crumpled when landing heavily on the rear wheel, kept them busy smoothing over the outer skin and strengthening the weak section. Also they carried out repairs on wing flaps and rudders.

A few electrical bods looked after the electric circuits, and a few ordinance bods worked at freeing any jammed gun belts.

All the crew together made the ship a vital part of the Fleet Air

Arm. We were able to repair, supply and serve the fleet aircraft carriers in any part of the world, being able to carry three complete squadrons of kites and men for replacement or occasional operational service, or ferry sixty kites which could be catapulted off to save time.

There were six port and starboard counter-flooding tanks which had been installed, then cleaned out and painted with red lead. Their seacocks and flooding valves were fitted and had extended spindles to the deck above. There was a simple small brass indicator installed on the bulkhead to indicate when the ship was in the upright position or to show how many degrees the ship was listing over to port or starboard. These positions were manned by ERAs at action stations.

At sea the counter-flooding tanks supplied the port and starboard engine rooms as separate units, so if one side failed the ship could steam homeward bound on one unit.

In the event of the ship being torn open by collision, torpedo or gunfire, flooding several watertight compartments on the starboard side and causing a list of about 20°, the oil fuel and water level in the double-bottom tanks would run up the ship's side in the form of a wedge shape. This would leave the starboard suction valves uncovered, causing the starboard pumps to suck in air then stop. The furnaces would die out and the steam pressure would drop like a stone, causing the whole starboard unit to shut down, including the main turbines. At this stage the port counter-flooding tanks would have been filled up to reduce the list to about 5° or under, causing the oil to flood back in the starboard tanks over the suction valves. Therefore if the starboard unit was undamaged it should be possible to raise steam to restart the starboard main turbines so that the ship could limp back to port with both props turning.

It also made it easier for damage control to plug up the leaks, to shore up the bulkheads to contain the flooding, to isolate broken pipes or blank them off, and to connect up the emergency electric cables and steam ring main with a flexible hosepipe. The Fleet Air Arm would then be able to move their aircraft (of about three tons) as required, or to continue any landing-on of aircraft or even to use the catapult to launch them off.

Several times we practised falling in at our various abandon-ship stations. Gun crews and control parties were exercised to close up at the double for first degree of readiness before action stations was sounded. The guns had to be fully manned quickly, instead of the crews getting caught up in bottlenecks at the bottoms of the ladders as everyone else hastened to get to their action station as fast as possible.

'Action stations' was liable to be sounded at any time of the day or night. If you had been fast asleep you had to leave your hammock unlashed. You might be having a shower or already on watch, but whatever you were doing you would have to get dressed then collect your gas mask, which contained anti-flash gear, goggles and lifebelt from your locker then hurry to your station as quickly as possible. There were several damage-control and fire parties to be manned in groups around the ship where there were cabinets filled with bonnets to cover up shell holes, blank flanges and clamps to block off broken steam or water mains, pipe cutters, stilsons, wedges, hand lamps, flood lamps, chain blocks, and a host of tools and packings. Also there were flexible pipes for connecting up steam and water lines, and cables to connect up the electric ring mains. Then there was a variety of tradesmen, such as shipwrights, EAs and ERAs, and a number of various hands to deal with any emergency that cropped up in their section. Some ERAs when not on watch manned the magazine-flooding valves as well as the six port and starboard counter-flooding tanks. These had small indicators to show the degrees of list to port or starboard if the ship was damaged and taking in water, so that it could be brought back into the upright position. All these positions were connected to damage-control headquarters by an emergency phone system (which generated its own power by turning a handle). It kept them informed of exactly what had happened or enabled them to issue orders.

Damage control's first job was to ensure all the bulkhead and hatch X doors were fully dogged with all six clips and Y doors were dogged with two clips and Z doors were usually kept shut. Also certain X and Y valves, ventilation valves and air trunking valves were shut, along with portholes with their deadlights, and scuttles. In the hangars and on the flight deck the Fleet Air Arm was responsible for raising the lifts to flight-deck level, for lowering the fire curtains to prevent the spread of fire, for the fire hydrants and hoses, the foam-making hoppers and the hangar sprinkling system. The main object of damage control was to isolate each set of compartments between the bulkheads so that any damage or fire could be contained without spreading to the adjoining compartments, so any flood of water would not rush through the ship. Y and Z doors would only be fully dogged in stormy weather to keep the heavy seas out.

As our bathroom was below sea level the washbowl drains would not flow over the side, so an unusual feature had to be installed. This consisted of a drain sump which was sucked dry by a water ejector worked off the fire main. A venturi tube was used to suck up all the water from the sump, discharging it overboard through a seacock above the water level. As this seacock was an X valve it had to be shut at action stations by a long spindle extended to a handwheel on the deck above. This was OK when the seawater was shut off to the ejector, but sometimes it was left on, causing the water to flow back into the sump which gradually filled the bathroom and changing room to a foot or so (depending how long it was before 'secure from action stations' was sounded off). The first man down the hatch was liable to get his feet wet after clanging down the metal ladder and not noticing the rooms were awash with the duckboards, large tin baths and wooden benches floating about.

A similar occurrence had happened on the old target ship, *Centurion*. She was wireless-controlled from an old escort destroyer, *Shikari*, which took the crew off when the battle waggon was in position for the fleet to shoot at the extra armour plate which had replaced her guns. At the end of the day when the crew had returned to their ship they often found that their quarters were awash with several feet of water and the first man down the ladder would have to tread warily to the darkened mess deck below.

The first time our bathroom was flooded after action stations I was due to go on watch and happened to be the first man down the ladder. I went clanging down the steps as usual, never dreaming that there was water lapping over the bottom rung. It came over my shoe when stepping onto it, and was amazed, and puzzled to know where it had come from. However, being in a hurry to change my gear, I managed to grab a tin bath, then gingerly lowered myself into the centre without it tipping up. Then worked my way under the archway into the changing room to my locker on the bottom row. The water had reached over the base, filled up my working shoes and wet the bottom of my overalls. They were carefully squeezed out and emptied my shoes, then grabbed my steaming cap before returning to the ladder and carefully climbing out with my gear without getting any wetter. However, before leaving the compartment I took a quick look round and noticed water was

159

bubbling up from the drain tank. This meant only one thing: the ejector discharge seacock had been left shut and wanted opening. This could be done from the deck above by a handwheel on an extended shaft. I turned it open before going down the engine room to change and keep my watch. As this became a regular occurrence, with some damage-control hand always shutting the seacock without shutting the ejector down, a hand was detailed off to take a look down in the room to ensure the ejector was shut down properly, thus preventing any more flooding.

The engineers' flight-deck party were responsible for slipping the keeps under the lifts to ensure that their armour-plated tops would withstand a direct hit by a 1,000-pound armour-piercing bomb without collapsing. If there was an air raid when the ship was in harbour, and half the ratings were ashore, the duty ERA would climb down several flights of ladders to the hydraulic-machinery space to raise the lifts from the bottom, where they acted as huge ventilation shafts for the hangars. He then slowly raised them with the auxiliary electric hydraulic pump to three inches above the flight deck before inserting the keeps. Then he lowered the lifts onto them, so they became a solid part of the flight deck (the lifts were often stowed in the same way after the Fleet Air Arm had completed their repairs for the day so the deck could be used for recreation).

'Action stations' was sounded off firstly for the gun crews and control parties to man their guns and supply them with ammunition. Unlike the normal ships where the magazines were directly under the gun turrets, all the magazines for the eight 4.5-inch guns, the sixteen 2-pounders and the thirteen 20-mm machine guns (also the Fleet Air Arm torpedoes, bombs, depth charges, and machine-gun belts) were kept in various other magazines for'ard in the hold below the platform deck.

Everything had to be lifted through two armour-plated hatches, which were both closed and dogged tight so they could only be entered by manholes which were shut tight after use.

The ammunition was then trucked over the mess deck to the after end to be lifted through another hatch into a passage where it was trucked through a bulkhead door into the lower hangar (all bulkhead doors were shut and dogged twice after using them so as to contain any flooding which might occur to prevent it spreading into the next compartment).

The ammunition was then trucked onto the for'ard lift, taken to the flight deck and trucked around the four quarters for the 4.5-inch guns mounted on sponsons. The smaller ammunition was supplied around the island structure and flight deck.

The ERAs manned the magazine-flooding valves, which were only opened if the magazines got overheated or were surrounded by fire. Also they manned the six port and starboard counter-flooding tanks only to be used to reduce a list to keep the ship on an even keel and to prevent the water and oil pumps losing suction, making it easier to control and steer the ship.

The chief stoker's fuelling party manned the for'ard base to look after the highly volatile aviation spirit, which was encased in three large metal containers surrounded by water. They also looked after the numerous port and starboard double-bottom oil-fuel tanks, which were all interconnected to the port and starboard boiler fuel pumps so as to be changed over when empty, or pumped out to the other side to keep the ship on an even keel and keep the red-hot furnaces roaring and burning brightly.

The main damage-control party consisted of a large cross section of artisans: namely, shipwrights, ERAs, stokers (engine room), EAs (electrical) and OAs (ordinance).

It was positioned towards the centre of the ship with a large cabinet and space which contained a vast variety of equipment to codge up any damage and to stop it spreading.

There were several lengths of suction hoses which could be coupled up to the fire and bilge pumps to keep the water level down in flooded compartments. There were also several large baulks of timber and wedges to prop up any bulging bulkheads when a compartment was full of water. There were also several large battery boxes with floodlights to get lights into damaged compartments when their supply was broken off from the switchboard.

There were several flexible steam pipes along with nuts and bolts and jointing material, which could be used on broken steam or water pipes. Also there was a variety of strops and chain blocks for lifting gear, as well as hammers and chisels and 7- and 14-pound lump hammers, spanners, crowbars, pipe cutters, hacksaws, and a special face mask with a long flexible hose to enable a man to go into a gas-filled compartment to shut off a valve or collect something that was required to save the ship.

The after party consisted of writers, cooks, stewards and a few sickbay staff and seamen. Their role was to replace the ill and injured. They would also make sure all X and Y doors were kept shut, or shut down any valves if the fire main was broken, or tackle a fire if it broke out.

In damage control the first thing to be done was to close all X and Y bulkhead doors and dog them twice. If any flooding occurred, or fire started, they could be fully clipped to contain the flood or fire. Also any air vents would be closed to starve the fire of oxygen to prevent it from becoming an inferno. In the event of steam or water pipes being broken the bulkhead valves would be shut to maintain the pressure in the system. If the damage was in one of the engine or boiler rooms the whole port or starboard unit, including one turbogenerator, could be shut down. They could also shut down one of the supply valves to the port or starboard ring main, which supplied the evaporators, the two fire and bilge pumps, the hydraulic lift and catapult pumps, as well as the two high-pressure air compressors, the steam for the hot-water calorifier and steam for the galley and its baking ovens. The other side could be used to steam the ship into port and also supply the other turbogenerator with steam for lighting and its ring main with power for the steering gear, anchor, cranes, refrigerator and many more electrical pumps and machinery run by electricity, not forgetting the lighting around the ship.

After a daily exercise the ship returned to Lamlash to anchor for the night. As the boilers and engines steamed in separate port and starboard units the order was rung down from the bridge, 'finished with main engines'. Both port and starboard engine rooms were shut down. The two starboard boilers were also shut down with one in the port boiler room, leaving the other one auxiliary with its main stops shut and the auxiliary superheated-steam and saturated-steam valves left open. They supplied the port turbogenerator and the port ring mains. The superheated steam went to two fire and bilge pumps and hydraulic pumps for the lift and catapult; the saturated steam went to the evaporators to produce our daily water supply, to the calorifiers to produce hot water and steam for the bakery ovens, and to the jet on the flight deck to indicate the way the wind was blowing.

Now as the electricians had a job to do on the port generator it was shut down and the starboard one should have been left running to supply the power and lighting for the ship, but someone had omitted to open the cross-connection valve which supplied the starboard generator and ring mains with steam, so it had shut down leaving the whole ship in darkness.

The first time it happened I was having my tea and it was my job to nip down below smartly and stumbled on some unforeseen object in the dark when groping my way through the passages which only had faint glimmers of light. It was a perilous journey without even a small torch, especially down the ladders. Not knowing which turbogenerator it was that had to be restarted I made for the after one, only to find it was the wrong choice and had been shut down. So I had to gingerly retrace my steps and make my way to the for'ard one, taking good care to locate the top rung of the ladders and grab the chain hand guide to prevent me crashing down to the bottom in the dark. By this time the steam pressure had been restored in the line, but the compartment was black except for a glimmer from the emergency lamp, which did nothing to light up the valves and controls which had to be shut down before the turbo could be restarted. The stoker of the watch had not appeared to aid me, so decided to try to start up the machine in the dark. First I had to shut all the valves down and reset them from the beginning. So groped my way, taking care to avoid any hot spots which could give me a nasty burn on my wrists or hands whilst resetting the vacuum trip valve and then latched it to remain open until a vacuum of 20 inches had been created in the condenser, which was still hot. Then the main steam inlet trip valve was screwed back to reset so that it could be cracked open to start the rotor spinning. The oil pump had to be cranked around like the devil to flood the turbine bearings. The mechanical pump took over to supply the oil pressure, which also drove the circulating water pump (which began to cool the condenser) and the extraction pump, which maintained half a glass of condensate water in the bottom of the condenser.

As the turbo was a self-contained unit, all three pumps were driven on one shaft geared up to the rotor. Soon the pilot lamps began to glow when the voltage needle swung up to 230 volts on the meter, lighting up the control board. A test tube of water was drawn off from the extraction-pump discharge and tested with two drops of silver nitrate. If contaminated with seawater from the numerous tube end glands of the condenser cooling tubes, it would change to a milky white. Fortunately the water remained clear. Now the turbo could be run up to full speed so that the vacuum trip latch could be taken off and the air ejector adjusted to 29.8 inches with the excess gland steam being adjusted so as not to heat up the bearings.

The switchboard was then informed by phone that the machine was ready for load. The EAs started building the load up by putting in the breakers, so the amps began to mount up on the ammeter until the machine was on full load, when the speed was adjusted. So I handed the machine back to the capable hands of the stoker, who had suddenly appeared, and gradually the compartments and messes were lit up once again.

Flight-deck accidents mostly occurred in fairly rough weather which none of the pilots had experienced before. The flight deck rose up and fell several feet, with the *Unicorn* turning out of the wind until the deck had been cleared. If the wind suddenly veered when the kites were landing, then the *Unicorn* would alter course to get back into the wind to allow the rest of the kites to land. As the pilots became familiar with their deck landings at sea they became a little cocky and over confident, causing a spate of minor accidents which kept the repair party busy.

The most common one was bouncing down too heavily on the deck, then missing all the arrester wires, often bursting a tyre, into the bargain, before running into the barrier which was usually put up part way to catch the kite on its legs to do as little damage as possible, depending on how fast it approached.

There were several incidents where a heavy landing would burst a tyre causing the kite to run to the edge of the flight deck, sometimes with the arrester hook restraining it from taking a big plunge over the side. One teetered on the edge of the flight deck with the flight-deck party hanging on to the fuselage and wings like grim death to allow the pilot to climb out and escape. They then recovered the kite if possible. Sometimes one would carry on over the side with a crash, bang, wallop, and a gasp of amazement going up from the spectators. Usually the pilot bobbed up to the surface with his Mae West life jacket inflated a few minutes later. He waited to be hauled out by the crash boat, which raced to the scene of the accident. The crash boat rang down 'full speed astern' on her engines for an emergency stop right beside the pilot, who was hauled out of the water sopping wet.

The higher speeds of the fighter aircraft made them more prone to accidents. One particular one I noticed when glancing through a porthole was a Seafire which suddenly tumbled over into the briny upside down, with the canopy still in place over the cockpit. The pilot managed to open it. I thought he was a goner and would never get out from inside the fuselage so rushed up on deck to find the aircraft had already sunk out of sight, but suddenly my heart jumped for joy as he had managed to undo his safety harness and bobbed up wearing his inflated Mae West life jacket. He waited to be picked up by the crash boat, sopping wet, but none the worse for his frightening experience.

Accidents caused the repair staff to be kept busy replacing broken propeller blades and burst tyres, and sorting out all the other complaints from all the fleet carriers, such as renewing or servicing the engines and testing them in the special shop. Sometimes the small lighter was sent over with a reconditioned aircraft to one of the fleet carriers or to collect a damage aircraft.

One afternoon I was sent for as the temperature of the cold room had suddenly shot up, which was not surprising really as the CO_2 machinery was a Weirs new design which had never been fully tested. (It was quite common for new machinery to have teething troubles.) This one was the first to occur and stemmed from the fact that the compressors had twin cylinders with the piston rods' glands sealed with non-freezing oil to hold the gas pressure in the system as the rods bobbed up and down through tight-fitting gland seals. Unfortunately no provision had been made for the small amount of oil that escaped into the system. It should have been collected in a small oil trap on the discharge side of the compressor but this had been omitted causing the oil to work its way through the grids (or evaporators) in the cold rooms, etc. It accumulated along with rust and water, which entered the system via the gas bottles, to form a complete blockage in the scale trap.

The stoker on watch told me that the compressor discharge was running hot at 180°F, so the first thing we did was to add a bottle of CO_2 gas to the system. It had no effect as the cold rooms were beginning to defrost, so the cause was other than lack of gas. By changing over the scale traps we were amazed to find the one in use was blocked up solid. The plant started to work normally, gradually bringing the room temperatures down to their correct readings. We felt quite pleased at having located the problem so easily, then all we had to do was to remove the offending scale trap, which needed a 3-inch ring spanner for unscrewing a large brass plug. It required a few hefty clouts with a hammer to break the joint seal, then after that it had to be dragged around as the threads were tight and it was hard to turn. After struggling awhile the plug was dragged onto its last thread. The worst was over, or so we thought, but we hadn't realised there was 200 or 300 pounds gas pressure behind the plug. As it was blissfully unscrewed it was expected to drop out into one's hand, instead of which it was hurled out like a cannonball. It knocked the spanner from my grasp, giving both hands a nasty jar which stung with pain as the spanner was forced from my grip. It sped across the compartment, just missing a copper cooling pipe and ending up against the ship's side with a resounding wallop, which terrified us both into the bargain.

I soon recovered from the sudden shock, then removed the fine gauze trap with the contents full of a frozen mixture of moisture, oil, and rust. It looked like the brown mixture in a tin of Kattomeat (as advertised on the telly). It was soon cleaned out, then screwed back into position.

The next job was to send for my boss to show him the contents of the trap and explain how dangerous the cap nut was when it was blown out with a terrific bang. He brought down the senior engineer (Spriggs) with him and I explained what had happened, and also told him about the oil separator used on a Hall's refrigerating system, which collected the surplus non-freezing oil from the piston-rod gland seal which was kept flooded with it. The senior engineer said he would look into the matter and take it up with Weirs, the makers, and also said he would have a moisture trap made in the workshop. The idea was that it should be fitted in between the charging valve and the bottle of CO_2 gas, so that when the gas was released to top up the system it would pass through a cartridge of silica gel, which would absorb the moisture. It worked quite well for the first two bottles of gas, then the cartridge was changed for a dry one. He arranged with the chief cook to have the wet cartridge dried out in the galley oven ready for future use. It was OK as far as it went, but still left me with a dread of a future repeat performance of the sudden explosive missile shooting across the room with a terrific bang.

However, I decided the only way forward to deal with this problem was to sleep on it. It caused me endless sleepless nights, with the problem mulling around my brain until I eventually fell asleep from mental exhaustion.

However, necessity is the mother of invention, and, after much searching for a solution to the problem, one morning after a good night's sleep a brainwave occurred to me out of the blue. It was so simple that it nearly caused me to tip out of my hammock with delight. So during the forenoon without seeking permission or approval I wasted no time in modifying the second scale trap. It was easy as it had not been used and had no pressure of gas behind it. The plug could be withdrawn without fear, and was quickly modified by filing three equally spaced tapered grooves across the first three threads, so that when the plug was unscrewed again it would release the gas pressure through the grooves before dropping into one's hand. Within an hour the modification was fully tested and was a huge success. The traps were then changed over, leaving the other trap with the gas behind it to be modified as soon as enough courage could be plucked up to tackle it.

Several weeks elapsed with nothing being mentioned about this highly dangerous maker's component, which could easily be a killer if at any time a stranger to the system from the duty watch was required to remove the scale trap and happened to be in the range of fire as the plug was hurled across the room.

By this time I was prepared for the sudden frightening shock, and borrowed a pair of gloves and hammered the plug free with a ring spanner. I then used an ordinary open-ended spanner to unscrew the plug gently, gripping it so it would fall on the deck with a clatter, not hurting my hands as it did when the plug shot out with a whoosh and a terrific bang.

The plug was quickly modified so that there was no fear of being blown out again with a kick like a mule. It was quickly replaced, and both traps could now be removed with safety.

Several days later I received an urgent call from the duty stoker that the refrigerating plant had sprung a leak. I had just finished my tea so put on my overalls and went to review the situation. Bill, the stoker of the watch, was on at the time and told me he had already added a bottle of gas to the system but it was gradually leaking away. However, it was not a very big leak as the candle on the deck was still alight. The compressor was only being run for short periods at the time so the situation was not desperate. Nevertheless the leak had to be located. There was no hissing gas to be heard so we started checking the piston-rod glands with a lighted taper. They got worn with the constant rubbing up and down and needed tightening up from time to time with a large C spanner. This had to be done very carefully, otherwise they would instantly overheat and discolour. Also, the rods would score which made matters worse as they would need nursing by applying a brush of oil and constantly brushing until they cooled off; or else they would get hot and discolour the rods.

Bill acquired a paintbrush and made up a solution of soapy water, which we applied to all the joints and pipes which we could reach around the system and condenser, but we found no leaks.

As the plant was already showing signs of shortage of gas, in desperation we changed over the compressors and condensers, isolating the one that had been in use, which we stopped.

Then we charged up the system again with another bottle of gas, noting the addition and change in the logbook. Then I informed Lieutenant E. Whitehead of the situation. We waited half an hour to see what would happen. There was no further sign of any leakage of gas. It looked suspiciously like a leak in the other condenser as its pressure gauge was showing a drop with its finger. So I left Bill to carry on his watch, then visited the compartment again before slinging my hammock, finding everything was working OK and the cold rooms had come down to their correct temperatures.

Next morning all was well, so we awaited a visit from the senior engineer, Lieutenant Commander Spriggs, to give his judgement as to what was to be done. After a short discussion he decided the condenser should be dismantled for pressure testing. It should have been an easy job; however, naval construction, which allowed a series of pipes to be installed in the most awkward places, especially near deckheads, in corners or around the machinery once it was bolted down in position on its bed, was the problem.

We soon had the high-pressure and circulating pipes removed, then unscrewed about fifteen $^5/_8$-inch Whitworth bolts so that we were able to break the flanged joint on the condenser door, so as to withdraw the coil of tubes about three quarters of the way out. After discovering the coil was barred from slipping the whole way out by a cooling pipe across its path, we undid two large nuts on the coil to remove the end door (which weighed abut 30 pounds and had a diameter of about six inches more than that of the coil). We expected this would enable the tubes to slip under the obstruction without more ado, only to find it needed lowering another inch before it would pass through.

There was nothing else for it but to draw out a set of chain blocks from the engineers' ready-use store to lower the condenser down a little. We removed three ¾-inch Whitworth securing bolts, then slacked off the fourth one which was in the far corner of the condenser. We then noticed that if we used this bolt as a fulcrum, we could lower the other end by removing the blocks from the centre to the end. This would allow the coil to tilt and slip right under the offending pipe. Success at last! We managed to get the coil out into the bottle compartment, then stopped for a stand-easy brew. We then blanked off one end of the pipe, connecting the other end up to the low-pressure air line, brushing soapy water around the two brazed joints where the two cupro-nickel pipe ends had been inserted into two screwed brass sleeves. They passed through the end door where they were secured by two large nuts, which held them in place so two high-pressure joints could be made for the inlet and outlet pipes. We located the leak on one of the brazed joints where a stream of bubbles issued forth. Then our engineer made arrangements to have the coil humped up several ladders, along the mess deck and through passages to the coppersmith's shop in the bows of the ship. It was then left for Jack Frost to re-braze the joints.

Whilst the coil was being repaired we cleaned up all the flanges of the cooling pipes and the condenser, cutting new rubber insertion joints for them. We also ran down all the nuts and bolts with taps and stocks and dies, then oiled the threads so that all the nuts turned easily. This saved a great deal of time when reassembling all the bits and pieces. Jack Frost soon completed the brazing and tested the joints with an air pressure of 2,500 pounds to make sure they were perfectly sound. Once satisfied, a party of stokers was sent to bring back the coil for reassembly, which was much easier than taking it down. We used two freshly annealed diamond-shaped copper rings so they would be soft to make a good gas-tight joint for the high-pressure pipe connections. We soon had the compressor back in good working order.

Convoy Duty

On 19 July 1943 steam was raised to be ready at 06.40 for 20 knots to slip the cable by 07.30 when the ship left harbour screened by a flotilla of destroyers, along with the battle waggon *Duke of York*, accompanied by USS *Alabama*, USS *South Dakota,* and the aircraft carriers *Illustrious* and *Renown* to carry out Operation Husky. It turned out to be an unsuccessful sortie along the Norwegian coast to divert the German's attention whilst our convoys made a safe journey to Murmansk. (We failed to make contact with the enemy forces.)

However, on 27 July *Unicorn*, along with a destroyer screen, the *Duke of York* and *South Dakota*, had embarked a squadron of specially prepared Seafires and Martlets (Hell Cats) for the operation. They were all tanked up by the chief stoker's fuelling party, and the armourers loaded up the machine guns with belts of bullets, all ready to take off to supply air cover for our convoys, which were being constantly attacked by German aircraft.

On 31 July our pilots were on patrol when they had a minor success in spotting and shooting down five BV 138 reconnaissance flying boats off the coast of Norway, which had been spying on the movements of our convoys and patrols to Russia. They were spotted after a tip off from British Intelligence, in an operation called Governor, that the German fleet was out.

On our return to Scapa Flow the winds were strong and squally at 70 knots. This made tying up to the buoy a nightmare. The thirty-three feet of combined height of both hangars above the upper deck must have made a fifty-foot freeboard above the water, causing the sheer sides of the ship to act as sails. Sudden gusts of wind blew the ship away from the buoy as the cable party tried to secure the cable so that the anchor chain could be lowered and attached to the buoy.

A cutter was launched, manned with a PO coxswain at the helm and a crew of strong seamen to row the boat. It landed two seamen buoy jumpers on top of the buoy to secure a long 3-inch cable which was lowered down and shackled on to secure the ship temporarily until the anchor chain could be passed down. (This was a simple job on the cross-channel ferries. Two men and a motor boat were used to drag an inch cable across to the buoy, then secure it so that the ferry could be winched out sideways into midstream in the River Lagan.) However, the bows kept yawing away from the buoy, causing the engine-room telegraphs to be worked overtime, and giving the throttle watchkeepers a strenuous time. (They obeyed eighty-four orders in all — mostly 'slow ahead 50 revs', 'stop', and 'slow astern 50 revs' — within half an hour.

Eventually the buoy jumpers secured the hawser temporarily so that the anchor chain could be lowered, then connected to the shackle with a split link by the blacksmith. Then a sudden gust of wind sprang up, catching the ship's side with such a force that it tugged on the hawser hard, tilting the buoy right over, causing the two jumpers to be tipped off into the sea out of harm's way. Then it happened — the hawser snapped, springing back like a whiplash. Fortunately the coxswain heard the snap and ordered his crew to row like the clappers as he steered the boat out of harm's way. If the cable had caught the cutter it would have sunk, as well as killing any man who happened to be sitting in its way. The coxswain then turned his boat about to fish out the two buoy jumpers with a boathook. They were cold and sopping wet and visibly shaken by their terrifying experience. Then they were taken back on board to be replaced by another pair of seamen. A 3½-inch hawser was unwound to be lowered down in place of the broken one.

Eventually it was secured on the shackle. This enabled the blacksmith to complete his task by securing the anchor chain to the shackle by a split chain link so the hawser could be removed.

The ship swung around the buoy for some while, which was usually the perks of the battleships depending on seniority of the captains. A duty trawler went around the ships, picking up several hundred liberty men. There was evening leave daily, extended to afternoon leave at weekends, to a large NAAFI canteen which had been purpose-built on the windswept island of Flotta. We could have a good stroll around the sheep tracks before going to buy big eats at the canteen. There was also a beer bar with a few billiard tables and dartboards; also a large cinema showed two different films each week and often had visits from stage artistes.

Eventually the ship cast off from the buoy, heading back to the Clyde area to fly off thirty kites with pilots and maintenance crews to returned to base. Six stringbags embarked with pilots and crews for convoy escort duties. Then thirty pilots landed-on their Seafires, with their personnel embarking later.

The ship then moved upriver to be provisioned for a month. The stores were filled up to capacity with the usual victuals, the various ship's tanks were filled to the brim, and the magazines were filled with ammunition. As usual the last collection of mail was piped to close several hours before proceeding to sea. A small team, including the padre, the jaunty and the crushers, had a big job of censoring the mail so that no hint of our whereabouts or wanderings was given away. There would be in the region of a thousand letters to be read through carefully and censored. Any offending long and short words were cut out so as not to give a single hint of our movements. A few of the worst ones used to look like blanks on a crossword puzzle in reverse or a stencil outfit by the time the censors had finished with them.

As usual the captain never informed us of our destination until we were nearly there, which was a wise precaution against careless talk. 'Walls have ears', so the saying goes, and often a German spy would hang around docklands and the pubs. A loose tongue could let a clue slip, or sometimes packing cases had their destination marked on them instead of reference numbers, or the time of a ship sailing was a useful clue which could lead to an organised reception committee in the form of a wolf pack of U-boats or dive-bombers lying in wait to sink our ships.

We set off outward bound from the Clyde area, steaming up around the north coast of Ireland, heading into the Atlantic on a southerly course streaming paravanes to protect the ship from floating mines and with degaussing gear switched on to avoid magnetic mines.

Each day at dusk 'darken ship' was piped over the tannoy. The hands closed all scuttles and deadlights, and all Y and Z doors leading to the upper decks, to prevent any chinks of light from showing around the ship, which would give its position away to any lurking

U-boat. Then close-range armaments hands were piped to close up for an hour, then again for an hour at dawn next day.

We joined a convoy with several small converted aircraft carriers (converted from banana boats, refrigeration ships or small tankers). They were nicknamed Woolworth carriers as they were easy and cheap to convert. HMS *Attacker*, *Battler*, *Hunter*, and *Stalker* all played an excellent part in providing our convoys with air cover with the old faithful stringbag that could take off in a storm to bomb, depth-charge or torpedo any menacing U-boats.

Our escorts consisted of two destroyers and four frigates. We carried thirty Seafires along with our six stringbags for use on voyage to patrol around our convoy and keep any lurking U-boat at bay.

Stringbags were kept fully fuelled. The armourer always checked the machine guns to ensure they were fully loaded and the bomb racks were stocked with rockets or depth charges, bombs or torpedoes, or whatever was required.

We proceeded at a speed of 12 knots, then after five and a half days at sea we drew level with the Iberian peninsula. We were on our way to the familiar haunt of Gibraltar, which most of us had visited before.

The convoy made an extra-wide sweep around Cape Trafalgar (the scene of Lord Nelson's victory against the combined forces of Napoleon and the Spanish on 21 October 1805). Then we pressed on, rounding Cape Marroqui, giving it a wide berth before entering the Strait of Gibraltar (which was thirty-five to fifty miles long by eight and a half to twenty-three miles wide).

Soon we were sailing over a large patch of water which rippled evenly at a speed of 3 knots. The colder water from the Atlantic steadily poured into the Mediterranean and steadily evaporated under the burning sun, with the result that it became more salty, and then flowed outward into the Atlantic.

Our ship, having the most senior captain, led the way, nosing into Algeciras Bay with the rest following. The bay was crammed full of merchantmen awaiting escort. As we passed by the naval patrol boats and other vessels there was the usual shrill piping of the bosun's call, standing to attention and saluting as the ship passed by them. Also, as we passed by, the merchant ships dipped their red ensigns (nicknamed red dusters, as many were old, tattered and dirty). Our ship acknowledged the custom by dipping our white ensign as a return salute.

We berthed inside the harbour alongside the dockyard with the small carriers tied up alongside the south mole, which was long enough to take all four ships. (It used to be part of an important coaling station which was often covered with fine black coal dust.)

The harbour was large enough to take the whole of the Mediterranean fleet, known as Force H, under the control of Admiral (Slim) Somerville.

In the dockyard there were three dry docks (large, medium and small) with a pumping station to drain them dry.

The equipment in the yard included tall shear legs (a crane for lifting in high masts), a donkey boiler to supply docked ships with steam for washing and cooking, large spare boiler drums, odd guns and turrets, a supply of metal and armour-plating, racks of pipes, and drums of oil all stacked up in various sizes.

The King's Bastion was a breakwater in the centre of the harbour with a passage at both ends. To the north was a mole which had five pens for the use of small boats. The rock was named after Jebel Tarik, a Moor who first captured it from Spain. The old rectangular Moorish Castle, standing on high ground next to the prison at the north end of the rock, bears witness to some ancient affray as the walls are pockmarked by cannon balls.

The town was protected by thick walls and heavy thick oak gates, having withstood numerous violent sieges. Large cannons were dragged up to the summit of the rock via long winding sloping paths with hairpin corners. Large iron rings had been set into the path sides to aid soldiers as they sweated heavily, straining to pull up the heavy cannons to the numerous galleries and vantage points around the rock.

Spain lay just across a long isthmus which had been converted into a small airstrip for RAF planes (it has now been greatly expanded to become an airport). The nearest town over the border was La Linea de la Concepción.

At the base of the sheer face of the rock lay the race course and to the left of it was the exit road which passed by Trafalgar Cemetery, which was full of Jersey lilies and freesias. Also, there were the graves of two brothers said to have been struck down by the same cannonball — which was a rare occurrence to say the least.

The main street ran for one mile along the side base of the rock, with a narrow gate and the governor's residence (guarded by two redcap sentries) at one end and another gateway at the other end.

The ancient battered buses, laden down to capacity so no bounce was left in their springs, chugged through these narrow spaces with barely an inch to spare on either side. Their roof racks were crammed with gear the Spaniards were taking home.

Halfway up the rock was where the curious Barbary tailless apes lived and were kept by an army corporal. The story goes that when the apes die off the British will leave the rock.

The rock had a narrow road running up it with extra-sharp hairpin bends where army lorries had to reverse to get round them. Also it was pierced with numerous galleries with gun emplacements, an emergency hospital, powerhouse, stores and magazines. A reservoir, which collected the town water from the flat concreted catchment area on the other side of the rock, was perched above Catalan Bay with its sole long fine sandy beach.

As the ship lay alongside for several days she took on oil, water and provisions (the NAAFI stores were topped up with fags and Nutty, etc.). So we took advantage of the make-and-mend time with leave in the evening.

We visited Rosia Bay, south of the dockyard, which was overlooked by the RN hospital. This bay was where Lord Nelson's flagship *Victory* returned limping into harbour dismasted after the Battle of Trafalgar. Spare masts, which were kept in the dockyard, were quickly fitted into place so the ship could return home to England with the great man's body preserved in a large cask of wine, to be buried with great pomp and ceremony with the church bells ringing throughout the land to celebrate this national hero. Although the great man had been struck down by a musket ball from a marine on the tops of the *Redoubtable* and was mortally wounded, his plan of action, which had been so brilliantly conceived, was strictly adhered to until 17.00 that day when the battle was over.

We carried on around the rock to Europa Point, where there is a lighthouse. It was quite cold, with a breeze from the Atlantic. This was the spot which formed part of the Pillars of Hercules, which in ancient times guarded the entrance to the Mediterranean. It was perched upon the 300-foot-high projecting terrace, together with the 100-foot-high cliffs off Ceuta (in Spanish Morocco, across the strait). We visited Catalan Bay for a swim, only to find it was sealed off with barbed-wire defences. So we returned to the ship with plenty of fruit (tomatoes, oranges, bananas, grapes and apples), all of which were very scarce at home.

175

Salerno

One morning I had an early call to change over the turbogenerator so that the EAs could change the brushes as they were sparking badly. After this I went up on the flight deck for half an hour, gazing across the Bay of Algeciras, which was packed full of ships, to enjoy the sweet scented air which wafted over the bay (probably coming from the cork trees). I wondered if any German spies were gazing across from the other side, watching the movements of our ships.

At the end of the day I went down below to keep the first watch, only to find my usual throttle watchkeeper, Tom, had been replaced by a young mechanician by the name of Staddon, who had joined the ship before leaving the UK. He had a photographic mind and knew all about the working of the ship's machinery. Unfortunately for him he was rather careless on the practical side, especially as he was a candidate for a warrant engineer officer.

We had completed the warming-up stage, which was to heat the turbines up to 160°F, then we shut the throttle valves opening up the gland steam and the air ejector to slowly raise the vacuum to 20 inches. Then we turned the turbines two revs ahead and two revs astern every three minutes. At this stage I had an urgent call on the blower from the refrigerating compartment that the condenser was getting hot and the cold rooms were beginning to defrost. Assuming nothing could go wrong I nipped down to locate the trouble without a relief, leaving the throttle watchkeeper in charge. Fortunately it was easy to locate the trouble as the circulating water pump suction was blocked up. So the stoker of the watch shut it down whilst I opened up the filter trap. It was a simple job undoing one screwed wing nut at one side of the top cover, then opening it up on the hinge

176

at the other side. Then I left the stoker to withdraw the grid from the centre to clear out the holes (which were choked up with bits of paper, driftwood, seaweed and jellyfish), box up the trap again, then open all the necessary valves to start up again.

I returned to the engine room within five minutes, feeling well pleased to have sorted it out so quickly, only to find Chief Mechanician Bradley was on the blower from the starboard engine room to give me a blast and inform me that our port turbine was silently spinning round, turning the prop shaft. This was showing on the repeat tachometer whilst my dozy watchkeeper had not spotted his own tacho turning. I shut the ahead throttle, then gave a blast of steam through the astern turbine to stop the shaft. It could have been worse but no damage was done. Then we completed our watch, having prepared the engine room for sea.

At 24.00 we were relieved by the middle-watch men, who took the ship out at dead of night. It was fully blacked out, without a chink of light showing from the doors and portholes round the hull and superstructure so we could not be detected. We threaded our way through the narrow shipping lane, leading our small convoy, veering to port then sailing due east, with our escorts taking up their stations, bound for an unknown destination in the Mediterranean. We passed by several small Spanish fishing boats. They were brightly lit up with three groups of large electric bulbs which shone down on the water to attract large shoals of sardines to the surface so they could be netted. We steamed on at high speed for several hours to be well out of sight of land before daybreak so as not to give our position away. We eventually passed Malta without incident, before meeting up with Force H from Gibraltar, units of the home fleet.

On the third day out our flotilla assembled to carry out Operation Campania in the Tyrrhenian Sea arriving off the Gulf of Salerno on 8 September during the first watch in the hours of darkness.

As dawn broke the ship's company went to action stations. The Fleet Air Arm prepared all the kites ready for take-off to form an air umbrella to protect the huge armada of ships and landing craft. The Allies, which consisted of the US army under Lieutenant General Mark Clark and the British X Corps started to land their thousands of troops from the landing craft, followed by huge supplies of tanks, guns, ammunition, etc., transported by the tank-landing craft. The British battleships and cruisers then opened up with a terrific bombardment, closely followed by dive-bombers from our fleet carriers to soften up any pockets of resistance. Operation Avalanche had begun.

Meanwhile, the *Unicorn,* along with the Woolworth carriers (*Attacker, Battler, Stalker* and *Hunter*), mustered seventy-eight Seafires in all between them. The small carriers each carried a dozen kites, which were formed into groups to form the umbrella to protect the whole of the shipping area during the hours of daylight by warding off any Jerry fighters or bomber attacks.

The hands were piped to flying stations from dawn to dusk. Our carrier steamed in and out of the wind to fly off our kites at 18 knots in the vast area of the Tyrrhenian Sea. We stayed in the background, well away from the main operation area, so that all five ships could work together. When all the kites were due for refuelling another batch of kites was assembled for take-off before the others could land back on again.

Fortunately the sea was calm, which was beneficial for the landings of these flimsy kites, as a heavy landing tended to crumple the tails up as they were far from robust. Once in the air they gave the advantage of speed and manoeuvrability to the Fleet Air Arm pilots against the Jerry bombers.

Our Fleet Air Arm repair staff was kept busy servicing all the kites. They were flown-on for repairing all the minor defects in the engines, fuselage, wings, flaps, rudder, etc. Burst tyres or broken props had to be replaced on their own ships as the kites were unfit for flying.

One marine officer landed his Seafire on an airstrip ashore to make some minor adjustment to his wing flaps, without which he would have been unable to land on the small patch of fight deck. He left his engine ticking over whilst he performed his task, which enabled him to land safely back on board without damage to his kite.

For the first few days there was little resistance. Everything went well for the Allies, with the British capturing the town of Salerno on 10 September. Our air umbrella allowed the landings to be carried out without any losses or interruptions. However, as each day ended the resistance increased as the Jerries rushed reinforcements to the front from surrounding areas.

Next day the Jerries launched a series of surprise attacks from Dornier 217 K2 bombers, which carried two Fitz X and HS radio-controlled glider bombs or missiles. They were very fast, with a maximum speed of 270 mph, increasing to 326 mph on releasing their loads. Their first two attacks came without any warning or any indication from which direction they had come. All the vessels, which were packed tightly in the bay, went to action stations with extra lookouts as well as gun crews, and control parties closed up. The defending fighter patrols had to be altered to ward off any more attacks, which continued throughout the next five days.

Not withstanding these new precautions, several missiles found their mark, causing a considerable amount of damage to the cruisers *Savannah* and *Uganda*, seriously damaging the battleship *Warspite* and sinking the hospital ship *Newfoundland* along with a transport vessel.

On Monday 13 September a huge detachment of German panzers was mustered to launch an overwhelming attack on the Allied troops, forcing them to retreat back to their beachhead whilst our supporting fleet opened up with a terrific round-the-clock bombardment. Missiles whistled over the heads of the troops for the next few days, while the Fleet Air Arm dive-bombers attacked alternately during lulls in the firing to soften up any strongholds of resistance. After this the Allies began to advance slowly again.

After a fortnight, with the successful conclusion of the landings, the fleet split up. The eastern part returned to Alexandria while Force H and the home fleet returned to Gibraltar. It was nearly a 1,000-mile trip (Gibraltar to Naples is 970 miles).

The *Unicorn* remained behind until the end of the month with three destroyers who had recently arrived after escorting a convoy of transport and supply vessels from Gibraltar. A Royal Naval auxiliary tanker refuelled the destroyers and the *Unicorn,* who spent their time slowly cruising up and down to give air-raid warnings to all the tank-landing craft and transports engaged in maintaining supplies and landing more troops.

A flight of Seafires were lined up behind the catapult ready for instant take-off when any dots showed up on the ship's radar screen which had a radius of thirty-five miles. After several scares no more aircraft arrived, so eventually the ship, along with her escorts, turned back towards Gibraltar, calling in at Algiers, which gleamed in the sunshine.

This city was once the headquarters in the Turkish era of piracy and slavery. It was situated on the seaward slopes of high fortified hills with the shore extending along a large semicircular bay. The kasbah (fortress) formed the apex of the triangular part of the old Arab town on the starboard side facing the harbour. The old part of the city contained a motley throng of Arabs, Moors, Jews and Europeans, and the prisons and palaces of the old Turkish rulers. The new part of the city was on the port side facing the harbour. It was modern, having been built by the French. It contained government offices, wharves, business buildings and several mosques. Two European suburbs were in the background. It was an extra-large harbour where all the ships were neatly tied up in rows, anchored ahead and astern.

We tied up in harbour during the forenoon, then a make and mend with leave for the port watch was piped in the afternoon. Some of the younger men took advantage of it to explore the kasbah with its ancient history and alluring influence. Most men preferred to wait and catch a later liberty boat when the sun was beginning to set and the locals had stirred from their siesta in the heat of the day. There was leave for the opposite watch next evening. We continued our voyage on the following forenoon.

Eventually the ship arrived back in Gibraltar and tied up alongside the inner wharf. This had just been completed and the engine room was in the process of shutting down when the second blackout occurred, causing all work down below to grind to a halt. The ship warmed up considerably as all the ventilation ceased. The switchboard was suddenly inundated with calls for the engineer's office as everyone groped around for the nearest handset in the dark. This jammed up all the lines.

The captain, who was changing to go ashore for an important meeting, was first to enquire what was going on. He was closely followed by the Fleet Air Arm repair staff, who were in danger of tripping over numerous articles scattered round the hangar decks. Then it was the cooks who were preparing the next meal in the galley, followed by the doctors in the sickbay who were treating minor ailments, the dentist who was filling a tooth, the supply ratings taking stock of their stores, the writers making up their pay ledgers, and the jaunty preparing his list of defaulters. There was a host of other complaints.

I was off watch at the time on deck gazing over the hindrail at all the ships at anchor in the Bay of Algeciras. Suddenly I heard a hubbub down below and nipped down to investigate. It was all in darkness. I groped my way down several ladders, closely followed by Commander E. Oliver in his white overalls and gloves and carrying a torch. He never said a word but aided me by lighting up the controls whilst I reset the steam valve, etc. We had the machine back on the board in five minutes flat, so the lighting and power was quickly restored and the fans could be restarted.

Next day lorryloads of supplies started arriving to fill up the empty stores. It was a vast undertaking which was spread out over the whole period we were there, as there was no direct passage to them. Before leaving, the pay bob took advantage of the glut of fresh vegetables and fruit which came over the border from Spain. When we left, our storerooms were fully stocked and our tanks of oil, water, aviation spirit, etc. were fully replenished.

The ship stopped alongside until the second week in November. The Fleet Air Arm repair party were kept busy repairing the damaged Seafires and other kites which needed maintenance and repairs around the carriers or on shore. Sometimes a working party was sent out with the necessary spares on the lighter to carry out repairs. Also, the lighter would bring back damaged kites to be worked on.

Once all the kites were serviceable, the ship joined a slow homeward-bound convoy, flying off the old faithful stringbags with rockets and depth charges to destroy any lurking U-boats. The Germans had recently acquired a new deadly accurate type of acoustic torpedo, which would home in on the noise of a thrashing propeller. However, with the combination of approaching winter storms and the patrols we reached home waters without incident then proceeded towards the Firth of Clyde to discharge the remaining Seafires and crews.

The ship anchored in her old spot, retaining her six stringbags and aircrews. During the next few weeks we steamed out several times to fly-on a variety of different aircraft — namely, a few Sea Hurricanes, Albacores, Martlets and Avengers. Also, some brand-new Fairey Fireflies and Barracudas arrived by road then were shipped out by lighter with their wings packed separately in packing cases. They were assembled by our repair staff to be flown off several times for testing. Then a crowd of spare aircrews arrived along with the pilots to be used for fleet replacements along with the kites when necessary. Once the ship had received her quota she weighed anchor to steam upriver.

One day when a gale had sprung up in harbour an anchor watch was kept below to prevent the ship from dragging her anchor and grounding on the rocks. I went down below to relieve Taff Gunney for the last dogwatch. After about a quarter of an hour the order 'finished with main engines' was rung down from the wheelhouse. We began to shut off the air ejectors and the gland steam, then the main bulkhead valve and main steam valve to auxiliaries. This caused a sudden drop in steam, which slowed down the circulating pump as if it were about to stop. Without more ado I swung round and noticed that the auxiliary superheated-steam valve was shut on the bulkhead, so I cracked it a quarter of a turn. This should have been enough to keep the pump ticking over, allowing any trapped hot water to escape from the line — or so I thought as the steam pressure came back to the normal 300 pounds.

However, everything seemed to be OK until suddenly Chief ERA Rodgers came dashing down the extra-long ladder two steps at a time, speechless, with his face as white as a sheet. He rushed over and shut the valve I had just cracked open. He then rushed back down the port boiler room to make sure everything was all right.

His action puzzled me. I was unaware he was working behind the bulkhead on remaking a joint on the steam pipe, along with Jonno and Willie Franks, in a confined space at the side of a boiler. They could have easily been scalded but fortunately they heard the roar of steam, dropped their spanners and jumped down off the grating out of harm's way. They were stunned by the unexpected occurrence, but not half as stunned as I was. I felt like I had been hit with a knockout blow from a boxing glove. It took me over a month to recover, when suddenly I realised my hasty action had not been needed as the steam pressure had jumped back to normal and was being delivered through the cross-connection valves from the starboard auxiliary boiler. We completed shutting down the engine room. Then had to explain my impulsive action to the Chief ERA, the boiler engineer and the senior engineer — how the sudden steam drop caused the circulating pump to whine as if about to stop. I looked around for the cause and picked the wrong one, opening the bulkhead valve, which was shut, and assumed the steam was flowing from the port side, never dreaming that the steam pipe on the other side had been removed to be rejointed. The first thing I was taught aboard ship — the golden rule — was that if one was working on any steam line, one should lash two steam valves between you and the job so that anyone wanting to open the steam valve should find out if the hidden job had been completed first. In this case not even one valve was lashed and the only indication that the steam line was open was a small note on the noticeboard, which was never usually made up in harbour. So as there was no damage done and there was carelessness on both sides, the matter was dropped. However, when entering our mess I had a strange feeling that everyone was watching me.

We prepared to set sail for the Far East to join the British East Indian fleet to aid in the defence of our crumbling empire against Japan, who had slavishly copied Western ideas since the turn of the century. The Japanese had ordered new warships from Armstrong Whitworth so they could copy them down to the last nut and bolt. Also they got the same company to produce blueprints for another warship, then kept the prints and cancelled the order, so they could build their own ships from them. Eventually they pulled that trick off once too often, so Armstrong Whitworth produced drawings for a ship which would founder in the first typhoon. The Japanese even bought a small steam trawler then stripped it down to the last rivet, to build exact copies.

The Japs showed total disregard for naval treaties, especially the London one of 1936, from which they withdrew as it limited the tonnage, number and sizes of battleships, aircraft carriers, destroyers and submarines, along with the tonnage and total armaments carried on each ship. The Japs also played their cards close to their chests and were extremely careful not to let any prying eyes of observers see the comings or goings of their fleet, or what they were producing on their slipways. When ready the ships slipped out under the cover of darkness into the vast Pacific Ocean miles away from any prying eyes.

They built three massive battleships bristling with nine 18.1-inch guns out of a total of sixty-one. The *Yamato* and *Mussashi* were completed, but the third ship, *Shinana*, was converted into an aircraft carrier. Also, they built five aircraft carriers (*Hosho*, *Soryu*, *Hiryu*, *Kagi* and *Akagi*); the largest ones carried over seventy aircraft each.

Some destroyers carried 24-inch-long lance torpedoes based on a design that the British Admiralty had tested some years before but had failed to perfect. However, the Japs had persevered, and fuelled them with oxygen so they left no telltale trail of bubbles behind them. They had a range of 24,000 yards at 48 knots, or a range of 44,000 yards at 36 knots, which was three times the range of our conventional torpedoes and far more accurate.

Their aircraft, which were mostly borne on carriers, were mostly based on German designs. Their performances of speed and bombloads were far superior to anything the Allies had out in the Pacific at the time (as shown to their credit at the splendid attack on Pearl Harbor and the sinking of the *Prince of Wales* and *Repulse*). Also, the pilots and aircrews had been trained to perfection.

However, the Japanese supply lines were stretched to their limit as their merchant ships plied over the Pacific Ocean trying to supply their newly acquired lands and islands dotted about far and wide. By January 1944 the Allies had sunk 294,902 tons of their shipping.

The Japs had acquired most of these islands without much resistance. They had occupied Malaya and Singapore with the greatest of ease and were now slowly driving the British forces towards Mandalay in Burma through the dense steamy jungle with our troops putting up a good show of stubborn resistance in their rearguard action.

The Japs had occupied Hong Kong as well as vast areas in Korea and China where they were battling to cut off the supply routes on the Burma Road heading for Calcutta, India.

They were in complete control of the Philippines, occupying many of the small islands. They also occupied Sumatra, Java and Bali in the Dutch East Indies along with Borneo and the greater part of New Guinea where they were encountering stiff resistance from the Aussies and Yanks, who were fighting stubbornly. Also they were threatening the coast of Northern Australia and Queensland. They had also attacked the Aleutian Isles and Dutch Harbour. They had fought several big sea battles (Midway, Coral Sea, Lombok Strait, Java Sea, Singapore and Leyte Gulf).

Fortunately for us their campaign was running out of steam, as their oil stocks were running low. Also they were failing to deliver regular supplies of armaments, food and medicine to their troops who consequently suffered from starvation diets and severe diseases (along with their prisoners) with nothing to ease their complaints. Nevertheless they were still fanatical and never gave up fighting. They fought with their last ounce of vigour to the last man in well-constructed defence lines where they could hold out for months (unlike our piffling defence lines in Malaya and Singapore where the Japs poured through like a dose of salts).

Their vast spread of fortified islands caused the Yanks terrific supply problems (called logistics) as each island required a separate battle to capture it. Supply dumps had to be set up throughout the Pacific before the front-line troops could be transported over thousands of miles to these heavily defended isolated spots. Then only after heavy naval bombardments and aircraft strikes could the first wave of troops be landed ashore from landing craft, closely followed by artillery, ammunition, tanks and food, and the other items needed to winkle out the enemy.

The Yankee aircraft-carrier forces had to grapple with a highly organised opposition protected by an umbrella of nippy little Zero fighters causing them a lot of bloody noses. Many of their aircraft were shot down in their first few attacks against the Jap carrier fleet. However, they soon learned from their mistakes, and along with the aid of brand-new mass-produced aircraft the Yanks were able to improve their technique before getting the upper hand against the Jap aircraft. Eventually, after a few successes, the boot was on the other foot, with the Japs being on the receiving end. Eventually the Japs began to lose some of their crack pilots and aircraft, which needed replacing. This was a scenario they had not allowed for.

As Christmas 1943 approached, the *Unicorn* was anchored in the upper reaches of the Firth of Clyde in Greenock near the tail of the bank, along with a large assembly of merchant and naval ships. Our ship was loading up with a vast range of supplies, which were handled by the chief, POs and store assistants who all came under the pay bob's department. The provisions and vitals came under the charge of Jack Dusty (a term loosely applied to chief and PO killicks and store assistants responsible for doling out the daily rations). The term was obviously derived from getting their navy-blue uniforms coated with white dust when handling sacks of flour.

Another set of store assistants took in a small load of tropical white gear for the ship's company and khaki for the Royal Marines and Fleet Air Arm.

One afternoon before the ship was due to sail a mass inoculation took place with everyone in the ship having large syringefuls of TABC (anti-typhoid and cholera vaccine), tetanus serum, and a general injection against tropical diseases. It was carried out in the for'ard section of the lower hangar (where we had our cinema shows). We were piped to muster by messes. As one was nearly finished another mess was piped. We lined up with our shirt sleeves rolled up for the massive dose of serum, which made one's arm quite sore when the hypodermic needle was plunged right in. When my turn came I placed my hand on my hip and turned my head away from the quack (doctor or surgeon). Afterwards I broke into a cold sweat with my arm throbbing, and felt quite groggy with a dull headache. The next day it had passed.

On a dark stormy December night when there was a strong gale blowing we were keeping a storm watch on *Unicorn*. Suddenly the duty man on watch cried out that the bows of a big ship were rapidly drifting towards our centre. It was the mighty 82,744-ton majestic leviathan, the liner *Queen Mary,* who had been at anchor on the soft mudflat off the tail of the bank when a sudden squall of gusty wind sprang up catching her massive superstructure side. This large area acted as a sail and blew her off her moorings. The anchor began to drag as its flukes failed to dig into the soft sandy mud. Fortunately the officer of the watch responded immediately. He rang from the bridge to the wheelhouse down below and ordered the steersman to swing the helm hard over. He ordered 'slow speed ahead' on the starboard engine, and 'slow speed astern' on the port engine, which swung the vessel round on its moorings. He then rang down 'stop on both engines', which allowed the mighty vessel to drift harmlessly down the side, missing us by about thirty feet, whilst her crew fought to bring her back under control.

As the storm abated we started to load ship. Another consignment of tropical gear indicated that we were outward bound for the tropics.

Then the final supplies arrived, including turkeys and ingredients for the Christmas puddings and mince pies.

On Christmas Day no one turned to except the usual harbour watchkeepers, and the cooks in the galley who cooked the dinner. The captain and his entourage visited all round the messes wishing everyone a happy Christmas. The cooks turned out the plum pudding, mince pies and Christmas cake.

On Tuesday 30 December, just before the New Year, the *Unicorn* weighed anchor and slipped her moorings on the Clyde to join forces with the battlecruiser *Renown* and the aircraft carrier *Illustrious* as well as the battleships *Queen Elizabeth* and *Valiant* from Scapa Flow and a destroyer escort from a secret rendezvous. We then made our way through the North Atlantic winter storms.

As usual the captain had received his sealed sailing orders for the first leg of the journey to Gibraltar, but he didn't let us know until we were nearly there. Then he broadcast to the ship's company, "This is the captain speaking. We are outward bound for Gibraltar." New sealed orders would be sent to him there, so we were completely left in the dark as to our final destination.

We settled down to a steady speed of 12 knots, with our bows rising some ten feet above the horizontal, then plunging another ten feet down into some terrific winter troughs. The pent-up anger of the high waves suddenly sent a thick carpet of white foam and seawater crashing down on the flight deck with an almighty roar.

The aircraft carrier *Illustrious* did not rise so far out of the water as it only had one hangar deck. Consequently it had sixteen and a half foot less freeboard. The battleships *Queen Elizabeth* and *Valiant*, with their heavy A and B for'ard turrets, bored into the waves as if about to submerge with the fo'c's'le fully awash. Heavy cruisers, such as *Edinburgh*, my first ship, rode over two and a half waves causing her to roll violently in heavy seas. Destroyers (sometimes shipping the odd wave, causing the mess decks to be awash and uncomfortable) would rise on the crest of a wave, then drop down into the trough, hitting the water with a sound like a thunderclap. Then the sharp bows would cleave their way through a huge bank of water ahead.

With the full force of the winter storms taking place it was almost impossible for any Jerry U-boats (patrolling in wolf packs) to mount an accurate attack on our ships, as the high waves would continually obscure the vision from their periscopes. Also, any tin fish they launched would be tossed off course by the strong currents and were just as liable to get one return than hit the target. Consequently the first part of our journey was free from any attacks.

After being at sea several days we passed out of the Atlantic over the ruffled water into the Strait of Gibraltar at the dead of night, then continued in an easterly direction, increasing our speed to 20 knots to be well out of sight of land by daybreak. We then settled down to 15 knots (a more economical speed for steaming). Throughout the day our ship remained at flying stations, sending off the occasional stringbag patrol armed with depth charges and rockets in search of any lurking U-boats or warships. Fortunately the Allied attack on Italy had denied the Jerries use of their forward naval and aircraft bases around Bari, Taranto and Reggio in the toe of Italy, and around Palermo, Messina and Catania in Sicily, as they were busy fighting a rearguard action.

We steamed from the Western Mediterranean eastwards towards Alexandria without meeting any opposition.

In this area there were a large number of feluccas sailing about. They were the largest sailing boats in the Mediterranean. They were decked to sit low in the water with high bows and raking sternposts. Also, they were rigged with three masts carrying large lateen sails on jibs set to collect as much wind as possible.

Our ship anchored in the large harbour of Alex (a shortened version of Alexandria) with a good view of a well-laid-out city. All the ships took on oil, stores and water ready for the next stage of our journey.

Smaller feluccas plied for hire around the harbour and also carried out some trafficking around the ships' sides selling Stella (the local brew of onion beer), fruit and other goods. Ropes were flung up to the portholes to be caught so the basket at the other end could be hauled. The cash was then lowered down to pay for the required goods. This had to be carried out when the master-at-arms and his POs (crushers) were not about, as it was an illegal practice.

On 15 January we all raised steam, weighed anchor, and headed in an easterly direction, passing close by the Nile Delta where all the rich soil was washed down, enabling the fellahin in their fields to irrigate and tend their bumper crops. We carried on to Port Said (the entrance to the Suez Canal, which is 101 miles long and thirty-three feet deep), where we awaited our turn to enter in order of our captain's or admiral's seniority. Once entered we proceeded in a southerly direction, passing through El Qahira, Ismailia and the Bitter Lakes with nothing around but mile after mile of sand.

All the ships were restricted to the slow speed of 5 knots as the bow wave at higher speeds would have washed away the soft sandy banks. Some ships had a deep draught of around twenty-eight to thirty feet so they were liable to suck in vast quantities of sand from the bottom by the suction of the main circulating pumps which cooled the main condensers. It would block many of the small banks of tubes which cooled the turbine exhaust steam back into feed water. (Consequently once clear of the canal the pumps would have to be run flat out to flush out the tubes.)

Any ship with a draught of thirty foot or over was liable to ground on the canal bottom, so they had to travel the long way around via the Cape of Good Hope.

We assembled off Port Suez under the escort of the destroyers

Pathfinder, *Paladin*, *Petard* and *Rocket*, then proceeded down the Gulf of Suez into the burning Red Sea, a length of 1,200 miles with nothing but sand on each side as far as the eye could see. The sun's rays beat down on the ship throughout the daylight hours, causing the ship's interior to heat up. The ventilation fans were speeded up to run flat out with all the portholes opened up until 'darken ship' was piped. All the deadlights and scuttles were shut throughout the hours of darkness. Everyone perspired more freely, causing a long queue at the separate halls' drinking fountain in the locker flat, which cooled the water with its own freezing unit.

The freezing coil was opened up in the cooling water tank for a supply of cool water for the mixing of the daily bread and also for the sickbay. The ice tank was brought into use with its twenty-four galvanised steel ice pans immersed in freezing brine. 14-pound blocks of ice were formed by freezing the water which was poured into each pan. Then it was broken up for a daily issue of ice to the messes to cool the tots of rum or grog.

By now the intense heat down below had become unbearable, especially in the boiler rooms. It had risen from 110° to 115° in the port room where the watches were split up into two hours as the men were becoming completely exhausted and dehydrated. The other parts of the ship, such as the engine and auxiliary rooms and magazines, rose up to 100° to 105°F. Now we were in the tropics a daily issue of lime juice and oatmeal was doled out to the engineering watchkeepers so that water and ice could be added to make a cool drink which was kept in large fannies hung up near to the air intakes to slake our thirst from time to time.

Our overalls soon became sopping wet as we kept watch down below. All supply and exhaust fans were speeded up to run flat out in our compartments when steaming to prevent the heat from rising. The turbine bearings began to heat up so the lubricating-oil coolers had to be opened up wide to keep the circulating oil temperature down. The extra-heavy weight of the two long prop shafts was too great for each of the single plumber-block bearings to bear, especially at high speeds. Along with the high ambient temperatures, this caused the white metal to heat up excessively to the danger level between 130° to 140°F. The stokers kept a strict half-hourly watch on them to ensure they did not overheat, especially when the shafts were turning near to their top speed. Once hot the shafts had to be slowed until they cooled down again. Also, as the plumber blocks were self-contained with their own oil sump and drag ring, which brought the oil up with it as the shaft turned, the oil had to be kept dead on half a glass. Otherwise overfilling would make it churn, then overheat, causing the bearing to heat up. Lieutenant Commander E. Spriggs had small copper coils made to be inserted into the sump, then coupled up to the fire main, so that water could trickle through then discharge into the bilge. This kept the oil in both sumps cool and prevented the bearings from getting hot. Every day or so the water had to be pumped out of the bilges. The heavy weight and turning of the prop shafts caused me to go down to the port stern gland with a large spanner, to nip it up now and then as a steady flow of water leaked in from it.

The consumption of fresh water shot up. With everyone spending long periods under the cool showers the total consumption jumped up to 110 tons a day, which worked out at about fifteen gallons per man. The water was rationed to several different hourly periods a day as the evaporators were already working flat out and could not cope with such a huge demand.

Eventually we came to Aden with its dull dried-up, burnt-out landscape. We passed by several Arab dhows (sailing ships carrying up to 200 tons of cargo, consisting of rice and fragrant spices). They sailed up and down the Arabian Sea, along the east coast of Africa, to Zanzibar, Madagascar and the west coast of India. They were picturesque craft with huge lateen sails, the top point of which extended skyward to catch every breath of wind possible. They were suspended on extra-long yardarms, which were drawn fully up to the top of the mast.

The ship veered hard to port into the Gulf of Aden with its sultry dead damp heat. In our off-duty hours we spent much of the time on the upper deck watching the flying fish scud over the wavelets of jade green.

On 21 January we were joined by more escorting destroyers, making a total of eleven in all. Then we carried out exercises with the fleet and the *Illustrious* in the Indian Ocean for the next few days, flying-off an odd assortment of kites (Fireflies, Martlets, Avengers and the ungainly looking Barracudas).

The fighters carried out high-speed mock strafing attacks, diving down, then the running the whole length of the ships to exercise the high-angle and close-range armaments. A handful of Swordfish practised their painfully slow suicidal approaches, closing in to 900 feet. This was their normal range for launching their 18-inch torpedoes at practically water level (zero altitude) at the correct angle so as to run at the correct depth to hit their target.

Then came the turn of the Barracudas. These newcomers to the fleet were exercised from *Illustrious,* plummeting down out of the sun, and demonstrating their superb diving qualities. Their massive air-brake flaps were suddenly operated to slow them down as they approached perilously close to the mast tops before the anti-aircraft guns could get them in their sights.

We then left the fleet which formed up into two columns heading south-east between the Laccadive and Maldive groups of islands some 1,400 miles away.

Cochin

The *Unicorn,* along with the old battlecruiser, *Renown,* as well as our two escorting destroyers, *Petard* and *Paladin,* broke off exercising. They headed for our first port of call in the Indian state of Cochin, of which Ernakulam was the capital, in Kerala Province in the south-west corner of India (the land of princes and paupers).

One forenoon before going down on watch I had a few minutes' breather in the cool fresh air on the upper deck watching the rapidly approaching coastline and the entrance to a vast lagoon in the direction we were heading. We were leading the way, being senior ship. It appeared to be surrounded by a large swampy area. This turned out to have a very hot and humid atmosphere, which made us sweat cobs.

The first things that loomed into sight on the starboard bank of the entrance were several curiously shaped rough wooden structures, which turned out to be fishing equipment with a net attached at the ends. I gazed at these structures from afar before going down below to relieve Taff Gunney.

The ship soon entered the lagoon, then suddenly 'stop' was rung down to pick up the pilot who was late arriving. The order 'slow ahead 50 revs' was rung down so the ship could proceed to the inland dock. We arrived at 09.30 when the usual flurry of orders was rung down on the engine telegraphs. We started manoeuvring with the turbine drains open — the usual practice to prevent any hot water from being drawn over with the steam from the boilers. This was liable to happen with the rapid opening of the throttle valves ahead and astern, mostly at 'slow speed 50 revs' and 'stop'. All the movements were noted down in the logbook by the ERA who was throttle watchkeeping.

After about a quarter of an hour the ship was safely tied up alongside the jetty. 'Finished with main engines' was rung down on the engine-room telegraphs. Now came the job of shutting down in the sweltering heat. First of all the auxiliary feed pump had to be started in the auxiliary steaming boiler room. Then we stopped the main feed pump and the air ejector, and shut off gland steam. The main steam line to auxiliaries was shut off, along with the main steam bulkhead valve, which was tripped shut then reset with all necessary auxiliary cross-connection valves open and all necessary drains cocks open. This left the main circulating condenser pump, extraction pump and lubricating-oil pump running to cool down the condenser, the feed water and the lubricating oil.

After half an hour the remaining pumps had done their job and so were shut down along with the contraflow valve on the main feed tank. The ventilation fan was eased down to slow speed and the exhaust fan was shut off. As we climbed the long ladder out of the engine room we were completely exhausted, but not half as much as the poor beggars of the chief stoker's boiler party, especially the boiler-room ERA who had the shutting-down watch in the terrific heat of both rooms.

I made my way to the bathroom then stripped off my sweat-sodden overalls, which I put in a bucket of disinfectant. I was just taking a refreshing cool shower when all the lights went out and the supply fans stopped, causing the whole of the ship's interior to heat up. There was nothing else for it but to grope around for my overalls, wring them out, then slip them on and tie up my shoes. I began to grope through the hot, dark and stuffy atmosphere of the passages and compartments and was sweating like a pig from the exertion of climbing up and down several ladders before I eventually landed up in the for'ard turbogenerator room, which turned out to be even hotter. The pressure on the steam line had just been restored, so that the throttle valve could be reset, then cracked open to restart the turbo once again. Then as the pilot lights began to glow, I noticed the room temperature had risen to 115°F. Immediately I switched on the power from a local switch to the supply and exhaust fans. Then as I was anxious about the meat in the cold rooms above, which was already showing signs of defrosting, so rang up the switchboard to report the generator was ready for load, and asked the EA to make up the switches for the refrigerating machinery first, as it was running flat out for twenty-four hours a day and I did not want any rotten meat on my slop chit.

I paused for a few minutes to make sure the machine had settled down OK before making my way down the hatch to the refrigerating room, and reset the regulator, then the inlet manifold valves to the cold rooms, etc., before restarting the condenser circulating pump and the compressor. I then waited a while to make sure the plant had settled down before returning it to the stoker on watch.

By then I was feeling lethargic, with a slight headache. I returned to the bathroom with all my energy drained away, so rested awhile on the stool talking to ERA Hill, one of the boiler-room ERAs, who had just recovered from the most excruciating unenviable job in the ship — shutting down three boilers and leaving one auxiliary, in temperatures between 110 and 120°F. This entailed shutting down three auxiliary saturated- and three superheated-steam stop valves and eight main stop valves. The boiling-hot handwheels were stiff to turn with lumps of cotton waste in his hands, so he tightened them with a wheel spanner to ensure no steam leaked. After that he had three forced-draught fans to shut down in the fan flat. This consisted of shutting each air louvre, which needed a hard shove. Then he shut each steam valve and pumped the oil around the turbo bearings until it had stopped. He then shut each exhaust valve and opened all the drains. By this time he was completely knackered and was looking like a wet rag, drained of all energy. He had to rest awhile in the slightly cooler air by the air inlet to regain his strength.

Then I stripped off my sweat-sodden overalls and shoes to continue my shower, only to find the rationed fresh water had been cut off, forcing me to use the seawater tap to mop down with.

Before dinner, hands were piped to fall in outside the pay office to change £10 sterling into rupees (there were twelve rupees to the £1). In the afternoon there was a make and mend with leave. So after a good rest, then washing and changing into my tropical white shirt, shorts, shoes and stockings, I sought out the officer on duty for permission to carry on ashore to have a good look around before sunset. I crossed over the dockyard in search of the ferry, which was moored at the far end, to have a shufti around the native village and the crude wooden constructions at the entrance to the harbour. The ferryman was curled up under a canvas awning fast asleep and it took me several minutes to arouse him from a deep slumber, and then encouraged him to scull me across the water to the other side. After boarding his grubby old boat, which hadn't received a lick of paint for many years, and sat down on the thwart watching him skilfully use his long oar, moving it from side to side with a slight circular motion of the wrists.

Soon the boat bumped alongside the far bank. After alighting and paying my fare and stepped out towards the village. Fortunately I found a rickshaw for hire, which was parked nearby with its owner resting in the shade. He agreed to take me to see a weird contraption which was about a mile down the narrow, dusty, bumpy road.

He set off pulling at a steady lope in the humid atmosphere. A small patch of sweat start showing on his back and it got bigger as we advanced. We eventually arrived at the water's edge where six of these contraptions lay. I alighted and asked him how much he wanted for his fare. He said eight annas, so gave him a rupee and told him to keep the change.

I went to examine one of these antiquated objects and found out they were for fishing. It consisted of a long triangular frame with its point pivoted at the base, standing upright with the two top ends several feet apart. The front one was attached to a large four-sided framework, which opened out at the ends to carry a large square fishing net. This was lowered or raised by a long rope with stones fastened to the back of it. When the structure was in use it was lowered to ground level, which allowed the fishing net to be immersed in the water, and was pulled out again when some fish had been caught. I was disappointed to find the nets were not in use, so there was nothing for it but to retrace my steps through the village. It smelt of decay with its strong smelly open drains and red stains of betel nut spat out all over the place. Most of the occupants were still slumbering in some dark corner or under a tree away from the sun rays. Others squatted cross-legged in front of their shops or dwellings on the shady side of the street. The swampy terrain around was very humid, making me feel very hot and sticky. I noticed that several old men had extra-thick swollen legs, which turned out to be caused by elephantiasis, a parasitic infection which blocks up the lymph channels and can cause gross enlargement of the legs or scrotum.

Feeling thirsty I hastened back to the ferry where the ferryman was waiting. I quickly boarded his boat, sat down and asked the man if he could drop me off at the other side of the dockyard near our ship as I had become hot and weary, so offered him double his fare which he gladly accepted. Once on board I was able to slake my thirst at the drinking fountain.

On the next day it was my turn for duty watch. I stopped aboard to attend fire party when it was piped at around 17.00; also to stand by for any snags on the turbogenerator or the CO_2 machinery, and to stow the lifts at flight-deck level when required.

I was taking a breather on the upper deck after dinner when I noticed a duty mess cook pour the contents of the gash bucket down the chute, and was surprised to see several young native children swimming in the water below, salvaging anything that was floating about which was edible.

After tea, whilst pacing up and down the flight deck, I paused to watch a small sailing coaster floating slowly past on the current. It was heavily laden with large logs and sacks of rice, all stacked neatly in an open hold subject to the sun rays and sea spray. A Tamil in a loincloth and turban was up the mast precariously balancing on the long yard which supported the large lateen sail he was unfurling. It started flapping violently in the wind whilst the other two members of the crew secured it below, then they adjusted it to catch the wind so it sailed away steadily.

Next day a small oil barge was towed alongside by a tug. It was just about large enough to replenish our double-bottom oil tanks in two trips. I noticed it had an ancient Tangee oil pump mounted midships. It had been made at the turn of the century (about 1896). It had been skilfully maintained by an Indian craftsman, and it worked perfectly without a trace of an oil leak anywhere. The hosepipe, which appeared to be equally old, had been bound up skilfully so that no leak appeared anywhere. Two squatting Indians in clean white sarongs controlled the pump and when the tanks were empty the barge was towed away.

Next morning we were rudely awakened at 05.30 to start a new type of working day (tropical routine) — arising before sunrise in the coolest part of the day, lashing up and stowing our hammocks, followed by an early breakfast, then turning to on our daily maintenance work together with inspections and examinations as laid down in the engineers' manual. If carried out to the letter this would have left us with little time to spend at sea. We had a ten-minute stand easy at mid-forenoon, then worked on until 12.30 dinner time (the hottest part of the day with the sun being directly above at its zenith). Afterwards we were free to get our heads down (or crash on the cushions to sleep off the tot, which made us drowsy).

There were many ribald remarks at dinner that day, as it appeared that orders were issued from the doctors in the sickbay to put an extra pinch of salt in the daily vegetables for dinner, making them almost inedible. It was necessary to make up for the loss of salt due to excess sweating, especially when working down below, or even when having a brisk rub after a cold shower when the sweat glands would open up allowing beads of sweat to pour out, especially on one's brow.

After tea, Tommo Thompson, Willie Franks, Alf Seldon and myself went ashore in white shirts and blue serge trousers. We caught an ancient ferry which lacked a good coat of paint. It was powered by a smelly old paraffin engine, which was packed full and overloaded so any rough water could have lapped over the gunwales then sunk it. The lower castes of people were crammed on the lower deck, so we climbed on the upper deck where there were several higher-caste women with their husbands. The women wore colourful saris and had red spots in the centres of their foreheads.

The vessel continued upriver, making a puther of black smoke until we arrived inland at Ernakulam where we all disembarked on the jetty. We groped our way around for an hour or so until it went dark. Then we found a café for a meal, finishing up with thick black coffee and sweetmeats, which we all enjoyed before returning to the ship.

Nagumo Attacks

From 1 until 12 April two forces consisting of Admiral Nagumo's air strike force (of five fleet aircraft carriers, four battleships, three cruisers and three destroyers) and the Malay force (of Admiral Ozawa, six cruisers, one light cruiser and four destroyers) entered the Bay of Bengal along the Indian coastline from Calcutta to Madras, sinking all ships that came into sight. There were many SOS messages sent out before the crews abandoned them.

Admiral Somerville got wind that the Jap fleet was in the area and prudently ordered his British eastern fleet to raise steam and weigh anchor to slip out of Colombo Harbour on exercise around the Maldive Islands. His four battleships, *Resolution, Revenge Ramillies* and *Royal Sovereign* were all ancient craft, built in 1913. They all suffered from the same complaint as the *Hood* with little in the way of anti-aircraft guns, and they had wafer-thin armoured upper decks which could not withstand long-distance plummeting shells, or dive-bombing. (The mighty *Hood* was blown up with one shell from the *Bismarck* with the terrifying loss of all her crew except three lucky ones. As the ship exploded into pieces guns and men were flung high into the air.)

Admiral Somerville had two aircraft carriers, *Formidable* and *Indomitable*, which carried eighty-four aircraft between them. They were both armed with sixteen 4.5-inch guns and forty-eight 2-pounders. Each carried a squadron of fighters. The five Jap carriers carried a total of 350 aircraft. They had a similar performance to our two carriers' Martlets, which would have been overwhelmed by their numbers. Also, the fleet would have been overwhelmed by a heavy attack. About half of the Jap aircraft would have been Val dive-bombers, which had already shown their ability by the sinking of our modern battleship *Prince of Wales* with eight 500-pound bombs, and the other half would be Zero fighters who could deal with the puny squadrons of our aircraft carriers. So our admiral made a wise decision to steam out of range.

Our carriers were ill-equipped as there were not enough Yankee Martlet fighters, which were a prototype with a speed of 310 mph. They could have replaced the painfully slow Swordfish which had to skim over the water to drop their torpedoes from 900 yards away from their target. It was like committing suicide if the guns opened fire on them, and they could only succeed if they came in out of the sun or had fighter protection. The other squadron they carried were Albacores, dive-bombers of which little was known.

Two county-class cruisers, the *Dorsetshire* and *Cornwall*, were left in dock having an extensive refit and boiler-cleaning after their long journey out east. They were to have some extra-short range 20-mm Oerlikon guns fitted to supply them with better anti-aircraft protection as all they had were four for'ard and four aft 8-inch guns for anti-aircraft work, which could be elevated to 70° using shrapnel. However, all the jobs opened up had to be boxed up rapidly, then steam was raised on two boilers for a rapid crash flash up with steam blowing everywhere to drain all the steam pipes, whilst all the other joints were made. As they steamed out slowly on two engines, they unfortunately left the Oerlikons behind on the jetty, which would have given them some extra defence. The engine-room watches worked hard to flash up and got all the jobs boxed up so all the engines could be used and both ships could increase their speed to 20 knots.

They had covered a good mileage on the second day out when unfortunately they were spotted by fifty-three Val dive-bombers who were very near their point of returning as their fuel tanks were nearly empty. The ships were like sitting ducks and hadn't a chance. The planes started bombing in quick succession, hitting the *Dorsetshire* with thirty-one bombs, which lifted her 10,000 tons up, until her bows were clean out of the water, before she sank. The *Cornwall* fared little better. She was hit by eight bombs, became a huge blaze then rolled over and sank.

Both ships had been overwhelmed in a quarter of an hour with the loss of 425 hands out of a total of around 1,400 hands. These ships had been the most spacious ships in the navy, with comfortable messes. They had been built before the top brass had recognised that 15-inch guns on battleships were obsolete, and that plenty of anti-aircraft guns were needed to take their place on big or little ships.

On 5 April Admiral Nagumo attacked Colombo Harbour. It was an Easter Sunday at 08.00 when the church bells were pealing. The city was still wet from a rain squall and it glistened in the sun. Radar had warned of the approaching aircraft. Only nineteen Hurricanes were able to take off from a small airstrip in time. They rapidly climbed to their maximum height to attack the enemy from out of the sun. (This was an old dodge developed in Malta by the Gloster Gladiators, *Faith*, *Hope* and *Charity*, puny biplane fighters of a bygone age, which answered the air-raid siren calls time and time again when the Jerry dive-bombers attacked Valletta. They climbed to their maximum height then dived down out of the sun to break up these attacks.)

The Hurricanes performed reasonably well, shooting down six out of the thirty-six superior Zeros, but they had to pay the full price of being slower than their opponents and being outnumbered. Consequently they were all shot down. Twelve stringbags, which had left the large airfield at Ratmalana, south-east of the city, empty, were flying to join their ship *Hermes* and were suddenly jumped on without warning. All were instantly shot down by the Zeros.

The Japs were disappointed as the airfield was empty and all the naval ships that mattered had left harbour. Their first strike of ninety-one Val dive-bombers, manoeuvred by the elite pilots of Pearl Harbor, went into the attack shooting up and strafing the hangars, offices, messes and runways of the airfield. Then they attacked the harbour, completely destroying the installations. They set the armed merchant cruiser, *Hector,* on fire, leaving it burning furiously as she settled on the bottom; and they sank the destroyer, *Tendedos,* by blowing off her stern. They also damaged the old coal-burning submarine depot ship, *Lucia*, along with the old monitor, *Erebus,* and caused damage to several merchant ships unloading in the harbour.

This was the end of the RAF as it was ill-equipped with old Hurricane aircraft (their best kites being used fighting the Germans). Also they had lost airstrips in Singapore and Hong Kong, and they had lost all their aircraft in the small airfields of Ceylon, leaving no suitable islands to attack Japan from. They needed to build new fully equipped bases, but quite simply we did not have enough merchant ships to transport all their requirements.

Four days later a float plane from the Jap cruiser *Tone* spotted the *Hermes*, which was an old original purpose-built aircraft carrier. She usually carried fifteen kites but had lost three while defending Ceylon. She carried six 5.5-inch surface guns and four 4-inch anti-aircraft guns and was totally lacking in short-range weapons. Her maximum designed speed was 25 knots. Her total complement of men was around 850. She was accompanied by an ancient greyhound of the sea in the form of a V and W Class 40-knot destroyer, HMS *Vampire,* which could only sail at that speed for short periods (she was lightly armed). Both ships were travelling south from Trinco when they suddenly reversed their course. A wave of Val (Aichi D3A) dive-bombers from the Japanese aircraft carriers *Akagi* (the flagship), *Hiryu* and *Soryu,* carrying well over 200 aircraft between them, homed in one after another in a constant stream. In less than ten minutes Admiral Nagumo's first strike force had dive-bombed *Hermes,* which was almost unprotected. Forty kites hit her with their 550-pound bombs. She sank within half an hour, quickly followed by the *Vampire. Hermes* lost a total of 302 men.

A second wave from Nagumo's carrier force of 100 dive-bombers struck at Trinco in the face of a strong opposition of ack-ack-gun defences, which put up a good barrier of flak. The Japs demolished cranes, workshops, ammunition dumps and fuel-storage tanks, which went up giving a spectacular firework display. They also damaged some small coasters, including a corvette and two small tankers. They then attacked China Bay, situated half a mile away, where they made mincemeat of twenty-two assorted vintage kites belonging to the RAF and Fleet Air Arm, none of which were capable of standing up to the Japanese aircraft. Nine Blenheim bombers from China Bay made a suicidal attack on one of the Jap carriers, but the conventional method of RAF bombing was not accurate enough to score any direct hits, and near misses were useless. Unfortunately five of the bombers were shot down without doing any damage.

Meanwhile, Admiral Ozawa's cruisers were having a field day sinking twenty-three merchant ships with a total gross tonnage of 100,000 tons, sailing between India and Burma.

Admiral Nagumo's carrier strike force had steamed over 50,000 miles since Pearl Harbor. His ships required boiler cleaning, fuel and oil. His aircraft required aviation spirit, which was low in the storage tanks. Although he had lost few of his aircraft, many of them required small repairs to damage caused by heavy landing and machine-gun fire. The supply of bombs was also getting low. His supplies of rice and food were running out. The hulls of his ships were fouled up with barnacles and other marine growth, which knocked off several knots from their top speed and also increased their oil consumption, cutting down the range they could travel. The shortage of oil would compel them to run at economical steaming, which varied from about 10 to 16 knots depending on the type of craft. Any more high-speed runs into the wind to fly-off aircraft was out of the question. The higher speeds of the carriers would use up to three times as much oil as the sea resistance rapidly built up beyond the economical point, and the tanks would run dry before reaching their home port. Down below in the boiler and engine rooms there were plenty of steam leaks on the steam glands and lines which needed repacking. Also water glands and pump glands needed tightening up. The boilers needed their twenty-eight days' cleaning, and firebricks needed renewal in their furnaces. So they were not in a good state to meet a Yankee task force. Even so they could have mustered enough dive-bombers to sink the weak British fleet.

Admiral Somerville had prudently put to sea on hearing the Japanese aircraft-carrier force had entered the Indian Ocean, and was 500 miles away when the dive-bombers attacked Colombo Harbour. He had left instructions for his two heavy cruisers, *Dorsetshire* and *Cornwall*, and small carrier, *Hermes,* to follow on behind, but unfortunately they were all sunk by Val dive-bombers. He decided to run and seek shelter in Bombay and Kilindini in Keyna.

Had another carrier arrived in time with three or four squadrons of our latest Barracuda dive-bombers, he would have been able to launch a surprise attack out of the sun on the Jap carriers. This could have done considerable damage before they departed for their home port, but unfortunately nothing arrived.

The British fleet were all due for docking to have their bottoms cleaned up and other big jobs done, so they did not arrive back in Ceylon until 4 September 1943.

By the time we had arrived at Ceylon to join the British eastern fleet Colombo Harbour had been fully restored to working order with very little Japanese bomb damage showing. It was the same story when we eventually arrived in the vast natural harbour of Trincomalee.

Colombo

As usual we were bound for an unknown destination. It turned out to be Ceylon, which is separated from India at the south-east tip by the twenty-miles-wide Palk Strait. It is a large island, 240 miles long by 140 miles wide, with an average temperature of 82°F. Colombo was the capital and the main seaport was Jaffna, 186 miles away in the far north of the island. Kandy (the old capital) was situated in the centre of the island. It was a small town with a population of 34,112 people of mostly Singhalese stock. Trincomalee is situated on the east coast some ninety-nine miles north-east of Kandy, and was mostly populated by Tamils. The population was 38,000 people. The Singhalese formed the ruling party, being better educated, and most of the men wore lungis (a skirt which could be worn short around the tops of their legs or let down to their ankles). They were Buddhists, whose priests went around with clean-shaven heads and bare feet, wearing brightly coloured saffron robes.

Ceylon produced several rare timbers such as ebony, satinwood and rosewood. It also had a large supply of semiprecious stones and gems — sapphires, rubies and pearls — from the Gulf of Mannar. Her main exports were tea, coconuts, cocoa and cinnamon.

Soon we were steaming down the west coast of Ceylon until eventually we arrived at Colombo, which had a population of 562,000 people. It was the chief harbour and is situated near the mouth of the River Kelani. The city lay around the harbour. Its centre was on the south side with broad avenues, the customs house, passenger jetty, belfry clock tower, a bank and a railway station. The main shopping centre was around the fort area and Galle Road had a large cinnamon plantation alongside, along with the civilian and local administrative centre run by the British. The Galle Face and long esplanade ran along a straight piece of coastline southward, facing the Indian Ocean.

Beyond this point was the start of the residential area where the top brass hung out. To the right of this area was Pettah which housed the town hall, the police station, the law courts with the gaol in close proximity, the fresh-fruit market and the railway junction and terminal. Beyond lay the native quarter on the outskirts. The area beyond Pettah was Kochikade, which lay behind the central position of the harbour. Northward above the harbour lay Fisher Hill. This was the start of a large area of shanty town in Mattakkuliya, which lay in the bend of the River Kelani Ganga.

The ship entered Colombo Harbour in the forenoon, tying up to the buoy near the centre so there was plenty of room for swinging around it. The senior engineer, Lieutenant Commander Spriggs, in white overalls complete with torch and gloves, suddenly climbed down the ladder making one of his rare appearances down below.

As there was a light breeze blowing it required over thirty-five engine movements to tie the ship safely to the buoy. So for the next half hour he had me running around hither and thither like a scalded cat owing to the vacuum reading in the condenser being 29.3 inches instead of 29.8 inches when manoeuvring astern. This was caused by the excessive clearances in the labyrinth packings which sealed the turbine shafts, and the temperature of the warm seawater being over 80°F. The engineer tried to improve that figure by speeding up the condenser circulating pump, running it flat out. This increased the gland steam pressure, which poured out of the glands only to heat up the turbine bearings and the circulating lubricating-oil to over 150°F. So I had to open up the spare cooler to drop the temperature.

As the vacuum reading had never budged he had me start the spare air ejector, but to no avail. By then the closed exhaust system had reached 20 pounds and was blowing to waste.

After 'finished with main engines' had been rung down, the engineer disappeared up the ladder leaving me, as limp as a wet rag and completely knackered, to shut down the engine room. It was the signal we had been waiting for to ease down the speed of the auxiliary machinery and make sure the auxiliary cross-connection valve was wide open. Then we shut down the main steam bulkhead valve, main steam to auxiliaries (opening drains on various lines as required), both air ejectors and gland steam, as well as the main feed pump. We left the extraction pump and main circulating pump running to cool down the condenser and condensate, then shut off the spare oil cooler, leaving the lubricating-oil pump running to cool down the turbine bearings. After half an hour we shut down all the pumps along with the contraflow valve which allowed water to flow to and from the main feed tank or condenser.

The order came through from the starboard engine room to pack up the watch. My stoker, throttle watchkeeper and myself climbed up the excessively long iron ladder then departed to our different bathrooms, only to find that the rationed water was still shut off. I climbed up on deck to find what sort of a place we had arrived in, and was still sweating like a pig, with beads of perspiration running down my brow and my saturated overalls sticking to my body.

When gazing over the handrail the first thing I noticed was a light golden-brown varnished Chinese junk, which was one of the workhorses of the Orient. These sailing vessels abound in the China Seas and beyond, but they are not usually so well cared for (being a tough trading ship). It was glistening in the sunshine against the blue sky and water. Suddenly the crew began to move around the deck then unfurled the three red batwing sails to hoist them. Then they weighed anchor. Soon she started to move, slowly gliding through the water as a light breeze filled her sails. She looked as pretty as a picture as her bows cut through the blue water, creating a small white-topped bow wave and a wake which she left behind as the water parted.

I sat down on a shady spot on the deck looking around the large 600-acre harbour, which was nearly empty except for the old rusty coal-fired liner, *Lucia*. She was used as a base and a submarine depot ship. She was tied up alongside the little-used coaling jetty, with the engraving dock and slipway alongside. At the south end of the harbour lay the customs house with the passenger jetty alongside. A little further along there was a host of small sturdy native sailing vessels which were tied up and connected together by short planks. A host of coolies loaded small barges, which passed through a narrow canal to Beira, a large inland lake with numerous warehouses and rail rolling stock to distribute the goods to their destination. The outer limits of the harbour were formed by three breakwaters, the centre one being some 4,000 feet long, with a medium-length one to the south-west and a short one attached to the land in the north-east.

Once I had cooled down the rationed water had been turned on again, so hastened down the ladder to strip off my smelly sweat-sodden overalls, leaving them in a bucket of disinfectant overnight to be wrung out before using them next day. I then had a long cool shower, which was a pleasant experience.

Having passed over the equator in the Near East the refrigerating plant could no longer be stopped for long periods throughout the day and night. It ran continually during the twenty-four hours with the pre-cooler being brought into use to add to the efficiency.

One day a batch of locally charged CO_2 bottles arrived on board the ship. They had been carelessly filled with an excessive amount of moisture along with traces of white coconut oil with the gas. This tended to choke up the system when the gas was discharged into it. The Sprigg's special filter could not cope with the extra damp as the gas passed through it. This meant that the scale trap would soon get choked up and would need to be cleaned out more often.

Although the local currency was in rupees it was not divided up into sixteen annas like the Indian rupee, but into 100 cents with 5-, 10-, 25- and 50-cent notes. As usual we had to muster at the pay office to change our £1 sterling into the local currency. At 15.00 the first batch of liberty men fell in for inspection. I followed on to catch the liberty boat which landed us on the customs jetty.

There was little activity ashore as most of the native population had not stirred from their daily siesta and were still resting out of the sun, which would soon begin to set. I heard an engine whistle which attracted me to the Fort Railway Station where I bought a ticket, then caught the train to Mount Lavinia. It was more or less a straight run for about half an hour down the west coast. It was an easy way of sightseeing, as the train stopped at several different villages, namely Kollupitiya, Bambalapitya, Wellawatta and Dehiwala.

The carriages were old and rickety, as well as hot and stuffy, except when the train was moving. It became quite pleasant with a light sea breeze floating through the open window where I sat as the train sped along the bumpy track with the usual clickerty-clack as the wheels crossed over the numerous line joints. It made a change to see the clean brown sand on the beach with the lapping waves breaking over it and tall coconut palms swaying in the breeze on the other side of the track. Except for a crowd of about twenty RAF bods who were returning to camp at Ratmalana, some seven miles out of town, I was the only other passenger on the train, so made for the beach, which was quite deserted. I had a swim before resting awhile in the shade of some tall coconut palms. Several outrigger fishing canoes were drawn well up on the beach. I watched the wavelets, with their white tops breaking, then looked miles out over the empty blue sea wondering where I should be at the same time next week.

After a pleasant half hour retraced my steps, passing by a coconut vendor with his barrow full of green nuts. He was dozing in the shade. I managed to stir some life back into him to buy a nut for fifty cents. He sliced the top off with his machete and handed me the shell full of deliciously cool milk to quench my thirst with.

On my return to the station, not knowing the time of the next train, an army lorry pulled up and the driver offered me a lift back into town. I gladly accepted and climbed up the high steps into the cab. It was a rather bumpy journey on a narrow dusty road, but we soon got back. I thanked him, then climbed out and shut the door so he could finish his journey to the barracks, then went for a long walk down the esplanade at Galle Face and turned off at a green path which led to the centre of Victoria Park. There was a small museum, which was closed. The training college, an asylum, a racecourse, a cricket ground, two cemeteries and a gaol were in the area, then kept straight ahead for a while before bearing left on a narrow road and passed a small hospital and gaol. In the distance were the railway terminus and junction which ran alongside the north end of Beira Lake where all the activity of handling goods for transport took place.

I carried on around the shore of the lake, passing by the law courts, before returning to the centre for some tea and sweetmeats. I then returned to the ship and had a shower as my body was feeling itchy after bathing in the seawater.

On my second run ashore I made for the Pettah area which was the native quarter, where Singhalese, Tamils, Moors, Afghans, Brahmins, Eurasians and Malays lived together. I then passed several churches and a Hindu temple with an elaborately carved square tower tapering towards the top with numerous carved coloured figures all the way up. It served a large Tamil community.

Seated on their haunches cross-legged were several beggars with bowls in hand, so dropped a few cent notes in as I passed by into the entrance hall, and noticed a pile of sandals in a corner (apparently everyone enters the temple barefooted). I was surprised to see a couple of men go to the fountain then dip their finger in the trough of water and spit back into the trough, which seemed to be a dirty habit to me. I did not venture into the temple itself, but noticed the floor was carpeted with men kneeling with bowed heads touching the floor. I beat a retreat to continue my wanderings, passing through into a fresh-food marketplace where everyone slumbered, huddled up, having their afternoon siesta. The next place I passed by was the town hall along with several other important buildings conveniently grouped together. I eventually reached a long street with open-fronted shops which were mostly owned by Tamil Indians. The Tamils were introduced into Ceylon by the British to work the tea and rubber plantations, and to farm the paddy fields.

There were all manner of businesses carried out in these shops in the forenoon, and then again after sunset. They continued well into the night, often by candle or oil light (the more wealthy owners could afford electric lights and fans). There were tailors (dressed in white seated at their treadle sewing machines); brass workers beat out brass plating into shapes for bowls and trays, then carefully tapped out elaborate patterns on them with a small hammer and chisel; and a casting maker blew air into his forge with hand bellows until it glowed a cherry red. When it was hot enough to melt a small crucible of molten brass, he carefully picked it up with a pair of long tongs, pouring the contents carefully into prepared black-sand moulds until they began to overflow. Then they were left to cool. He produced such useful objects as plain or fancy candleholders. I bought a pair of cobras rearing up on their tails ready to strike, with candleholders on top of their heads. He also produced various types of gods, Buddhas, elephants, figures and other animals. There were numerous craftsmen: woodcarvers, carpenters, goldsmiths and silversmiths, potters, shoemakers, cobblers, and tinkers who made all manner of simple household gadgets from scraps of wood and tin. They used old light bulbs, removing the filaments and replacing them with wicks so as to use them as small oil lamps.

On my return journey, after passing by another mosque with an octagonal clock tower and an attractive patterned facade, I bought several oranges to slake my thirst (not liking the look of a grubby native drink shop). I also purchased some tropical fruit: a mango (which tasted like turpentine), and something that had been recommended to me by my father, who said the only place to eat it was in a bath — it was a durian, which was taken in the mess to cut open with a knife. It let out a foul stink when the hard rind was penetrated and someone shouted, "What a smell!" so it was instantly taken outside to throw overboard. However, my curiosity got the better of me, so scraping a little of the pulp and finding it was delicious, so ate the lot, then went down to the bathroom to wash my hands and face to get rid of the smell.

On the last day, after changing into my tropical white shirt and serge trousers, I caught the first liberty boat, which was piped away at 16.00. As usual it landed us on the ocean-liner jetty. I passed a belfry where a native woman in a colourful sari sat on the steps splitting open cashew nuts which she sold to passers-by. A little further along by the bank a native street trader had set out his stall in a painstaking way with an impressive array of goods, such as buttons, reels of cotton, pencils, ties, cigarette lighters and watches, etc. in a small square of the pavement about the size of a hammock cover.

After wandering around several broad avenues I found a shop with bolts of silk material, which I wanted a length of for a dress for Ellen, my girlfriend. The shopkeeper bade me sit down and handed me a clean glass and a bottle of orangeade which was cool from his fridge. He showed me half a dozen different colours and patterns to choose from. The one that caught my eye cost ninety rupees, which seemed excessively dear to me, so I got up to leave. He induced me to stay, then started to haggle, which was something entirely new to me. However, he was a wily old fox and baffled me with flannel until I became quite dizzy, and was confused by the rate of exchange, which was twelve rupees to the pound, so came away feeling I had paid too much, then wandered around to find something to eat. The sun was rapidly beginning to set, unlike at home where it takes an hour or so. In the tropics night descends rapidly, causing the buildings and unlit streets to look entirely different. Not wanting to get lost in the dark I hired a rickshaw to take me back to the dockside.

We left Colombo at the end of January for a short trip of about 350 miles to Trincomalee. We arrived there on 2 February 1944.

Trincomalee

After completing their escort duties, the two destroyers left us to make our way into the vast natural harbour of Trincomalee on the north-east coast of Ceylon. We tied up in a large isolated creek on the opposite side to the *Adamant* (a submarine repair and depot ship). We were now attached to the East Indian fleet, as a back-up force which was gathering strength to attack Japanese shipping.

Now that the ship was stationary the flight deck became red-hot with the sun rays beating down upon it all day long. The mess decks were becoming unpleasantly hot without the cooling breeze caused by the for'ard motion of the ship and despite the fact that the ventilation fans were now running flat out by day and night.

On Saturday 12 February 1944 the two destroyers that had been our escort, bringing us safely to harbour, answered an SOS in the Indian Ocean. They sailed away at high speed. A troopship, *Khedive Ismail*, had been sunk with 2,000 men killed by the explosion or trapped below as the vessel sank quickly after settling down in the water. As the destroyers set about rescuing the survivors the Jap sub I-27 was lurking about to make another kill. It was spotted by the destroyers who gave chase and depth-charged it so it sank to the bottom never to surface again.

The *Adamant* was a large depot ship with tiny main engines, which had living quarters and locker spaces for the crews of about a dozen subs (five of which were generally tied up alongside). It had large workshops for repairs and servicing, and kept the submarines topped up with diesel oil, stores and torpedoes. The crews were able to relax on board in the spacious and comfortable messes. There were large lockers to stow their surplus gear, large bathrooms with showers and extra-large galleys to cook their food.

A Chinese houseboat was tied up astern, connected by a narrow plank for extra-cool sleeping quarters for some of the sub crews.

The subs went on regular patrols for several weeks and we always looked out for their return to see if they were flying the Jolly Roger (a flag with the skull and crossbones painted on it) from the top of the periscope. This indicated that they had made a kill with a torpedo sinking a Jap ship.

We soon settled down to the daily tropical routine: completing all our work in the forenoon with the rest of the day off. On Sundays we all assembled on the flight deck for divisions along with a short church service. There was afternoon leave for excursions ashore in tropical shorts and shirts. On evening leave we would go for a ration of beer at the makeshift canteen wearing tropical shirts and No. 2 blue serge trousers. This was drunk from rough-rimmed makeshift glasses. They were made from empty bottles by filling them with a pint of oil then plunging them into boiling water. This caused the neck of the bottle to break off evenly in a circle at the top of the oil level, leaving a rough rim.

We often went ashore for a wander around the native town in the late afternoon before dusk. Most of us bought souvenirs from the goldsmith's shop which always had a glittering display of semiprecious stones mounted in necklaces, bracelets and rings which soon began to lose their shine. Another shop sold neatly carved black ebony elephants with ivory toenails and tusks.

As the weeks rolled slowly by a number of events happened. Owing to our badly aligned propeller shafts the main engine's double-helical crown and pinion wheels had begun to flake off into tiny slivers of metal. Chief ERA Williams and ERA Jack Frost removed the top of the gear casing to hone the roughness off the several hundred long teeth with carborundum stones. It was a long tedious job needing great care to remove all flakes and grit to ensure no foreign matter escaped through the filter into the system. It could have played havoc with the turbine bearings, scoring the soft white metal which would heat up excessively then run out. If that happened the main engine would have to be stopped.

I had not been in the tropics long before a rash of prickly heat developed across my back. It stung like a thousand needles in my skin. Also an ulcer developed on my left leg and it refused to heal for several months.

The ship acquired a duck (or DUKW) from the Yanks. It was a

handy amphibious craft. It could be lowered over the side, and contained up to about twenty men. A propeller could be engaged and the rudder was worked from the one steering wheel so it could act as a motor boat which, with its tyres deflated, could be run up onto the beach. As soon as the tyres touched terra firma they were all automatically pumped up so it could be driven on dry land like a normal transport wagon.

At night it felt so hot in my hammock that it was hard to get to sleep. A louvre was about nine inches away from my head and it crossed my mind that if the jet of air could be directed on my head it would probably give me better night's sleep without the tossing and turning. One night a simple idea came to me. That was to get hold of an old stocking and thread a lace round the top so it would fasten onto the louvre. I cut away the toe part and tied another lace to it to direct the warm air towards my face, keeping my head much cooler and free from sweating. After that I had many a good night's sleep.

The ship had not been there long before the cockroaches multiplied in their thousands, especially in the pantries and galleys where they were often found crawling over the food or dead in the soup or porridge. It made one queasy to look at them. The only solution was not to look too hard when fishing them out.

They also clambered up into our lockers, swarming out every time the doors were opened. I even found one alive in an air chamber of a fire and bilge pump. It was a puzzle as to how it got in there.

We often looked across to the upper deck of the *Adamant,* which was always a hive of industry. Torpedoes were often being prepared for use. They had to be topped up with high-pressure air, then have the engines and gyroscopes tested, then finally the warhead was screwed into position. They were then lifted by crane and lowered over the side to the for'ard or aft hatches of the innermost sub (there were generally four or five tied up abreast of one another with a narrow gangplank between each). Once the inner sub was fully oiled and loaded it had to be moved to allow the next one to move alongside to be fuelled up with diesel oil, whose haunting smell wafted over so we got a constant whiff of it.

There were usually about five subs alongside, belonging to two classes. First were the T boats, which consisted of names like *Thunderbolt* (formerly *Thetis*), *Taku, Tempest, Trusty, Tally-Ho, Tiptoe, Templar* and *Truculent.*[1] All of these carried a crew of

212

sixty-one men and were armed with eleven 21-inch torpedoes, with a range of 8,000 nautical miles at 14¾ knots. Also there was a Dutch submarine attached to the ship. Then there were the smaller S boats, with names like *Sealion, Seawolf, Sirdar, Sceptre* and *Strongbow,* and a crew of forty-eight men, carrying seven torpedoes with a range of 6,000 nautical miles at 14¾ knots.

One forenoon ERA Drinnan came rushing up to me all excited to tell me he had just seen a PO with bare legs riding on a torpedo. Being curious I nipped up the ladder to the upper deck to have a shufti, only to be disappointed. The torpedo had just been lifted by crane out of the ship and was being towed to the outer sub with a PO riding on it to prevent it bumping into anything on its way to a torpedo tube. I had expected it to be charging round the bay.

Another day when working below water level, tending my refrigerating plant, there was a terrific explosion but fortunately the lights did not go out. Although shocked my curiosity compelled me to down tools and take big steps up the ladders to the upper deck to find out what was amiss. Apparently what had happened was that a PO was testing the after torpedo tubes by blowing them out, and was unaware the tube he was working on contained a torpedo. It was blown out and started running quietly for about a mile across the bay where an empty oil tanker was anchored. Several onlookers saw its telltale white streak run across the bay then strike a centre tank of the tanker with a blinding flash, tearing a big hole in her side. Fortunately she did not sink or catch fire, but the water washed out her tank and the whole bay was covered with a thin black scum, which prevented any swimming over the ship's sides for about a month until the water was clear.

Fortunately no one was hurt or killed by the explosion, but someone was for the high jump and would have to carry the can at the naval enquiry for this terrible gaffe which put this valuable tanker out of commission. It was the most valuable oil-supply boat in the harbour.

After tea, if no work of servicing or repairing kites was in progress the lifts were raised to flight-deck level so the deck could be used as a recreation space. Occasionally the Fleet Air Arm would occupy it to change an engine for one that had been tested down below on the engine bed, or to carry out repairs on the fuselage or undercarriage, or test the air flaps, etc. Often a marine corporal would exercise a party of defaulters with half an hour's drill on the deck. Sometimes it was used for a game of deck hockey.

The deck was always hot from the sun rays beating on it all day long and no one dare touch it with a bare hand or foot. After tea, when the sun began to set, a large crowd would wend its weary way up several sets of ladders. Usually a slight breeze would spring up, which made it cooler on the flight deck and more pleasant than the mess decks below.

A party of messmates, Alf Seldon, Willie Franks, Scouser Tommo and myself, would often pace up and down the deck together, or assemble around the Welsh Wizard, Robbo (Stoker PO Roberts), who spun amusing yarns by the hour.

The joke of it was that when he went ashore he would go to the nearest pub, starting off with a friendly conversation, but as he downed his first few jars of ale his speech became glib. He reverted to the lower-deck vernacular, which was highly insulting and deeply wounding, especially to a sensitive person. Robbo would use phrases like 'You bloody shower of springboks' or 'Aussie bastards', which would soon get under anyone's skin. Consequently he caused a fracas with everybody joining in hurling glasses about and overturning tables until the police or naval patrol arrived to arrest him. Sometimes he was chucked out by a burly landlord or customer who gave him a couple of black eyes or bruises. Once back on board he was locked up in a cell for the night then charged with creating a disturbance — all because of the way he spoke, although no particular offence was meant.

Early one morning Ben sent for me with an urgent message. The refrigerating plant was gradually losing gas and the room temperatures had suddenly shot up 10°F above the normal working temperature. Fortunately we were working tropical routine, starting the day by lashing up our hammocks and stowing them in the netting (or bin) at 05.30. I dressed then went down to sort things out, and decided to start up No. 2 compressor then isolate No. 1 compressor, suspecting a high-pressure joint might be leaking. Ben connected up a bottle of gas to the system.

After half an hour we found the system was holding its charge of gas but needed another charge of gas putting in. No. 1 condenser pressure gauge was steadily dropping. After slipping down to the bathroom for a wash and shave, then went to the mess for my breakfast. I then changed into my overalls to go down and locate the leak with a solution of soapy water, which we applied all round the necessary high-pressure joints so that any leak would be shown up by blowing out a stream of bubbles. We found none, so I sent Fred, who had just come down to relieve Ben, to report the incident to the engineer. He came down to see what should be done. After looking around he agreed with us that the leak must be in the condenser and gave orders for us to remove it. We checked over the compressor and room temperatures to make sure they were dropping before starting the job. It should have been a doddle, but owing to the usual style of Admiralty layout, with the pipes and stanchions built around the condensers, it was not as easy as it looked. However, we soon removed the obstructing cooling water pipes and high-pressure gas pipes and all the bolts around the condenser door flange. But the flange joint was stuck solid and defied all our efforts to break it. We had to draw a set of chain blocks from the store along with some strops, and rig them up to get a steady pull on the door. It yielded with a bang, dragging the coil behind it. We then dragged the coil out halfway until it encountered an obstruction. The condenser shell had to be lowered at one end by removing three securing bolts and using the fourth bolt as a pivot. The coil could then be lowered to slide out under the obstructing pipe to be removed. It was then taken up several flights of steps to the coppersmith's shop to be pressure tested by Willie Franks (the coppersmith). He soon found the leak at the end where a screwed sleeve had been brazed on. He re-brazed the leak and retested the coil at 2,000 pounds pressure to ensure the coil was gastight. Then the stokers party humped it back down again so we could slip it back into the condenser shell, then box it up ready for use. This weakness occurred later on No. 2 condenser, so we slackened off the forcing bolts which were seized up so that it could be removed more easily later on when the coil needed removing.

A new batch of oil drums arrived in the ship. They were drawn out by a supply rating from the general stores in small five-gallon drums. They had obviously been supplied by a different maker, whose name had been omitted from the drums. Once the stoker started to fill the gland-seal pump with it on the refrigerating compressor the new oil gave nothing but trouble as it was not up to standard. It did not have the same viscosity (thick and sticky) as the usual supplier's oil. It went through the glands like a dose of salts instead of sealing them, causing them to need to be constantly tightened up. Also, it accumulated in the evaporator grids, then along with the moisture brought in with the gas from the bottles and the rust in the pipes it soon began to affect the cold room's temperature, which began to rise. Finally it blocked up the scale traps solid. They had to be changed over constantly, with one trap being removed to clear out what looked like a large light-brown lump of honey.

It was at this stage I realised something was seriously amiss, so tested it between thumb and finger only to discover that it lacked stickiness. I reported it to my engineer who came down with the senior engineer. I showed them the contents of the scale trap. They then weighed up the position, and sent a signal around the fleet for non-freezing oil from the usual makers.

Meanwhile we struggled on for the rest of the week the best way we could. I had numerous calls to tighten up the leaking piston-rod glands, which would not hold the gas in for long, or to clear out the blocked-up scale traps, whilst the watchkeepers struggled to keep the cold-room temperatures down. Also we had to bring the second compressor into use.

Eventually two drums of the right oil were located on the *Queen Elizabeth*, so one of our motor boats was sent over to collect them. It returned promptly and the drums were hoisted aboard by the crane. Soon after we were able to open a drum, then test it to make sure it was the right stuff. Once satisfied we wasted no time in draining out the oil seal pumps then refilling them with the new oil. We marked the old drums U.S. (short for useless), so they would not be used again except as a last resort in an emergency. The gland gas leaks improved immediately, but it took a considerable time for all the oil to work itself around the system to the scale traps, where it was gradually removed so the plant could settle down to normal running.

It was discovered that the port main condenser inlet sluice valve had jammed wide open, so a routine inspection of water tubes and ferrules and the renewing of zinc slabs to reduce corrosion could not be carried out. The situation could have become serious if any of the water tubes began to leak as the feed water would have become contaminated.

The senior engineer came up with the brainwave of remedying the situation without going into dry dock. He consulted the chippies to construct a flat board five or six feet square, then he had a soft rubber cushion of about three to three and a half feet diameter attached around the centre standing 3 or 4 inches proud of the board.

The diving party was assembled in white polo-neck pullovers, then lowered over the side along with the cutter complete with their gear. It was towed to the required spot above the sluice valve, where it was secured. Chief ERA Fred Crate (one of the very few artisan divers) was to carry out the operation. He was dressed in a diving suit with his heavy leaded boots. Then the Sieb Gorman air pump was manned. The heavy diving helmet was lifted over his head then secured to the suit. A small glass porthole was screwed into position and the pumping began. He was then helped over the stern onto a short ladder into the water where he grasped the wooden blank which had been lowered down to him. Then the air hose was paid out as Fred disappeared under the water, taking the strange wooden object with him to cover up the large orifice in the hull. All one could see from the upper deck was a stream of bubbles rising from the top of his helmet whilst the two seamen cranked the pump in the centre of the cutter below. It was a tricky job to manoeuvre the blank in because of its buoyancy. Fred held it in position for about ten minutes until the water from the condenser above had drained into the bilges, reducing the weight on the top side of the blank. The sea pressure outside the hull held the blank firmly in position, completely sealing the inlet, which turned out to be a neat idea. It enabled the sluice valve to be freed. Had it failed it would have flooded the engine room.

As Fred's job was completed he suddenly bobbed up to the surface where he was aided up the ladder. He then had his helmet removed followed by his weighted boots and other gear.

Chief ERA Bungy Williams and his engine-room party started to remove the large copper pipe to get at the sluice valve. It was taken to pieces to clean out the slide and working surfaces along with the valve, and to have the spindles removed. It was then taken to the machine shop to have the threaded block cut off then drilled out so that the seized-up square threads could be machined out. The new spindle, which had been turned up on the lathe, was screwed into the block, which was inserted into the sluice valve to operate it.

Whilst this part of the operation was taking place the engine-room party removed the inspection doors to examine the condenser tube plate, ferrules and tubes, also to replace any worn-out zinc slabs (fitted to prevent corrosion). They then boxed up the condenser once again. They ran down the nuts and bolts, oiling them so they screwed together easily and cleaned all the flange faces and cut new rubber insertion joints in readiness for an easy reassembly.

In the afternoon, being on duty watch along with several others we went down to reassemble the job whilst the others were free to go ashore. We boxed up the job, completing it within two hours, then flooded the condenser up again by opening both the inlet and outlet sluice valves. We also pumped out the bilges. With the weight of the water being equalised on both sides of the blank it was easily removed by a rope which had been attached. Then it was hoisted back on board out of harm's way.

Ted Perkins and myself sat for our chief ERA's exam and failed through lack of sea time and experience.

One day I had a recurrence of my childhood complaint of acidosis, and was confined to the sickbay for a fortnight, constantly vomiting and bringing up everything I ate. It completely baffled the surgeon commander and his staff as it was quite a rare occurrence, but it soon faded away.

One day there was a terrific row over the destroyer *Quadrant,* which had been lent to the Aussie navy and was tied up at anchor with one boiler steaming auxiliary to give light, heat, power and hot water to the ship. It ran dry owing to the stoker PO's negligence. It blacked out the ship with disastrous results. The first row of water tubes distorted and hung down in the furnace with blobs of metal melted on the floor (looking more like Aladdin's cave with stalagmites and stalactites). There was a court of enquiry and a court martial for putting the boat out of action. Fortunately with the boiler steaming auxiliary, only one sprayer out of nine had been in use. The furnace was not fully glowing with red-hot bricks, so the damage was not as great as it could have been. After a fortnight beside the repair ship, where the boilermakers worked round the clock, she was ready for service once again.

One day, 8 August 1944, a large new prefabricated Yankee floating dock arrived. It had been hastily constructed and welded together in Bombay, then towed around by three large tugs to be secured in a deep part of the bay. The battleship *Queen Elizabeth* was the first and last ship to enter the dock once it had been sunk then pumped dry to lift the ship out of the water. Then she had been secured by props around her sides. The usual examinations on the propellers, rudder and seacocks were taking place, with the hull being scraped free of marine growth and barnacles. All of a sudden there was a terrific noise of steel being torn apart. It was heard all over the harbour. The dock caved in under the enormous weight of the ship (being in the region of some 38,000 tons). Everything had been progressing smoothly when a great tidal wave swept over the dock's bottom carrying all the workers and their equipment with it, sweeping them off their feet as the massive hull plunged back into the water. We never heard how many casualties there were or if all the men survived. Several magazines were flooded as their seacocks had been removed for inspection to make sure their seals were watertight.

This loss of the dock was a blow to maintaining the East Indian fleet as all the big ships had to travel to Bombay, some 1,450 miles away. The dry dock in Colombo was too small to take aircraft carriers and battleships, which all needed regular attention to keep the ships' hulls clean to maintain full efficiency for fuel consumption to the last knot. The only other docks in the area were Singapore and Hong Kong, both of which were still in the hands of the Japs.

After running about a year, the condenser seawater pump suddenly developed a serious problem. The roller bearings collapsed causing the glands to leak and to run noisily. It was stopped and the spare pump was started whilst the offending pump was taken down to the fitting shop to be stripped down, and all the old packing was taken out and all the old grease removed. It was found that the bright hardened steel polished ball race had been attacked and eaten away, and a black powdery substance was left in its place. It was a mystery as to what had happened, as no one had seen the like of it before. We all knew that seawater attacked metal pipes harshly but special corrosion pieces had been inserted to counteract the corrosion on them.

The pump was then reassembled with new gland packings and roller bearings, which were packed with Stauffers C grease according to Admiralty requirements. The pump was placed into position then tested. It worked quite well, but the spare pump was left running giving several months' trouble free service, except once or twice when the sea suction grid got chocked up with bits of flotsam and seaweed. This was easily cleared by shutting the seacock and the pump suction valve then withdrawing the grid to remove the rubbish.

The incident was soon forgotten until some months later, when sticking in my yearly supply of amendments into my engineering manual, I came across a paragraph which highlighted a roller-bearing failure in circulating pumps. It stated that the careless mixing of Stauffers C and Belmoline RB (which was the grease for electric-motor bearings) caused a chemical reaction to take place and the failure of the bearing.

The next forenoon, on going down to check the refrigerating machinery as usual, I found one of my stokers on watch was about to use the grease gun, so asked him what grease it had been filled with, and much to my horror he produced a tin of Belmoline RB from out of a corner. He told me that as far as he knew it was the right grease to use. So being nearly empty it was ditched overboard and a new tin of Stauffers C was drawn from the engineers' store.

All three stoker watchkeepers were given strict instructions on no account to use any other grease. Also the grease gun was cleaned out then refilled with Stauffers C grease. The spare pump was brought into use whilst the second pump's roller bearings were examined. They showed no signs of discolouration, consequently they were cleared out and refilled with clean grease.

I'm happy to say, the pumps gave splendid service without more ado once the mystery had been solved. Later it turned out that the watchkeepers had been overenthusiatic with the grease gun, filling it with any old grease that came to hand — which simply was not good enough.

After six months in Trincomalee we were sent up into the hills to the naval rest camp at Detalawa, called HMS Wolf, for a week's leave. It was a long journey in a hot carriage with the windows wide open. The train passed within a few miles of Anuradhapura where an offshoot of the holy bo tree remains, under which Buddha received his inspiration some 2,500 years ago. We carried on down the line, passing through Galoya Junction onto the Colombo line to Maho where two Aussie POs joined us. The train then branched off to Polgahawela, then through Peradeniya Junction to Badella where the line split up. One branch led to Kandy (where the famous Buddhist Temple of the Holy Tooth lies), and the other track led to Nuwara Eliya, eventually rising to 4,000 feet with the track curving around almost in a spiral during the final ascent.

About one hour before arriving we could see the camp down in a large fertile valley full of tea plantations and paddy fields.

When we reached the valley a couple of trucks were waiting to take us to the camp.

My messmates, Alf Seldon, Willie Franks and myself, spent the day roaming around the village. We watched the cobbler deftly slicing bits of leather then nailing them on to soles and heels of shoes, which he positioned on his last to hammer in the nails. Then he rasped them level to the uppers before staining them or stitching new straps on to sandals.

We noticed a few cars and taxis which had some curious repairs carried out on their tyres as new ones were unobtainable. Some had thick leather patches sewn onto them over a bad crack, while some side cracks were bolted together with nuts and bolts and a plate inside or outside the tyre.

The weather was comparatively cool and pleasant compared with the bloody hot mess decks on board ship. Also the temperature in the evening was pleasantly cool. In the camp we had our own little cubicle to sleep in. One night I was awakened by the terrific buzzing of a mosquito as it zoomed down on a dive-bombing attack, so just managed to pull the sheet over my head, which remained buried for some time until the drone of the attacker had faded away.

At 06.30 there was a friendly knock on the door by the native char wallah bearing a nice cup of tea with a slice of lemon in it instead of milk. After drinking the tea I leisurely got up, washed and shaved, then went in the dining hall for breakfast.

There was a slight haze hanging over the hills, and the early morning dew glistened on the trees and shrubs all around. It was the coolest part of the day as the sun began to rise giving off its gentle heat on our bare arms. Later it rose fully, burning like fire in the heat of the day. Wisps of acrid smoke could be seen dotted all around, drifting upwards from the many stovepipe chimneys with their wood fires.

We visited a Brooke Bond tea plantation in Nuwara Eliya. In the engine house was a small paraffin single-cylinder engine which drove a belt turning the overhead shafts and pulleys to drive all the machinery.

Near the engine, neatly laid out on the deck, was an old crankshaft, con rod and cast-iron piston, which was as impressive as a jewel in a crown. It had been carelessly dropped so the skirt was cracked, but it had been cleverly knitted together by a big lump of brass, inserted by a native craftsman. It bore the slight score marks of recent use after having been replaced by a new one after a year's successful running up and down the cylinder.

The newly plucked leaves were spread out on large hessian trays (they were known as tats). The leaves were then exposed to the sun and air and were constantly turned to dry out to a certain stage of withering — for a few hours or a day, depending on the weather. Then they were roasted in a large iron pot before being fed into the leaf-rolling machine.

The next process was to spread the leaves out for fermentation with liquid added for further roasting in the iron pot. Then finally they were dried over charcoal fires, aided by a Sirocco Belfast-built fan tea dryer. At the end of the process the tea was sifted by a mechanical sifter, shaking it gently into sizes, and sorted into three separate piles on the hut floor — thick, medium, and very fine, which was nearly dust — before being packed away in light plywood tea chests.

The tea pluckers were usually Indian Tamil women with large baskets over their shoulders, supported by a wide strap over their heads (still depicted on the Brooke Bond tea packets of today). They plucked the two topmost leaves along with the shoot, working a three-hour shift each day. At the end of their labour a tally clerk weighed the contents of each basket, logging down the weight for weekly payment.

The tea pluckers lived on the edge of the estate in small whitewashed huts. We were shown around a native foreman's living room, which contained a window, bed, table, chairs and an oil lamp. It was kept neat and tidy by his wife. We also looked at a native tea worker's kitchen, which was a small clean room kept neat and tidy with a simple wood-burning stove. A woman in white was stoking it up with dead tea-bush wood until it glowed a fiery red, then she squatted down pouring a mixture of batter to bake a chapatti on top of the hotplate to make the family's meal.

Another day Alf, Willie and myself wandered around the paddy fields, which were irrigated by channels. Each plot was separated from the others by a strip of land in between. They were kept flooded for the growing period of 150 to 200 days after the young rice plants had been set out in rows in the thick mud under the water. After this the water was cut off to allow the plants to dry off and ripen in the sun before the stalks were cut down so the grains of rice could be extracted. Paddy (unhusked rice) loses valuable vitamins in the polishing.

As we walked around the paddy fields I happened to plunge a stick in the murky water. Suddenly a snake shot out and slithered quickly out of sight much to my amazement. When passing through a narrow passage of shrubs, suddenly a large black snake slithered out of a large hollow tree trunk where it had been coiled up resting. I froze with terror until it harmlessly slid out of sight, so carried on but the others refused to follow, so I had to retrace my footsteps.

Later we passed by some children whose mother was breaking up stones to fill up the potholes in the road. They were playing with what looked like bootlaces but they were killing baby cobras by grinding their heads in the gritty surface of the road.

One of the bods in camp also had an unusual snake experience. He was fast asleep in bed one night after having a few jars of ale when he was awakened by the char wallah and sensed that he had acquired a bed mate.

He froze with horror as he realised it was a snake. It took him several minutes to recover, then he jumped out of bed in fear as the char wallah dealt calmly with the situation. Without more ado he got rid of what turned out to be a large cobra, which had been attracted by the warmth of the bed.

We paid our daily visit to the canteen for tea and biscuits, but were wary of the cane chairs, which were full of bugs hidden away in the nooks and crannies. One ATS girl sat herself down on one, then jumped up suddenly only to find she had been violently bitten several times all over. A pongo grabbed the chair, then thumped it down hard on the ground dislodging a pile of bugs, which fell on the floor only to be crushed by his big boots, before he sat down without any further bites.

One day a hawker showed us his silver wares, and we all bought neat little broaches off him. As we were dealing with him a Catholic priest walked by and the hawker stepped back, lowering his head and cringing with fear, so goodness knows what he must have told him.

One day about twenty of us took a truck ride up to the top of the mountain, some 6,000 feet above sea level, where we got a splendid view of the surroundings hills and countryside. It was flat on top and looked like an English scene on a hot summer's day. Lower down a small babbling brook was stocked with trout for fishing.

We all collected a packed lunch from the dining hall then set off in the truck with benches in the back. It turned out to be quite an adventure as the native driver was very erratic and took several chances. The route was a very rough mountain track, which started off with several sharp hairpin bends and then developed into a steep pass cut into the mountain side. It wound its way upward with a sheer drop of several hundred feet below.

It was extremely bumpy in the back and we were nearly thrown out several times. Once the back wheel of the truck slipped over the edge, bringing us to a grinding halt and giving us a nasty jolt. We all had to clamber out carefully to avoid the truck tipping over the brink. It was a hair-raising experience, especially when looking down below.

We soon managed to lever and push the suspended wheel back onto the track so that the tyre gripped once more to allow the sturdy Ford V8 engine to drive us forward until we came to the next obstruction, which was several large boulders strewn about our way. We had to dismount again to remove the landslide before proceeding on the perilous journey until arriving at the top in one piece. We alighted to take in the fantastic view. Then we collected our packed lunches and followed a small path across green fields. A small freshwater babbling brook meandered alongside with the occasional trout swimming into view. After two miles we came to a small hotel where we brewed up then had our lunch.

We made the return journey in record time. It appeared as if the driver had lost all sense of caution and never thought of applying the brakes as we whizzed down the slopes, bouncing and bumping all over the place. Not daring to look around we started to sing some of the old songs such as, 'The Beer Barrel Polka', 'Run Rabbit Run', 'Kiss Me Goodnight, Sergeant Major', 'Lili Marlene', 'Bless 'Em All', and 'My Bonnie Lies over the Ocean', to fill in the time until eventually we arrived back badly shaken but still in one piece.

One afternoon we stumbled on a Buddhist temple in a clearing of the woods. It had three large sitting golden Buddhas, with several clean-shaven, bald-headed and barefooted monks in saffron-coloured robes carrying out their daily chores.

After a pleasant break we caught the train at 08.00 to travel upcountry on our return to the ship. After an hour's travel we could still see the camp standing out slightly above us in the background. As noon approached the sun was at its zenith, shining brightly and making the train hot and stuffy. When the train stopped at points and stations we could feel the heat pour in, making us all hot and sweaty. When we arrived back in Trincomalee we were exhausted.

Several naval transport trucks were waiting to take us back to the jetty to catch the liberty boat, which had a long run journey to the small creek where the *Unicorn* lay.

One afternoon a few days later it started to thunder. Then brilliant flashes of forked lightning struck the wires connected up to the smoke floats planted all around the harbour to form a smokescreen in case of an air attack. Suddenly a blanket of smoke built up around the harbour, reducing the visibility to nil during the next half hour so that we could barely see across to the *Adamant* anchored several hundred feet away.

Another time I had climbed up the numerous steps to the flight deck to take a breather after a dhobi session in the heat down below. All of a sudden the heavens opened. The monsoons had arrived. It started to rain heavily, soaking me to the skin as I beat a hasty retreat over the deck to seek the shelter of the island doorway. It fell so hard, like stair rods, hurting my face as the raindrops bounced off the deck like small rubber balls, cooling the red-hot deck in minutes. It was quite enjoyable to feel the sudden coolness in the air, and to watch the smooth surface of the water in the bay erupt into large splashes and the tall waving palm leaves being dragged down by the sudden weight of water.

A solitary native, clad in his loincloth, paddled his dugout canoe for all he was worth, making for cover on the shore. He made little progress as the canoe started filling up rapidly to the gunwales, by which time it was completely waterlogged. He had to abandon it in the centre of the bay, then swim for the shore.

After gazing around for five minutes or so it was rapidly beginning to feel quite cold, so I went down to dry off.

Bombay

As the Japs were steadily retreating and fighting a bitter rearguard action, often to the last man, the Yanks gradually flushed them out from island to island using some of them as stepping-off bases in the Pacific as they moved towards Japan.

Consequently the British eastern fleet's advance base of Trincomalee (Ceylon) was thousands of miles away from the battle area and was no longer a suitable base for waging war against the Japanese across the vast distances of the Pacific Ocean. Unknown to us the brass hats had decided to abolish the British eastern fleet on 23 November 1944, and remove the fleet to an unknown base. This turned out to be Sydney, Australia, which was the nearest seaport with docks where our fleet could be repaired. Arrangements were being made to divert enough supply ships to keep our ships at sea for three months at a time. Our ship was to take an important part by being attached to the fleet train. A new naval transit camp was to be set up at Warwick Farm, New South Wales, occupying the racecourse — which was the only suitable place. It had power and water on tap, and an area large enough to erect 100 bell tents. It supplied replacements, which would be transported to the fleet in the battle area by the fleet train, and would bridge the gap to the vast sea area surrounding Japan.

Consequently on 25 November 1944 our ship raised steam then weighed anchor to proceed to an unknown destination. We steamed in a southerly direction around the coast of Ceylon then headed northwards towards Bombay, where we were surprised to land about six days later after an uneventful trip of 1,450 miles. The only vessel we passed on our journey (heading the other way) was a brewery ship. It was the only one of its kind and made beer on the spot, thus

226

saving a great deal of space required for shipping out barrels of beer. It was heading out to Trincomalee to supply the troops.

The ship rounded Colaba Point, which formed one side of Back Bay, and which was shaped like a massive talon with a long and a short claw.

I had the afternoon watch in the port engine room and we had the usual flurry of orders on the telegraph from the wheelhouse below the bridge until the ship was safely tied up alongside in the Government dockyard. Then the order 'finished with main engines' was rung down.

The ship's hull had become encrusted with barnacles and marine growth after her long months in harbour. This caused a drag on the hull, reducing her speed and increasing her fuel consumption. She had to go into dry dock to have the marine growth scraped off, then the ship's bottom was coated with red antifouling paint to retard any future growth, and various corrosion pieces around the propeller shaft and rudder were examined. Once completed the ship was ready to undertake its long mysterious journey.

Whilst in Trincomalee we had been building up our shattered remnants of the eastern fleet before moving to our new base in Sydney, New South Wales, to operate in the vast Pacific Ocean. This is the largest stretch of water in the world, covering 40% of the earth's surface, with an area of 64,186,300 square miles. It extends 7,000 miles from Cape Prince of Wales in the Bering Strait in the north and passes by Australia, New Zealand and Cape Horn in the south. Along the west seaboard of North America, from Alaska and the Aleutian Isles, past Vancouver in Canada, Portland, San Francisco, Los Angeles and California to the Panama Canal, the Pacific continues along the whole coastline of South America. It passes Lima in Peru and Santiago in Chile, then on beyond Cape Horn to the Southern Isles. It has a maximum breadth of 10,000 miles. On the other side the Pacific laps the vast continent of Asia along its eastern coastline, from that bitterly cold area of Siberia in Russia, past Japan, China, Korea, the Philippines, Indo-China, Malaya, Sumatra, Australia and New Zealand.

The American naval base, being situated well out towards the centre of these huge waters, was ideally situated at Pearl Harbor, Honolulu. The trading routes were long and arduous. Vancouver to Sydney, via Pearl Harbor, is a distance of 6,780 miles. Pearl Harbor to Auckland, New Zealand is a distance of 3,826 miles. Wellington,

New Zealand to London, via the stormy Cape Horn, is a distance of 11,970 miles. Vladivostok, Russia is 4,401 miles from Vancouver. Vancouver to Yokohama, Japan is 4,320 miles. Tokyo to London, via the stormy Cape Horn, is 11,970 miles. Tokyo to London, via the Suez Canal, is 9,562 miles. Tokyo to Singapore is 2,890 miles and to Hong Kong 1,585 miles (both cities were still occupied by the Japs). Tokyo to Sydney is some 4,420 miles.

Bombay is on the west coast of India. It had come into the possession of the British Crown in June 1661 as part of the dowry of Catherine of Braganza on her marriage to Charles II.

It was a hell of a city and seaport, founded on an island eight and a half miles long by two and a half miles wide.

It was the administrative centre for the whole of the country, being ruled by fewer than 500,000 whites of the British Raj. It was a fantastic undertaking as the population of India was 390,000,000 people covering a vast area. The main means of transport was the slow black buffalo, especially along the west coast, and an extra-long rail system which connected up a few major cities.

Bombay was the sole port where the Royal Mail liners docked from the West. Nearby was the vast Victorian Gothic post office which handled all the country's internal and external mail.

A little to the north lay Crawford Market, which was the entrance to the native area on the fringe of the city, with the Mumbadevi Tank (an important watering place), and the Great Jami Masjid (a famous temple). The stables of the great Bhendi Bazaar, where some of the finest horses in the East were sold, was also situated in the area. India's population had disgustingly rich rajahs, with fabulous palaces, tremendous wealth and jewels, at the top end of the scale. Its class-ridden society was disunited by politics, race, language and class distinction. The untouchables — road sweepers and beggars — were of the lowest order.

Bombay was a densely overpopulated area where my dad had landed some thirty years before. He served with the RAMC at Fyzerbad, up in the hills, where they dealt with heatstroke casualties by slinging them into a bath of ice-cold water.

In the heat of the afternoon the temperature rose to 86°F, then at night it dropped about 12°F.

The inhabitants sought shade from the burning midday sun. Shopkeepers slumped down in front of their shops when they were on the shady side of the street; or retired to the backs of their shops with small electric fans to keep them cool if facing the sun. They left their front doors wide open. The more prosperous employed a punkah wallah to pull a cord up and down which operated a punkah, which swung to and fro on the ceiling; or they had a long four-bladed fan which turned slowly to keep the air circulating. Many other inhabitants squatted on the pavements or in the gutters or under jacaranda or pepper trees.

By 14.30 we had shut down the port engine room, then showered and changed. Half an hour later I mustered in a long queue outside the pay office to change my £15 worth of ackers (cash) for a pile of rupee notes.

I then climbed the two flights of steps to the mess for tea and noticed the absence of the cooling breeze created by the for'ard motion of the ship. The passages and mess decks heated up again along with the armour-plated flight deck as they absorbed the rays of the sun.

After tea changed my togs in preparation for a run ashore. Before going, several dhobi wallahs climbed up the gangway in brightly coloured saris to collect soiled clothing from the messes. Several of us handed a neat little lass our bundles of dirty linen and overalls with some trepidation as to whether they would be seen again or if we would get the right gear back. She promised to return them next day, then marked them in various letters with an indelible pencil before bundling them into a sack and carried on to the next customers until she had collected her quota.

After sunset, when the temperature dropped a little, she would take the clothes down to the river to bash them against some smooth stones to clean and remove the dirt, which must have shortened their life considerably. Then she would take them home to dry, then iron them and spread them on the ground to air as it was still warm from the sun.

Next day, true to her word, she returned my washing neatly ironed in a bundle, and I gladly paid her with several rupees. Also was pleased to find that they were the right garments. I told her to call again after the ship had undocked when another bundle would be ready for her. My mattress cover, hammock covers and overalls were due for changing and would need a good deal of hard scrubbing. Another bundle was made up including these items. It saved me a lot of time and energy as I would have had to scrub them on the bathroom tiles in the sweltering heat with only four small louvres for ventilation, in the nude and sweating like a pig. Also the ironing was much better than I could do in the mess.

Leave had been piped at 16.00 so I made my way to the jaunty's office to tick my name off before seeking out the officer on duty on the quarterdeck for permission to carry on ashore. I saluted him; and he returned, saying, "Carry on, Chief." I then ambled off down the gangplank.

I had only taken a few hundred steps along the jetty when two smartly dressed young Indians wearing white sarongs and turbans accosted me, grabbing both my hands simultaneously. They then deftly started to manicure the nails on each hand, which made my blood boil. I lost my temper and dragged both hands free although the scalpels they were using could have given me a nasty cut, and let go a string of naval oaths, the choicest I could lay my tongue to, then carried on down the road without more ado.

Later on after cooling down I examined their handiwork, finding they had each trimmed a nail and a half on each hand quite neatly. I would not have minded them completing the job had they approached me in a proper manner.

As I wandered around the old fort area the shopkeepers were just beginning to stir from their long afternoon siesta.

A gharry driver was crouched down at the base of a large tree which shaded him and his horse from the fierce sun. I eventually roused him to take me around the most important commercial and official buildings in that area of Bombay. We started off by passing Victoria Railway Station, the terminus of the Great Indian Peninsula Railway, which lay north of the fort area. We then bore left, passing by one of the several hospitals which treated lepers, then continued to Esplanade Road. This suddenly opened out into a square with a large, round island with the Queen's statue in the centre. We then carried on driving past the fort area down Esplanade Road to the junction of Hornby Road at Flora Fountain and to where it is crossed by Churchgate Street. We passed by many large buildings of note (the Elphinstone College, the Mechanics Institute, the General Post Office and Telegraph Offices, the Cathedral of St Thomas, the Public Works Office, the Rajabai Clock Tower, the university, the Government Secretariat, the museum, and the Court of Justice). Then we carried on to the far side of town to see the five gruesome Parsee Towers of Silence between the Cambella and Malabar hills where my dad had visited all those years before. He told me that they laid out their dead bodies completely stripped of all clothes and possessions on wide tapering circular steps. Then vultures, which would perch on top of the highest trees, descended on their daily prey and squabbled over the choicest bits of skin, eyes, intestines and offal until only the skeleton remained to be bleached by the sun.

We continued down the short peninsula of land forming part of Back Bay to see the impressive Government House and to look across the bay at Colaba Point to the lighthouse, the lunatic asylum, Colaba Station and Bombay Yacht Club. We then returned to the start where I paid the driver.

I found a small café and had curried meat and rice for the main part of the meal. It was so hot and fiery that it nearly burnt the roof out of my mouth. It must have been nearly rotten as curry is used extensively to disguise the taste of bad food.

As I made my way back to the ship through the old fort area the darkness had suddenly descended. Many of the pavements and side streets were beginning to fill up with the residents who lived and slept on the hard surface of the pavements. Suddenly I heard the groan of a woman in labour, then later a sharp scream as her friend assisted her during the painful episode.

Most of the shops had come back to life. A tailor was cutting up material by the bright glow from a paraffin lamp. He then stitched it together with a treadle sewing machine.

One man was seated at his bench sewing gold thread onto RN cap badges, assisted by electric light, whilst the cobbler was busy at his last repairing shoes and sandals. The baker was at his oven baking bread and chapattis on a hotplate. Other shops also sold their daily wares.

Next morning steam was raised down below so the ship could be manoeuvred into dry dock, then secured centrally on the keel blocks. The dock gates were then shut so enough water could be pumped out to allow the ship's keel to rest firmly on the blocks. She could then be shored up in the upright position with props and wedges to hold her firm whilst the dock was completely emptied. After this a party of seamen emptied the contents of the cool and cold rooms whilst the stoker and myself shut down the refrigerating plant. Then the ship's company was billeted ashore as the dockside facilities were inadequate for such a large number of men.

All the heads, bathrooms and galleys were shut down along with the engines and boilers, but several parties were left on board to deal with various requirements. The EAs with the torpedomen mates had to shut off all the motors on the various ventilation systems throughout the ship. They also broke down the various power and lighting circuits on the switchboard, then tripped the main breakers so that my stoker and I could shut down the turbogenerator. This left the ship in total darkness so that finally the auxiliary boiler had to be shut down in the dark leaving the PO and the two stokers of the watch to grope their way to the upper deck through the boiling-hot passages.

All that remained to be done was for a party of ERAs and stokers to fit the flooding bonnets underneath the magazine-flooding valves on the bottom of the hull once the dock floor was pumped dry. Then they were connected to the water hydrants ashore by long canvas hoses along with the fire main to flood a magazine or fight a fire if the cause arose.

Strings of lights were hung up by the dockyard in a few passages or where there was any work to be done.

Once completed we washed and changed in a small bathroom on the dockside. Then, along with our suitcases which we had already prepacked, we clambered up on the back of a large army lorry. This took us to the European Transport Garrison, which generally was used for the comings and goings of troops between India and Blighty.

On our arrival, after a short trip, we disembarked from the lorry and were shown our billets. The sleeping quarters ran level with the seafront around Back Bay on a narrow strip of land towards Colaba Point. They were large and airy. The cool night air, brought in by a gentle sea breeze, circulated around a long row of charpoys under thatched roofs, making the atmosphere just comfortably warm enough for sleeping (unlike our own mess decks where we were packed like sardines in a hot stuffy atmosphere where one was uncomfortable and hot causing many a restless night).

Being in a transit camp we had no duties to perform, so we could while away most of our time in the sergeants' mess or we were free to leave the camp after dinner until 22.00 by just ticking off in the guardroom.

Curious to explore the native quarter to see a few mysteries of the East (such as a young boy climbing up the rope in the Indian rope-trick, and the snake charmers) we washed and changed, leaving the camp at 14.30. We went out in search of a gharry, eventually finding one along with the driver fast asleep with his horse in a shady spot under a jacaranda tree.

It took a considerable effort to rouse him from his deep slumber, then explain to him exactly where I wanted to go. Eventually he agreed to take me north beyond Crawford Market for twenty rupees. It was a foolhardy adventure, on which I could have easily been beaten up or robbed, or got lost without anyone from the ship knowing my whereabouts. But still, being young and inexperienced the thought never crossed my mind that my white uniform would stick out amongst thousands of brown-skinned people.

We started off with the old nag being urged into a steady trot. We advanced northward for several miles towards the native quarters. The buildings became more sordid and shabby the further we advanced. The streets were beginning to fill up as the sun began to set.

As we were making little progress I decided to pay the driver off then get out to walk. The stench became ever more overpowering, and the hot dusty air was nearly suffocating, causing me to sweat like a pig. The perspiration rolled off my head, soaking my cap band and body, so that my white shirt became as damp as a mop rag.

Having wandered down the main street the stench of sweating people, garlic, cow dung and filth became most objectionable. It was the end of the day when every coolie and cotton-mill workers, who were low-caste Hindus, came pouring out of their sweatshops, factories and stifling tenement buildings in small groups. They gabbled away in a strange language. The pavements became overcrowded with humanity who pushed and jostled one another so they flowed into the gutters and roadway where sweetmeat and other vendors tried to sell their wares.

Meantime, I was becoming extremely anxious, never realising that my white tropical gear stuck out like a sore finger. It struck me that I was a long way from barracks and might have difficulty finding my way back. Fortunately it was a straight road, so having come so far I pressed on for nearly a mile, being jostled about by the milling crowd in an alarming manner. I observed various strange sights. An ancient overloaded tram came into sight crammed full of passengers, some with their heads sticking out of the window, so they were unable to move or get on or off. The conductor was unable to collect all his fares. The tram driver's job became a nightmare. As the tram slowly rumbled along, he constantly clanged his bell to warn all manner of vehicles to clear the track. Slow ox carts, wheelbarrows, rickshaws and handcarts trundled slowly along, blocking the track. One old man was pushing a wheelbarrow in which was seated an ugly old woman.

Some men were clad in the scantiest bits of rags and walked around in their bare feet. Some were heavily pockmarked, with crater-like scars, having survived a smallpox epidemic. Many women wore cheap colourful or white saris, which had once been clean and attractive but now were stained and worn. Other women had deep staring brown eyes which seemed to be following my footsteps as I passed by, and suddenly came to an abrupt halt as a dozen humpbacked sacred cows, with loose skin that encased their skeletons, with most of their ribs showing through, staggered out of a side road impeding all progress, as no one dared drive them out of the way. A multitude of people built up all around and caused a huge blockage that hemmed me in, making it hard to move. There was nothing for it but to turn back and try to retrace my steps, and forced my way through the crowd, being jostled in the most alarming manner. It caused a sudden spasm of alarm to run down my spine as it was rapidly approaching nightfall. Soon the curtain of darkness would spread over the ill-lit area, making it difficult to distinguish one building from another, so one could easily have got lost. Also it had never struck me to tell the driver to await my return, so expected he would have gone, so there would be a long tiring walk back to camp, providing I did not get lost. However, my luck held and after a long half-hour struggle, the crowd began to taper off, allowing me to press on until the horse and driver came into sight. They were a joy to behold as I was hot and bothered and needed a rest. The driver had anticipated my return and had rested himself and his horse in the shade.

He dropped me at Victoria Station and was paid off with an extra rupee for waiting. Being dehydrated my first job was to purchase a cool drink from a coconut vendor. He sliced off the top of the nut with the greatest of ease and handed me the nut to soothe my parched throat. The station was an extra-large building, looking more like a palace than a station with its fine architecture (a large dome on top in the centre with small domes and short steeples attached to them around it). This was the terminus of the Great Indian Railway, a network extending for hundreds of miles, and catering for all classes. The passengers were cooped up in hot stuffy dusty carriages for hours on end. Some took a perilous ride on the roof, clutching their possessions and hanging on like grim death and having to put up with the sun, dust or an occasional rainstorm.

Being sweaty and grimy I went to have a shufti after purchasing a platform ticket for one rupee in the spacious booking hall. I had a quick look round and noticed the first-class waiting room had conveniences attached. I then spotted a shower room attached to the second-class conveniences. It contained six showers, which cost two rupees with soap and a towel provided. This was just the job after all the excitement with the sweat and grime of the day. I availed myself of the service and enjoyed a long cool shower. Then I wandered around several of the platforms packed full of passengers with their children and baggage until I came across a buffet where I purchased a large pot of lemon char and a good meal.

On my way out I noticed a platform at the far side. It was well lit and had a red carpet, so made my way over to have a shufti to find out what was happening. On drawing near the stationmaster in all his finery approached me to tell me to clear off, but, after telling him of my curiosity, he told me that the Nizam of Hyderabad's personal train was due to arrive at any minute. He kindly offered me a seat in his office with a grandstand view of the colourful spectacle through the open window.

The Nizam's major-domo, resplendent like the entire train crew in royal livery, gave the guests a warm welcome as armed retainers with lances lined the platform. Apparently the guests were going on a forty-eight hour journey to the Nizam's summer palace for a fortnight's entertainment.

Within a quarter of an hour everyone was comfortably seated as the train left the platform. I thanked the stationmaster for the loan of his seat.

On the way back I paused to rest awhile on a stone seat near to a hanging garden which was filled with jacarandas, begonias and bougainvillea. Nearby, the branches of a large pepper tree hung down low over an old Sikh with a long flowing beard who slept soundly. The garden was mostly in the shadows of the Taj Mahal Hotel. It was floodlit for the wealthy patrons so its colours did not show up to their best advantage, but it was a mass of colour when seen in the daylight.

The Taj Mahal Hotel was reputed to be one of the finest in the East. The large spacious rooms were cooled by large open windows and old-fashioned DC punkahs with four long blades which whirred around slowly overhead creating a cooling draught. It was considered to be the twin of Raffles Hotel, Singapore, which was like a large honeypot. It was an attractive rendezvous for the big nobs of the Middle East, Sumatra, Borneo, Ceylon, Madagascar, Medan, Delhi, and the Malay States, with numerous rubber planters passing through the doors.

I was just about to continue my journey when a long red carpet was rolled out and clipped on to the steps and across the pavement. The first man to use it was an Indian prince who was just departing with his escort, a Sikh bodyguard of a dozen men all clad in scarlet uniforms and gold turbans carrying ten-foot lance poles with small fluttering pennants at the ends. He stepped into his large Silver Cloud Rolls-Royce open tourer, then sped off leaving his guard to make their own arrangements to follow him.

Shortly after, several other Indian princes, jewel merchants and top brass turned up in all manner of transport. There were several ancient Rolls-Royce and Bentley cars, old taxis, numerous gharries and the odd palanquin. They were followed by a steady stream of guests. The women in their fine-silk party frocks and jewellery and the menfolk in evening or mess dress.

Being curious to see how the other half lived I tarried awhile to watch the arrivals and the old taxis empty their passengers then chug away. Some of the couples were accompanied by their Indian servants in white livery with red sashes and turbans, who addressed their employers as sahib or memsahib.

One palanquin, borne by four native servants, was lowered at the bottom of the steps. It contained a high-caste woman with a red dot in the centre of her forehead, wearing a black sari with many silver bracelets. She stepped out then loped superbly up the steps, then glided with the smooth easy motion of a cobra along the red carpet before disappearing into the building.

On gazing through a large window I could see all the guests assembling in little groups for their usual round of drinks and chats. The bartender was in the background mixing their favourite tipples of gimlets, gin slings and chota pegs, handling enough booze to sink a medium-sized ship.

As there was a lull in the arrivals I went over to have a word with the doorman. He told me these parties usually went on until the crack of dawn, which did not surprise me one bit. I bade him farewell, then departed, returning to depot down an unlit road.

On Saturday afternoon after dinner I rested awhile before going ashore on daily leave, then made my way to Bombay Central Station where a steam train had just pulled into the platform. Most of the carriages were third class with hard wooden seats which were packed far beyond their capacity to suffocation point. Hitchhikers had climbed onto the roof and were hanging on like limpets, many with their sole possessions in sacks or bundles. One even had a small kid goat with its head sticking out of a sack. Others seated themselves on the buffers. Some managed to wedge themselves in between the framework underneath near the wheels, and some hung on to the handles as they stood on the side steps.

All of these hangers-on took their own lives into their hands. Some were badly hurt when the engine suddenly ground to a halt, hitting the buffers with terrific jerk, dislodging many of them from their positions.

Suddenly the doors swung open with all the passengers alighting from the carriages, so the platform was suddenly swarming with families. The fathers were fussing around looking for their baggage and offspring that had got lost in the crowd. To add to the confusion the mail van was being unloaded with the bags being flung out then piled on to waiting trucks. Within half an hour the crowd had dispersed after being loaded up into numerous waiting gharries and taxis.

As soon as the baggage and mail had been emptied from the vans the train was shunted into the sidings where the cleaners got to work brushing the carriages out, preparing them for the next trip. The native wheeltapper with his long light hammer tapped each carriage wheel, which gave a sharp ring when sounded. One gave a dull thud, which indicated the steel tyre was cracked, so the carriage had to be separated then shunted away out of service. Several dwarf black goats, feeding on a piece of scrubland nearby, lifted their heads from time to time as if to see what was going on.

The engine was shunted to the shed whilst the usual procedures were carried out (cleaning out the firebox, ash box and soot box, and doing the immediate small repairs which needed attention). Several leaking glands required tightening up, and piston-rod packings needed adjusting so they were a neat fit on the rods to keep the steam pressure from escaping. The heavy cast-iron brake blocks were well worn down and required changing. The leaves of a heavy spring had broken off so the spring needed changing and the water injector needed its cones cleaning and tightening up. The water was running to waste as it was delivered into the boiler with it usual contented song.

Then the tender was filled up with coal and water, and the fire was relit to raise steam. Another engine was being prepared to leave the shed by the driver. He was going all round the drip-feed bearings with his oil can, and a bottle of thick black cylinder oil to fill the box which contained several small pumps which supplied the cylinders and valves at different points. The stoker spread the fire, shovelling the coal evenly all round the firebox to get a large roaring red fire. The safety valves began to lift with a full head of steam.

Soon the engine left the shed to pick up half a dozen third-class carriages, then pull them into the platform where another two second-class carriages were coupled to the back along with a guard's van. They were luxurious carriages of unusual design with attendant servants from the state railways serving ice-cooled drinks which were kept in large wooden barrels similar to the type used by the old Italian ice-cream vendors of long ago.

A party of eighty semi-invalids boarded these coaches bound for Deolali in the Western Ghats (mountain ranges) surrounded by vivid green gum trees, colourful shrubs and flowers, set in amongst neatly manicured lawns.

They were going to recuperate in the tranquillity of the floating houseboats on the lakes of Kashmir, with the luxury of sleeping in cool charpoys (beds) with mosquito nets, and barber wallahs coming to shave them before rising next morning.

The third-class compartments were rammed jammed full of passengers, many having the upper parts of their bodies hanging out of any window they could open. The atmosphere inside was suffocating, with the added stench of sweating bodies in far worse conditions than a cattle truck.

As usual the hitchhikers secured their perilous positions on the outside, hanging on like limpets just as the train was about to start off. They were vulnerable to all sorts of hazards, such as loose stones flying up from the track; dust, soot and sparks getting into their eyes from the engine funnel; clouds of steam from leaking pipes; the cruel sun rays that beat down on their skins; the occasional monsoon rains soaked them; or dust storms which choked them. The only advantage they seemed to have was plenty of cool breeze when the train started moving.

Then I wandered around the docks, which covered an area of several square miles of land. It was a bustling area with several different types of docks. One basin was full of native craft. They traded along the southern coastline of India, then across the Arabian Sea and Indian Ocean. The place was full of coolies loading and unloading the different craft as they bobbed up and down in the water. They walked barefooted over narrow gangplanks with heavy sacks of rice, etc. on their backs to fill up the small holds or empty them.

Liners from the West berthed nearby the Gateway to India and were mostly Royal Mail vessels, which delivered all incoming and outgoing mail to and from the West to the large General Post Office which was situated nearby.

The landing stages, wharves and warehouses were stacked with bulging mailbags, trunks and cases awaiting the next liner to call so that they could be shipped out.

There was a crowd of Muslims with their beards dyed a fresh red, which was a sign that they were pilgrims returning from the holy city of Mecca. They were just disembarking from an overcrowded ferry boat.

I watched a medium-sized merchant steamship preparing to unload. It had just tied up alongside and the Goanese crew was coiling up the ropes before opening up the hatches.

Two donkeymen were preparing their Clarke Chapman steam winches by draining the water from the steam lines. There was a loud hammering as they vibrated with trapped water which tried to escape followed by a loud hissing of steam as the line had warmed up. Then the drains were eased down so the winches were ready for use. The derricks were unfastened then swung out into position as the donkeymen and winchmen worked together raising and lowering the crane hooks with their large cargo nets as required. The donkey engines revved and clattered away at full speed. They suddenly reversed when required, so the cargo net could be loaded in the hold then unloaded on the deck. Gangs of coolies could take the sacks down the gangplanks to a long line of waiting bullock carts. Large boxes or crates were lifted out later with slings, then swung out over the ship's side onto the jetty.

Nearby there was a railway siding where I noticed a train arriving. It pulled up with the usual squeal of brakes, then a sudden jerk as it hit the buffers, throwing the for'ard-facing passengers off their seats. When I was just about to leave, an unusual sight met my eyes. As the passengers were alighting on the platform they were all dishevelled with red stains about their eyes, noses, ears, throats and mouths, and their garments stained with long red streaks.

Being curious to know what had happened I strolled over to find out. The train had arrived from Poona, its last stop after travelling several days from Madras on the east coast. On its long journey over the vast Deccan Plateau, situated centrally on the huge Indian peninsula, it had encountered a terrific dust storm. The fine red dust like talcum powder had penetrated through fine copper screens (fitted into the open windows to supposedly keep out the dust and flies). In this instance it had penetrated every nook and cranny, leaving a film of red dust on the seats, floor and passengers.

This storm had lasted many hours, completely coating the inside and outside of the train with dust, making it impossible for any hitchhikers to hang on. It was followed by a terrific rainstorm which washed all the rain dust from the outside of the carriages, but the damp penetrated the compartments, causing red streaks on the passengers' faces and clothing as well as tiny rivulets on the floor which ended up with red blobs.

When wandering past the engine I noticed it was unlike our engines at home. Louvres fitted to the sides admitted air and kept out rain, dust and the burning sun rays. They totally enclosed the footplate, which was already as hot as an oven with heat from the boiler and furnace. This must have added to the discomfort of the driver and stoker.

During the height of the storms they would be unable to see where they were going through the tiny cab windows; they couldn't see when to stop at signals or stations to fuel up or water the engine, or to change over engine crews. They had to rely on fog signals, placed on the lines to go off with a bang as the wheels ran over them, which warned the driver when to stop.

I retraced my steps searching for a café for a cup of tea and a bite to eat before returning to barracks.

On Sunday afternoon I wandered around the immediate vicinity of the barracks which was sparsely populated, paid a brief visit to various places, starting off at Colaba Point, then on to the observatory and the English cemetery. (I was surprised to note that many of the occupants had died young — mostly in their mid-thirties. Their lives must have been short and sweet.) I then wandered through the tidy churchyard of St John, which was a small church with a lovely stained-glass window of the crucifixion. It also housed several regimental flags.

I wandered over to Sasson Dock where many of the small sailing boats were tied up and there was much activity of loading and unloading.

Finally ended up close by Bombay Yacht Club in Back Bay, where I spent a couple of hours watching the yachts in a slack wind lazily tacking, turning about and manoeuvring trying to catch the wind in their sails. In a shady spot on the beach, under some swaying palms, then stripped off and had a couple of short swims in the pleasantly warm water before returning to barracks.

Next morning we returned to the ship in an advance party required for undocking and removing the flooding bonnets and flashing up the auxiliary boiler. Later we started up the for'ard turbogenerator so lighting and power could be restored to the ship. Meals were sent down and we slept aboard so as to prepare the boilers and engines for manoeuvring out of dock the next morning. Then we shut it down again once the ship had been secured alongside. Then the rest of the crew returned to the ship to help with the storing.

I had a last run ashore with Taff Drinkwater. After wandering round for a while we finished up in an air-conditioned cinema. It was one of the best in the city and quite expensive. The seating was comfortable, and the atmosphere was cool and pleasant compared with the high temperature outside. Unfortunately I must have sat in a slight draught and I later developed severe colic pains in the intestines. It was an old film that we had seen before but it was nevertheless enjoyable. The Pathé Gazette News was a bit more hopeful than it had previously been.

As we stepped out of the foyer into the dark night air there was a confusion of smells. The heat rose up from the street and surrounded us, just like the heat from a large hot oven when the door is suddenly opened.

It was a strange scene outside as we wandered around in the dark. Quite a number of the city natives had lain down on the hard pavements or gutters to go to sleep in their grubby white loincloths or sarongs. It impeded our progress somewhat as we could barely make out their outlines in the dark so we could step over them.

Behind us we could hear the sound of slapping feet against the cool grey slabs of slate pavement, not knowing if they were being made by friend or foe. Once we had accustomed ourselves to the night atmosphere it seemed almost cool with the false coolness of the west coast of India, until we had walked on about a mile with suffocation and sweat taking hold of us.

My stomach ache persisted, but all the buildings looked the same in the dark shadows and I was unable to find a convenience anywhere, so asked a waiter in a café and he directed me to a loo in the back of a large block of buildings. It was pitch black but I groped around to find a small cubicle. It contained a native convenience with two foot holes in the floor with a hole in the centre. Afterwards we sat down to enjoy a chicken and rice meal. It was a little too hot for me, being flavoured with curry. I washed it down with strong sweet black coffee.

After strolling back to the ship through the dockland area, stepping over more sleeping natives on the hard warm pavements as we walked carefully along the badly lit streets, we arrived back on board shortly after 22.30. I was met by ERA Johnson (Jonno, for short), who was duty watch and was having trouble starting up the refrigerating plant, which was my part of ship.

It appeared the pressure gauges were not registering any pressure as the cocks had become blocked. He had sent for Lieutenant Whitehead, who had decided to turn the job over to me.

I thought I knew what was wrong and went down below to fix it.

I thought I would have the machinery running within half an hour. I knew exactly what to do with the pressure gauges because they were only cracked open to prevent the needles from fluctuating wildly to give a steady reading. All that was required was to open them up wide, with the pressure shooting up to 1,000 pounds on all the gauges around the system.

This meant there was no more room in the condenser to compress any more gas, but had failed to realise this. It was a new factor which had crept into the starting-up of the plant, and it had failed to sink in fully to my sluggish brain. The temperature of the rooms was shooting up to 105°F, the same as the ambient temperature, causing the gas in the grids to increase in volume. This meant the normal settings for the regulating and inlet valves were too small to cope with such a large volume of extra gas.

To get back to the story, the machinery was prepared for starting up in the normal manner as in the cold northern waters. The first thing to be done was to light the candle on the deck, then make sure that the ventilation system was running with the exhaust fan started up to draw any escaping CO_2 gas via the suction trunking which was fitted a couple of inches above the deck level. The next job was to open up the inlet and outlet seacocks then start up the circulating pump to cool the condenser gases, and then prepared the regulator to set at three turns open, with the manifold inlet valves one and a half turns open (which was wider than usual) and finally pumped up the gland sea oil and opened up the compressor inlet and discharge valves wide.

Then by turning the handle of the electric starter a few notches I imagined that I would soon be soundly asleep, but to my horror and amazement that was not to be. The motor only turned a few revs before the overload trip cut out, stopping it dead. Three times it was tried but to no avail. It simply refused to budge.

My tired brain pondered over what to do next as it was essential that the plant should run in order that the rooms would be cold enough for loading up next forenoon. Should the engineer or senior engineer or the duty EA be shaken?

That was the question, but they would be difficult to locate at that time of night. I would have a great deal of explaining to do before they could fully understand the problem. They were unfamiliar with the fine adjustments of the system, so a great deal of time would be wasted. There was nothing to do but plod on with the job.

A nifty idea sprang to my mind in a sudden flash of inspiration, which would prevent the overload gear from tripping out. I would start the machine up notch by notch, with the inlet valve shut off until the compressor had reached its full revs. It worked like a dream until the valve was reopened. Then suddenly the plan went hopelessly awry. Before I could look to see the pressure-gauge readings, the gas in the condenser must have reached the danger mark and blew out the safety disc at 1,800 pounds per square inch pressure with a terrific bang and a hiss which rent the air. My head began to throb as I reeled back in amazement. The gas should have started to cool down to drop the pressure, and it was alarming to see a large cloud of frozen white gas suddenly fill up the room. It had already extinguished the candle and it made me wonder how long it would be before I became unconscious.

Fortunately my instinct came to my aid and guided my hand to trip out the breaker to stop the compressor, which would ease down the volume of escaping gas. I then shut the discharge and suction valves, with the aid of a ratchet spanner on the valve spindles, to prevent further loss of gas. This was accomplished by a supreme lightning effort from my weary body, and hardly dared to breathe until I had rushed out through the door then shut it tight behind me to allow the exhaust fan to remove all traces of gas from the room. This operation must have taken several minutes, but there were no ill effects from the slightly toxic heavy gas, so paused for a few minutes to try to think how to overcome this green rub, which was a bitter blow that looked like taking several hours to sort out. It was rapidly approaching eight bells and was already knackered, mentally exhausted and bleary-eyed. It had already been an extra-long tropical day, so much so that I could have easily dropped down on the spot and gone to sleep on the hard deck.

However, some action had to be taken before the meat arrived next forenoon.

Finally my decision was to stagger slowly through the darkened mess deck. It was full of tightly slung hammocks in rows with little space between them, all filled with sweating stokers, some tossing about in their sleep and snoring. The stifling atmosphere caused my brow to sweat profusely. Then, after staggering up the flights of steps, I eventually reached the upper deck and made for the water side of the ship where there was a slight breeze which wafted the warm air around without the pungent city smells. It was much more pleasant than the hot stifling decks below, so dumped my body down on a fairlead which overlooked a huge inland bay, and gazed for several minutes at the moonbeams glistening on the water, lighting up small native craft as they slid slowly into harbour. Their sails were lined against the shadows, with a faint blue velvet sky above, lit up by stars glittering like diamonds.

After five minutes I began to relax and enjoy the scene. I turned over all the possible steps and alternatives in my mind as to how to combat the latest problem. There were no instructions in the maker's handbook or the engineers' manual as to how to deal with such a situation. Lieutenant Whitehead, the officer in charge, couldn't care less as he had no interest in the job. Consequently he was unfamiliar with the practical working of the plant, which he left to me. He let me down as at the very least he could have popped down to see what was happening and organised the watchkeepers to stand by the job and work their shifts, as it was impossible for me to find them in the dark when everyone was tucked up in their hammocks.

There was nothing else for it but to visualise the disaster that had occurred in the system so that I got a clear mental picture. Suddenly an idea flashed through my mind as to how I could overcome this unusual setback. It was so simple that it could not fail to work.

The City Hall clock chimed out the midnight hour in the distance, so, after enjoying another ten minutes, and having got my second wind, I descended down below to the bathroom. There was just a trickle of water left in the pipeline to swill my face and wipe around my sticky body before changing into my overalls, which made me slightly more comfortable and renewed my flagging vigour a little.

The first thing to do was to enter the bottle room to rummage in the spare box for a new safety disc, so opened the door into the adjoining compartment which was the CO_2-compressor room, to fit the safety disc and relit the candle in the corner of the room. It flickered but remained alight, indicating that all the gas had been extracted.

So far so good! Now came the most important part of the plan. I opened up all the valves wide, including the regulator and manifold discharge valves, to ensure the gas flowed freely through the system without any back pressure, to be cooled in the condenser until the volume was reduced to the working level.

It was imperative that the freezing was in good working order for the next forenoon so the cold rooms were frozen for restocking. Now all that had to be done was to notch up the starting handle until the compressor was running at full speed without the least sign of any protest. The gas circulated freely around the system until the condenser began to cool it far too quickly. This meant that the spring-loaded safety valve had not done its job, as it should have shut tight once the condenser pressure had been reduced to 1,000 pounds. It stuck open and it allowed a great deal more gas to escape than it should have done.

Soon it became crystal clear that the loss of gas had been much greater than anticipated as the discharge side of the compressor heated up. It was sucking in too much hot gas, causing the discharge side to heat up. Because of the loss of gas I had to shut all the discharge valves except the two to the cold room, which was the biggest and needed cooling first. I also shut down the regulator slightly to increase the pressure in the condenser slightly. There was nothing else for it but to press on and charge up the system as quickly as possible. I removed the first CO_2 bottle from the racks and attached a clamp. I slung it up with a strop to the spring-balance scales, which indicated 180 pounds on the dial — its weight when full. It was then connected up via a small-bore copper pipe to the charging valve on the low-pressure (evaporator) side of the system. The two small valves were opened to allow the gas to flow from the bottle into the system. This took about fifteen minutes. When the bottle was three quarters empty the bottom froze up. This meant a long trek to the auxiliary steaming boiler room, up and down five flights of steps, for a bucket of hot water to heat up the bottom of the bottle to expel the remaining gas. The weight on the scales had dropped to 140 pounds, and 40 pounds had been added to the system. Whilst down below the SPO told me to come down at 02.00 for a cup of kye.

Meanwhile the empty bottle was removed, marked with a piece of chalk and replaced on the rack so that the next bottle could be slung up in its place. Also a flat iron electric heater was routed out to keep the bucket of water hot and save the long trip. The bottom of the second bottle was immersed until it was empty and then the valves were shut off ready for replacing. The regulator was then adjusted then I went down to join the SPO for a cup of kye, which was invigorating. I asked him if I could borrow his stoker for five minutes every three quarters of an hour to help me change the bottles over. Whilst I removed one, he replaced it with another, thus saving me a lot of time and energy. By 06.00 we had emptied five bottles into the system. I then adjusted all the discharge valves and reset the regulator before going in search of the regulating chief stoker to detail a watchkeeper off to get down as soon as possible, and went for a nice cool shower and changed my overalls into the rig of the day, and then went down to instruct the watchkeeper to keep adding more gas until the compressor ran cool and the rooms were freezing properly.

Meanwhile the hands had been called at 05.30 to lash up and stow, as the ship was working tropical routine, and the duty krusher would tour around the mess decks with his unwelcome cry of, "Wakey, wakey! Rise and shine!" The sun was burning your bloody eyes out, and anyone who failed to respond quickly would have the slip knot tugged at the foot of his hammock so it let him fall down on the deck with a thud. He had the job of re-slinging his hammock and packing in the mattress, etc. before it could be lashed up and stowed away in the bin. Once all the hammocks had been stowed out of the way the cooks of messes laid out the tables for breakfast as the hands were piped to fall in at 06.30, then work until 12.30 when it was dinner time. If they were not on duty watch they were free for the rest of the day, so then went up to the drinking fountain in the locker flat for a long cool drink to slake my thirst before going down to the mess for breakfast. I had two cups of tea, some scrambled egg, a piece of bacon, and a piece of toast and marmalade. I then waited until the mess was clear to tell Chief ERA Rodgers that the safety disc had blown on the refrigerating plant, causing the loss of half its charge of CO_2 gas, and that I had been up all night replacing it. He agreed I should sleep on the cushions in the corner of the mess for the rest of the day after I had rechecked the plant and opened up the pre-cooler (a device to add efficiency to the plant). I also had to find out how much more gas the watchkeeper had added to the plant, and found he had added another five bottles, making a total of 400 pounds added.

I then set the cool room and cold rooms, the ice tank and cool-water tank (for the galley), manifold inlet valves and regulator, also examined all the temperatures to ensure they were all beginning to freeze. I then left instructions for the watchkeeper to give me a shake in the mess if anything went wrong. I made myself comfortable and crashed down on the cushions, sleeping soundly until teatime. After this I went for a good swill down in the bathroom before checking the logbook and long-distance temperature recorder to find out if the temperatures were dropping steadily. Once satisfied climbed up onto the flight deck for a stroll along the deck with my oppos.

During the next few days I kept a watchful eye on the cold rooms to ensure they were brought down below -18°C.

Durban

As usual we left Bombay ignorant of our destination, but with a deep lasting impression of its heat, stench and the sweet smells of Eastern spices. I will never forget the countless millions, often in the streets in filth and squalor, many with deeply pockmarked faces and wrinkled skin, with dark-brown sunken eyes and long black hair. Many were blind, with diseased limbs withered away or extra-fat. Also there were those who slept and died on the hard stone pavements, or in gutters and alleyways of the city, whose only possessions were the rags that covered their bodies.

Little children begged with their tiny hands held out, crying out, "One anna, no mamma, no dadda," It was enough to soften anyone's hard heart, but once you had given to one, a crowd of children descended on you like a swarm of bees. It was impossible to give to all.

We steamed south-west down the Indian coast, heading for Addu Atoll, Gan. Admiral Slim Somerville had first sought shelter here with his British East Indian fleet, which consisted mainly of ancient ships. It was vastly inferior to the large Japanese fleet with its greatly superior air arm with high-performance kites. They could have easily sunk his lot had they extended their search beyond the Indian Ocean, but fortunately their oil fuel and supplies ran low so they were forced to return to harbour.

We had only been outward bound for two days when a sad event occurred. A young cherry-faced West Country stoker, who was one of my turbogenerator watchkeepers, suddenly died of heat exhaustion, which was a great shock to us all.

Next day the funeral service was held on the quarterdeck by the padre with the captain reading the lesson. Then, as was customary, his body which had been sewn up in his weighted hammock was then slid overboard from under the Union Jack and committed to the deep. The master-at-arms had all his belongings collected to be sold off at a masthead auction at highly inflated prices. The proceeds were then sent to his next of kin along with his personal effects.

A few days later we arrived at Gan, which is a large flat coral island, only about three feet above sea level, with tall coconut palms swaying in a warm gentle breeze. It is one of a large cluster of Maldive islands which varies in height from three to twenty feet above sea level. The main island was Malé, where the sultan resided. The group was attached to Ceylon and lies 500 miles south-west of it. It is only a few degrees off the equator, and had a population of 30,000 inhabitants, who lived in an unhealthy climate, exporting cowrie shells, coconuts and coir. Gan is situated in the southern group of islands. Addu Atoll is a vast natural harbour, formed by a large barrier reef with huge breakers from the Indian Ocean crashing down on it. The entrance was barely wide enough for us to sail through, so soundings had to be taken by lead weights on the end of ropes to ensure the hull did not run aground in shallow water. Soon we were clear of the reef and the ship entered a huge blue lagoon where she anchored. We dropped the hook close by a battered old merchantman which was floating in a most unusual position with its bows sunk well down in the water. On closer examination it was noticed all her deck cargo had been shifted for'ard to allow a staging to be erected aft round the propeller, which had one blade broken off and was above the water. Four men of the engineers' party, stripped to the waist in shorts, were taking it in turns to hit a large ring spanner with a 14-pound hammer. The sweat poured from their brows as each stroke struck home without any visual signs of movement; the ringing blows resounded around the lagoon. Eventually after a quarter of an hour the boss nut began to move little by little until it could be unscrewed by hand. Once removed a strongback was screwed into the propeller boss to force it off the taper. It did not budge for several minutes until it yielded with a terrific bang. The worst of the job was now over, so the old propeller was removed to allow the spare one to take its place after it had been slung up then secured by screwing up the boss nut.

For the next two days the ship lay at anchor. The crew was piped to bathe over the side, and also played several games of water polo. The cutter was rigged and lowered to sail around the lovely clear lagoon for parties to land ashore. It was deserted except for a few native huts and outrigger canoes drawn well up on the beach of white sand. Otherwise there was no sign of life as the village lay out of sight on the north of the island.

In the evening we raised steam then departed from the atoll heading to our unknown destination (Durban). Soon we were crossing the equator. As it was wartime we omitted the first part of the ceremony, which was to stop the ship to allow King Neptune and his court to come aboard to sentence the whole ship's company for trespassing in his kingdom. His court was set up on the flight deck in front of a large canvas tank, constructed by the shipwrights (which was filled with water from the fire main). A hinged ducking stool was built above the level of the tank. A large crowd gathered to see King Neptune, decked out with his crown and seaweed about him, along with his court dressed as dolphins, sealions and walruses. He sentenced each man in the ship to be lathered with a big paintbrush, then shaved with a large wooden razor, then tipped backward into the tank where he was ducked half a dozen times by several burly matelots until he reached the other side of the tank and struggled out half drowned with sore eyes and nostrils. Everyone wore a pair of shorts with no shoes as the deck was cooled by a gentle breeze which filtered through the windbreak, which had been raised to reduce the draught.

We steamed on for several days before preparing a Firefly and the flight deck for a take-off after a balloon had been flown off to observe the wind speed and weather conditions. The HO navigator had lost his bearings on Madagascar, so the Firefly was manned then flown off to locate the long island. On its return to the ship our course was quickly altered. We headed for Tamatave (the main port) where we were to drop off a party of officials. Afterwards the ship proceeded in a southerly direction. We spent Christmas at sea before arriving at Durban, Natal, South Africa.

As we docked a lady in white welcomed us with several patriotic songs from the dockside as the ship berthed alongside.

The ship docked for boiler cleaning, oil-fuel-tank cleaning and fumigating to get rid of the millions of cockroaches. They were even in the lockers, where we could see them running over our clean white clothing.

Durban was situated on the long coastline of the Indian Ocean, around the large natural harbour of Natal Bay. Some twenty-two miles away lay the Valley of 1,000 Hills, where nearby lay a traditional Zulu kraal (a South African native village). The kraal had a commanding view over the vast valley which was shrouded by early morning and evening mists. It was once inhabited by legendary cannibal tribes.

The hottest months in Durban were from December to March (when the maximum daily temperature rises to 86°F). The average temperature was 73° to 80°F. Minimum temperature was 48° to 57°F, which was a subtropical climate — warm to hot, humid to rainy. In summer the days are often humid causing emotional depression and physical discomfort.

Afternoon leave was piped from 14.00, so I hastened to change my English sterling to the local currency before making my way ashore to explore the place. I got lost once or twice before finding my way down to the Victoria Embankment, which runs for several miles around part of Natal Bay. I eventually came to the statue of Dick King on horseback. He was a local hero from the Battle of Congella. On 23 May 1842 a small British garrison force, under the command of Captain Charlton Smith, mounted what was thought to be a surprise attack on the trekkers' camp. But the commander committed a terrible blunder as there was a full moon shining that night which lit up the soldiers' red coats. They glowed like beacons in the dark. As the advancing men crashed their way through the bush so the sound alerted the Boer sentries who gave the alarm to their comrades. They immediately laid an ambush, hiding amongst the bayside mangroves and picking off the soldiers one by one until there were fifty casualties. The soldiers were unable to return fire so the retreat was then sounded to call the unit back into the old fort, carrying the badly wounded with them. The Boers then besieged the British garrison and could have starved it into submission, had not Dick King and his black retainer Ndongeni volunteered to ride 625 miles bareback to Grahamstown for relief. They were rowed across Natal Bay in a small boat with muffled oars, well out of view of the Boers, to start their famous ride. They endured terrific discomfort due to the strong sun and soreness from being constantly jogged up and down on a horse without stirrups or saddle. They reached their destination after a journey lasting ten days. Dick King was in a state of collapse but was able to alert the garrison, who immediately sent a detachment of soldiers to relieve the fort.

I then turned up Gardiner Street past Farewell Square to the post office and went as far as the old Durban Railway Station (which was purely functional with a plain platform, booking office and without a roof). I went around the back of the post office to the City Hall (built in white stone resembling Belfast City Hall, which was designed by the same architect who built the white stone town hall in Stockport, Cheshire, not a stone's throw from where I was born), eventually ending up on Soldiers Way. I took the right turn to the unimpressive remains of the old fort, which I examined briefly before arriving at the North Beach, where I sat down to rest in a cool shelter before going in search of big eats (a large meal).

Another afternoon I set off for the beach to bathe in the warm Indian Ocean. I then lay out to rest in the shade. When Mr and Mrs Invernizzi (Robin and Marion) turned up with their son to build some sandcastles on the beach they invited me to join them.

We soon got talking about home, and I was greatly surprised to find they came from the same neck of the woods as I did. In fact they were from the next town over the county boundary, some three miles from my home. I had served my five-year apprenticeship there at Mirlees Diesel Engines in Hazel Grove (which was commonly called at that time Bullock Smithy). The tramlines ran through there to the Rising Sun, which was the terminus. (When the tramlines were laid several of the locals blackleaded them outside their houses, or so the story goes.)

We had become quite friendly and we were beginning to move off before sunset. They then invited me to visit them any time I was free, and Marion said she would make up a bed for me to sleep there.

We went to their home where Marion made us an evening meal, after which we sat outside at the back in the cool of the evening in the dark.

Apparently they had emigrated from England a few years before the war started, having come out to better themselves as work was scarce and wages were low. Robin had been in the building trade as a carpenter and had lost many hours' work by being rained off, or due to frost and snow in the winter.

I stopped with them for several nights and during our stay we discussed everything in general, especially conditions at home, the shortage of food, clothes and furniture, and the loss of many dwelling houses due to bombing. Also, many of our ships had been sunk, leaving no room to import luxury goods. We also discussed when the war was likely to be over.

Marion and Robin had been great cyclists and knew the county of Cheshire like the backs of their hands. They also knew the city of Chester, surrounded by its Roman walls, and its famous old black and white timbered buildings in which were covered arcades called the famous Rows. They also remembered boating on the river.

They knew the Peak District area — including Buxton Spa with its Victorian sandstone crescent houses, theatre and pavilion gardens. They also knew the Cat and Fiddle Inn, one of the highest in the country in the centre of huge black peat moors which stretched for miles around. It is often cut off in winter by a heavy fall of snow on the Macclesfield to Buxton road. Wild Boar Clough is a few miles away in a pleasant valley where the boars used to roam on the edge of Macclesfield Forest. There are miles and miles of drystone walling over the hills and dales, dividing numerous small plots, farms and roads skilfully assembled to withstand the harsh elements. There was Ashford-in-the-Water with its sheep dip on the riverbank. Then a little further down the River Wye is the market town of Bakewell, famous for its tarts and its narrow stone bridge. The pleasant meandering river attracts crowds of visitors along its banks and the cricket green is also popular.

They recalled the many stone-built villages and hamlets, such as Stoney Middleton and Tideswell, where on different weeks throughout the summer each village would decorate its wells, then hold a ceremony. Large religious pictures were drawn out on large trays of damp clay then filled in by most of the villagers who followed the outlines, skilfully pressing in thousands of petals in numerous colours (blue hydrangeas were a favourite). Also mosses and small fir cones were stuck on to add to the colour. When finished they looked like works of art. They also knew the village of Eyam, where the plague from London had been transported in a parcel of cloth. This caused several deaths until the local rector took it in hand and forbade anyone to enter or leave the village. Any food coming into the village was paid for by leaving money soaked in vinegar on a certain stone near the church.

After some good discussions we usually turned in about 22.30, then I had a good rest between nice cool sheets.

In the morning we would rise at 06.00 to wash and shave, then have a round of toast and marmalade, washed down with a cup of tea. I then set off to the ship with Robin. We passed by the railway, which was stirring into life. The engines were being prepared in the shed for their heavy daily tasks. At the bottom of the hill we both went our separate ways for another round of our daily work.

Invitations were sent out for the ship's company to stay and be entertained by the English residents in their homes scattered over a large area in and around the city. At the weekend the first half of the crew had leave to be transported to their homes. Young Syd Chaffey, an ERA coppersmith, and myself were picked for the first batch and mustered early Friday morning at the jaunty's office for our leave tickets and travelling warrants. We packed a few things in our hand grips before making our way down to the railway station. A group of Fleet Air Arm bods joined the same train bound for Richmond, a small country town some sixty miles away in the heart of the fruit-growing area.

Eventually an old narrow-gauge steam train arrived. We all piled into the rickety coaches which stopped at numerous small stations and halts on the way.

We eventually arrived at Pietermaritzburg, a small Victorian city and the capital of Natal (once the Place of the Elephant). It was a good example of Victorian architecture with iron railings and atmosphere. We changed over to a waiting train, then continued our journey down a branch line to Richmond in the heart of vast acres of fruit farms.

We all alighted. The Fleet Air Arm bods were met by a truck, which took then to a large orange farm two miles out of town.

We were welcomed by Mrs Le Fevré (Rita), whose husband was away with the South African forces in the Middle East. We climbed into a large white Chevrolet car to be taken to her home just outside the town. Once there we were introduced to her daughter, Margaret, and her friend, Corrie Voss (a young nurse from Lusaka in Northern Rhodesia, who had prepared a light meal with a pot of tea.

After this we had a stroll around. In the front of the house stood a large dense thicket where an old Zulu retainer lived in a small grass hut. He mounted guard with his fearsome-looking assegai (sharp-pointed spear). He would not let strangers pass through the gate without Rita's approval, so she had to point us out as friends and not foes. We walked a mile up the road without meeting a soul. On our return the old Zulu was at the gate with his assegai. He let us enter with a broad grin on his face.

The bungalow had large high cool rooms with a stoep (or verandah) at the rear. Unfortunately the privy was an old-fashioned thunderbox variety with a hole in the ground, and was situated down a long path at the bottom of the garden. It was inconvenient for nightly calls, causing my mate to resort to an unusual stratagem, which baffled me after our first night's sleep. When arising I noticed his shoe was full of water (apparently he did not fancy a trip outside in the dark).

After a tasty evening meal we retired to the stoep, which was large and airy, to listen to the evening news on the wireless in the cool of the evening. The news was at last becoming more hopeful. Our troops were advancing on all European fronts, our bombers were making massive raids on Germany and the Russians were driving the Jerries out of their country. At 22.30 we retired, wishing our hostess goodnight.

After a good night's sleep we were awakened at 09.00 by the aroma of eggs and bacon from the kitchen as Rita was busy cooking the breakfast. We hastened to get washed and shaved so we could get tucking into our breakfast. It tasted good compared with the mass-produced stuff that was dished out on board, which had to be prepared several hours before, then kept warmed up, and which tasted hard and rubbery by the time it reached the table. We finished off with toast and butter, which was severely rationed at home and on board ship (in the region of half an ounce a week). Along with plenty of marmalade, it was washed down with enjoyable cups of coffee. We then helped Rita with the washing-up and did several odd jobs about the house.

As Rita was responsible for keeping the old Zulu, he came around the back to the kitchen for his meals. She also looked after his health and he came round for Rita to dress a nasty-looking burst ulcer on top of his head, which she bathed with a bowl of hot water. She took great care to stand at arm's length as his head was verminous with several fleas hopping around in his hair as she cleaned and dressed the wound. (Doctors charged the earth to attend black servants as they were often verminous.)

The next job to do was the weekly shopping. Before we could go we had to push-start the car as the battery was flat. So first we had to call at the garage for a new one. All the proprietor had was an old one which was well past its best. He was too busy to fit it so we took it with us. We went around several small well-stocked stores for the goods we required, then returned home for a light lunch and a rest during the heat of the day.

Later Syd and I borrowed some old clothes and an overall to work on the car. Fortunately Rita's husband had left a good selection of tools behind. So we were able to change the battery over, only to find it was in poor condition, and short of acid, but it was a little better than the other one. We removed it and carefully drained the acid from the battery cells into a jug, then carefully washed out the sediment with warm water to prevent the build-up of zinc paste, which would short-circuit the cells. We then added the acid from the dud battery to that in the jug, so there was plenty to refill the cells with before ditching the sediment left over in the bottom of the jug. Then we replaced the battery and found it would just turn the engine over, but needed recharging with the trickle charger for twenty-four hours. After this we tested it and found it started the engine with ease. (We were told it gave good service for two months until a new one was obtained.)

We then cleaned and checked the distributor and sparking plugs to make sure the engine started easily, then cleaned up for the evening meal before retiring to the stoep for our usual discussion. We talked about the minute rations that the people at home were living on, and the lack of fruit (such as oranges, apples, bananas, tomatoes, grapes, etc.). We were told we could pick as much fruit as we liked when wandering around the orange groves and apple orchards.

Then Rita came up with a remark that annoyed and puzzled me. She said I did not *live,* being an introvert with a lack of energy and exuberance. I did not dash around like an extrovert with tons of energy to get things done, consequently I led a pretty dull existence, never doing or achieving much.

Afterwards Syd and I went for a long walk up the country lane, aided by the light of the stars and the silvery moonbeams, which cast their shadows all around.

It was eerie without a soul about, only the loud chirping of cicadas, the croaking of frogs and the lights of the fireflies, which glowed in the dark as they fluttered overhead. Also several fruit bats fluttered silently by, silhouetted in the half-light out on their nocturnal raids into the orange groves. On our return we were confronted by the faithful Zulu at the gate with his treacherous-looking assegai in his hand. His sensitive ears had heard our footsteps. He smiled then let us through.

As it had been a long tiring day we wasted no time in getting into bed and were asleep as soon as our heads touched the pillows.

Sunday was another lovely sunny day, so we hastened to get up then had our breakfast.

The first thing we did was to cheek the batteries, replacing the one from the garage in the car, which started the engine up easily; with a bit of luck it would last a month or so with the other one as a standby. Then we noticed the offside front tyre was bald and was liable to puncture on some of the rough country roads, so we changed it for a spare. After this we washed the car ready for a trip out to see the countryside and surrounding landscapes.

At one stage we stopped for a word with a friendly farmer who allowed us to pick several sweet juicy oranges to quench our thirst. We carried on to meet several of Rita's friends, and arrived back home in time for the evening meal, which had been prepared by Margaret and Corrie.

It was another pleasant day on Monday, so we hastened over breakfast, then walked downtown to look around at the well-stocked stores which were stocked with essentials to supply the farming community. We called in a hardware shop to purchase a tap washer. The assistant had to rummage through a lot of pigeonholes to find one, as such things were not in great demand. We quickly made our way back home, then quickly replaced the cold-water-tap washer, which stopped the drip. Water was a precious commodity.

Then the phone rang. It was the friendly young Boer from the fruit farm where the Fleet Air Arm bods were stopping. He wanted us to make up a foursome at tennis. So we were run two miles up the road in the car for a knock-up on the tennis court. Syd was an average player but I had never played before. The two South Africans were well practised, so it wasn't much of a game. I was playing patball whilst our opponents returned the balls over the net just like whizzing cannonballs — so fast that I could barely see them, let alone hit them back again. After an hour's exercise in the boiling sun we packed up, then returned for lunch before relaxing in an easy chair on the stoep.

After the evening meal we packed our grips ready for an early start. At 21.30 we made our way to the only pub for a party that several of the locals had laid on for us. There was plenty of drink and we had a jolly sing-song and a knees-up until chucking-out time at 23.00. Mary (whose husband and son were away with the South

African forces in the Middle East) played the piano. The solitary local policeman, who originated from County Kerry in Ireland, was busy cracking corny jokes (having kissed the Blarney Stone) in his lilting Irish accent.

After closing time we continued the party at Mary's house until 02.30. Then we packed up — not before time, though, as we were tired out. One member of the party was soundly asleep and had to be carried home, whilst another was getting highly obnoxious and aggressive. We wasted no time in getting to bed, as we had to be awake at 06.00 for an early breakfast then catch our train half an hour later.

We were still bleary-eyed when Rita bundled us down to the station in the car just in time to hear the little train puffing in alongside the platform. We just had time to thank her for the hospitality and wish her goodbye before the engine started to puff out of the station.

The carriage bumped and rattled us to sleep until the train suddenly ground to a halt at Pietermaritzburg, rudely waking us from our deep sleep.

As there was an hour to wait for a connection we had a quick look around the old part of the small Victorian city. Strange to relate, it had been founded in 1837 by the Voortrekkers, who had little time for the British.

As we were very thirsty we looked around for a tea shop, but none were open so early in the morning. We did manage to obtain a glass of water and a couple of oranges from a helpful housewife before catching our train back to Durban.

We arrived back at the ship in time to relieve the second batch of crew, who were due for a few days' leave at noon. Then we had to get things sorted out as the ship was to be fumigated next day to kill off millions of cockroaches, which multiplied daily in their thousands.

All sections of the ship, especially the galleys, pantries and messes, were sealed off then fumigated. Everyone not required for duty was bundled off to the local naval camp in the country a few miles out of town as nothing could be cooked on board until forty-eight hours had elapsed and the seals were broken. After this thick carpets of cockroaches covered the decks and crunched when trodden on as they were being swept up.

A Stoker PO's Story

At the barracks I came across a stoker PO who had survived the massive torpedoing and bombing of the ill-fated *Prince of Wales* and *Repulse* off the coast of Malaya, only to be taken prisoner by the Japs when they stormed the so-called impregnable city of Singapore. He had a fantastic story to relate.

On Wednesday 10 December 1941, at 06.30, the Japs prepared their twenty-second land-based air flotilla, consisting of thirty-four Nell bombers and fifty-one Betty torpedo bombers on an airstrip near Saigon (which they had just marched in and seized without any opposition). They started bombing up and fuelling up ready for their 800-mile flight to protect their landings at Kota Bharu. The pilots were briefed as to what course they should take before being split up into ten flights and sent off at intervals.

Just before 11.00 the ship's radar warned Force Z of an imminent attack, and the direction from which it was coming. All the gun crews were ready, closed up at action stations, with their guns trained and brought to bear in the right direction. Also the force was ordered to speed up to 25 knots and to open fire as soon as the aircraft came into their sights. The first attack by bombers was easily repulsed. The second attack was by torpedo bombers and was also repulsed by the *Prince of Wales* and *Repulse* combing the torpedoes so that they ran harmlessly down past the ships' sides. But in the third attack the *Repulse* was struck in her steering gear, which quickly sealed her fate. She became an easy target and was quickly dispatched by three more torpedoes before listing to 65°, rolling over and sinking. Soon after, the *Prince of Wales* fared little better. A single torpedo wrecked her steering gear and bent the port outer propeller shaft, which was still being driven around by its turbine. It could not be stopped quickly enough to prevent it tearing the gland out of her hull, leaving a large hole which allowed over 2,500 tons of water to flood in. The ship drifted helplessly onward on a course of its own. Also, the power failed to her anti-aircraft guns, which remained silent. The ship was doomed, unable to defend herself. In the next attack she was hit by another five torpedoes and sank within two hours.

The survivors, including this stoker PO, were taken prisoner in Singapore and sent to the notorious hellhole of Changi.

He survived the rigours of the overcrowded camp, but he still bore the signs of ill-treatment and malnutrition. In the camp they were on a starvation diet of a handful of rice a day. They suffered greatly from severe dysentery, malaria, beriberi, tropical ulcers (which would not heal) and prickly heat (which felt like hundreds of small pricks stabbing into one's skin). There was a very high death rate, and no drugs or medication to ease their suffering. The Japs ensured that the prisoners never received any Red Cross parcels sent from home.

He told me an amazing yarn about being imprisoned for six months. The Japs decided that the prisoners should be set to work on the docks at Keluang near the capital of Malaysia, or should be forced to march through the whole length of the country (some 700 miles) then on through Siam to build a railway bridge over the River Kwai. They marched up to twenty miles a day, most of it while the sun was at its hottest. Even a well-kitted-up man, fully shod and protected against the sun would have found it difficult to walk so far under such appalling conditions, let alone thousands of ill-clad men clothed in tattered rags, mostly without hats, with worn-through boots or barefooted. They were forced to trudge over hot rough stony and dusty roads, often feeling the end of a rifle butt if they faltered. All suffered from malnutrition and became dehydrated through lack of water. Their scrawny bodies showed all their bones through their loose-hanging flesh. There was an appalling death rate as the men dropped like flies, too weak to continue the horrific journey.

As they were approaching Malacca the column ground to a sudden halt. One of the Jap guards up front was seized with an attack of malaria and beriberi. He dropped down shaking with fever whilst the two rear guards hastened for'ard to aid their ailing comrade. In the confusion Stoker PO Arthur, along with stokers

Ben and Charlie, moved to one side as if to relieve themselves. After realising they had not been missed they seized the opportunity to slip out of sight in the rubber plantation. There they lay doggo, never daring to move until the rest of the long column began to advance slowly towards Kuala Lumpur.

Then the tiny band of men set off into the forest, well off the beaten track, following their noses and hoping to hear the sea roaring or see the seashore. After struggling on through the woods, for what they thought was about six miles, they flung themselves down thirsty and hungry for the night.

Next morning they noticed there had been a heavy dew, which they licked from the leaves to moisten their parched mouths before setting off again towards the golden sand which they could see from afar. Then they thought they could hear the rollers breaking faintly on the seashore. Soon they came across a coconut palm. It had shed a couple of nuts with some milk in, which they could hear when shaken. But the thick fibre casing was too hard to remove so they had to carry on without opening them. Soon they came across a date palm loaded with strings of dates and managed to climb up on one another's backs to reach them. They ate them sparingly and carried a string with them for future consumption. They took note of the palm's position for future use. Fortunately a small stream ran nearby, gurgling away as it made its way to the beach. They all lay down to take some long refreshing drinks, then waded in to cool their tired feet. They followed the stream down to the beach where they did some beachcombing along the tidemark. After an hour they had collected several useful items, such as plastic bottles with tops on so they could store some drink and some driftwood with nails from which they were able to make a couple of crude spears. They tried their hand at catching fish in the clear blue warm water, but it was far from easy. After an hour they were totally exhausted and had only managed to catch two small fish. They ripped them open with their fingers and ate them raw, which was a very good start for three worn-out hungry men.

As the days passed by their weary bodies gradually improved with the small but regular diet of fish along with a supply of dates and wild bananas, which they tried to supplement with wild fruits, nuts, berries, leaves and roots.

Anything they didn't know was tested carefully by taking a nibble and immediately spitting out anything bitter or distasteful. With the more promising food they waited for a full day to see if they had any ill effects before trying a bigger sample. They lit a fire by rubbing two dry sticks together to cook their fish, but soon realised the streak of rising smoke was a dead giveaway during the day as it could be seen for miles around. As they were leaving their footprints in the sand, they made a half-mile detour over a rocky surface further along the beach to prevent anyone finding their hideout. To avoid being seen by someone who could betray their presence to any Jap patrols they ventured out for a couple of hours at sunrise and again before sunset, lying low in the heat of the day.

As they became stronger they began to explore the terrain for several miles around, coming into contact with a small kampong where some friendly villagers lived. They showed them some simple arts of living, such as weaving matting from coconut-palm leaves and making ropes from the nut fibre. They showed them how to break open the thick husks, which protected the inner nut, so as to get at the milk. They were also shown how to climb up a coconut palm, some sixty feet, to detach the nuts. This was later left to Charlie, being the youngest and lightest member of the party (he did it in his bare feet).

The villagers told them that a half-caste Portuguese, who had a violent temper, had lived in the area with two native assistants. He used to supply them with fish from time to time but had not been seen in the area during the last month. They never ventured near his dwelling place as he carried a shotgun which they could occasionally hear banging off in the distance.

The trio decided to look him up, and eventually found his hidden hut along with a small tool shed equipped with a bench and vice and a good selection of tools. It was well off the beaten track so it was fairly safe. There were signs that the place had recently been inhabited, but there was no trace of any of the men, so it was assumed that the Japs had captured or shot them. They waited a week in case anyone turned up, before rummaging through the little treasure trove for anything that would be useful.

They borrowed a small fishing net to increase their catches. Two of them waded out in the bay right up to their necks, then trawled by dragging the net between them and closing in together to trap any fish they had caught. They soon learnt which were the best fish and which were poisonous and gave them a violent tummy ache.

They also borrowed the saw to cut half a dozen small logs to make a raft and paddle so that one end of the fishing net could be towed out into deeper water to increase their catch of bigger fish, some of which they hung up to dry on bamboo sticks in the sun.

They were all poor swimmers. Being Northerners from cotton-mill towns they had had little opportunity to learn to swim. However, they had to be able to swim 200 feet of the breaststroke as it was a necessary part of joining the Royal Navy. They had been taught in Devonport Barracks baths by an instructor. Now they had plenty of time to practise swimming and diving off the rocks on the far side of the bay and could hold their breath under water for about a minute, which improved their health considerably.

After exploring the terrain for some time they discovered the kampong was about five miles off the beaten track from Malacca, which was occasionally visited by a Japanese patrol based at Kuala Lumpur. If the patrol happened to stumble on the kampong, careless talk by the residents, children or a visitor, could betray their presence and they would be taken prisoner or shot. The villagers would be brutally tortured for harbouring them. So the trio decided it would be prudent to keep away from the village as much as possible.

They decided to appoint Ali and his sister, Mary, to be their agents and work on commission on what they sold or bartered their fish for. Also, one or the other would collect their fish early on a Wednesday or Saturday morning at an arranged meeting place. They would barter any fresh fish around the village and dry any surplus fish to take to market on a Saturday morning along with any surplus fruit and veg grown on the allotments.

Fortunately Ali spoke English quite well and after several weeks' trading he took Mary and his handcart down to the market. Mary went shopping in town for three pairs of sandals, which were made from old rubber tyres but were hard-wearing. These were the first items she purchased for the trio, and as more money was accumulated she managed to fit the trio up with shorts, shirts and finally straw hats to protect them from the sun.

Ali had a part-time job in a small boatyard and was quite reliable. Gradually he was able to supply the trio with most of their needs.

The first month passed by without any sign of the owner returning, so they started to use anything they found suitable in the hut. They started off by preparing a small sunbaked plot of land at the back with the spade, fork and rake that they had found in the shed. They were surprised to find some yam tubers deep down in good condition, so they collected them and stored them in a sack for future use. Then they removed the eyes of the tubers with a small piece of flesh attached, then set them out in rows and fertilised them with seaweed. They watered them daily until they had grown to full size and were ready to eat. Seeds of greens and carrots were obtained in the village to be sown in an extended plot down one side of the hut.

The yams were peeled like potatoes and boiled for about half an hour in a small boiler set into the wall with a grate and chimney. They had collected a pile of dry driftwood from the beach then started a fire in the grate by directing sun rays through a broken piece of magnifying glass onto a piece of dry wood. It soon started to smoulder and glow and was gently blown on until it burst into flames. This was usually done towards sunset so that the rising smoke could not attract attention from afar. When the yams were ready they were spooned out of the boiler to cool before eating. They had a slightly sweet taste but were not very exciting to eat without any gravy. However, they helped to fill up the empty spaces.

One evening they watched a large turtle struggle ashore and dig a large hole well past the tidemark. It laid over 100 eggs by the light of the moon, then covered them up with sand before leaving them to hatch and struggling back into the sea. They mentioned the fact to Ali who told them turtle eggs were quite valuable for their oil, so they carefully dug them up and Ali sold them in town. With the money he bought a small skiff for them so that they could catch more fish.

In the shed they found several parts belonging to an engine (the carburettor, magneto, cylinder head and sparking plugs), but there was no sign of any engine or boat which they belonged to.

A few days later they walked to the far end of the bay where they found a concealed cove behind some rocks. It was obvious the cove had been used by the missing Portuguse trader. There was a small landing stage with fishing nets, traps and various pieces of ropes, etc., which were dumped well up on the beach past the tidemark. He had built a small store for his paraffin oil, oars, rowlocks, rudder and various other small items which he kept locked up. Obviously this had been his base where he worked to supply several small places down the coast with fresh fish.

The trio were just about to depart when Arthur spotted a small anchor embedded in the sand with a rope running down towards the sea. They tugged at it but it refused to yield, so they waded out about fifty feet and swam out another fifty feet and noticed the outline of a fairly big boat about five feet down which was broad in the beam. They dived down to investigate. After six short dives they found it appeared to be sound, without any apparent damage, so they thought it had been swamped in a gale or heavy monsoon rains and was obviously stuck in the mud.

Next day they revisited the site with the keys for the store and found it contained ten 5-gallon drums of paraffin (half of which were empty), also the oars, etc. and a can of lubricating oil. They could not believe the boat was seaworthy. They had another diving session but they were unable to find any serious damage.

The finding of the boat brought new interest into their lives as they had reached a stage where they were living quite well on a simple boring diet.

Now they were beginning to put on a little weight and regain a little strength. Even Charlie, the smallest and lightest member of the trio, had managed to climb up his first palm tree barefooted to detach half a dozen coconuts for long cool drinks.

That evening after bedding down on hard layers in their hideout they were all excited about the possibility of salvaging the boat. They had a long discussion on how to drag the boat free of the sticking mud. The challenge occupied their minds. They were worried about how their folks were faring back home. They had heard nothing since the tragic loss of the *Prince of Wales* and had had no means of informing them that they had escaped from Changi prison and were hiding out with their health improving on a diet of fish and veg. Also the fear of being recaptured again by the Japs was forever in their minds, especially if there were patrols in the town of Malacca. The boat had been kept afloat in deep water so the owner could take it out at any time without waiting for high tide. It had been fairly well kept, which meant beaching it now and again to scrape the marine growth off the bottom and repaint it. This meant he must have had some method of heaving it up the beach.

However, to get back to the discussion, several ideas sprang to mind to salvage the boat. The first one was to roll the boat over and release cans of air under it. The trapped air would eventually lift the boat clear of the mud so it could be easily hauled ashore. After much thought they decided it was easier said than done as the boat, being about fourteen feet long, was much too heavy for three weak men to turn over. Also, it would not be easy to empty the cans of air under the hull. There was a suggestion to lash empty air-filled drums to the thwarts, but it would take far too many cans to lift the boat and they had not got enough. Ben had noticed four 3-inch metal pipes about eighteen inches long hanging about and suggested that they could be inserted under the keel to raise it out of the sticking mud, so they decided to try to salvage the boat using this method.

During the next week they set about making a heavy mallet out of a tree root that had been washed up on the beach and they shaped it round by burning all the small roots off. They also burned a hole in the centre with a red-hot spike they had found, and inserted a long shaft made from a suitable tree branch. After this they picked up a long piece of driftwood and shaped it into two long wedges with a saw. They were 4 inches wide by 3 inches thick and had long tapers so that when they were hammered together under the stern they would raise the keel six inches out of the mud.

Once completed the trio started making shallow dives to wedge the stern up with the mallet, then they inserted the two metal pipes evenly spaced below the keel. They knocked out the wedges and repeated the process under the bows. They inserted the other two pipes so they were all evenly spaced underneath. Then they were able to heave the boat six foot forward off the two after pipes, which were reinserted under the bows.

They kept on repeating this process until they were all completely knackered. After stowing their gear away they rested up for a couple of days knowing that they had cracked it, and that the hardest part of the job had been completed.

In between times the trio set about using their skiff to search around the bay with their newly found traps to find out where the best place was for crabs and squids. They eventually found them near the rocks. They had to experiment with different bait to improve their catch of half a dozen a week. Also, they were able to improve their catch of fish by cutting in half one of the big nets they had found, and using one piece to trawl between the raft and the skiff, they rowed out into deeper water where they could net several more different varieties of fish. Later on they used the skiff for rowing to strengthen their arms to row the bigger boat.

After a few days' toil they managed to tug the boat about forty-two feet in all, with the bows just jutting out of the water. Next day with another heave the gunwales stood six inches clear of the water. Charlie had the bright idea of pulling the bung out of the hole to allow the water level in the boat to drop to the sea level. It continued to drain as it was dragged up into shallow water. However, after another heave, the level in the boat only dropped an inch, and it suddenly occurred to them that the quickest way to empty the boat was to bail it out. They replaced the bung and found two empty cans to start the bailing. Within an hour the boat began to float. Within another hour they were able to drag the boat to within twenty feet of the shore, where it grounded.

Next day they bailed it dry and beached it just above the tidemark on the far side near the rocks and covered it over with palm leaves so it could not be seen easily from afar. They tidied up the area where they had been working by removing all the footprints which would have advertised their presence. Any Jap patrol, stumbling on the area, would have destroyed their boat and searched around to try to trace the owners.

The trio decided to review their situation and decided to continue working on the boat as it would occupy their minds. They thought about attempting the trip across the Indian Ocean but they were worried about being picked up in the busy Malacca Strait by a Jap naval patrol or facing a storm. The one big thing in their favour would be the monsoon winds that gave a steady blow in the direction they wanted to travel.

It appeared that the Japs were too busy fighting to bother occupying isolated places, so as long as they took no risks it would be fairly safe to stay put.

All these thoughts would often turn around in their minds in the long dark evenings as they rested on their hard beds on the ground. They wondered if they would dare to pluck up courage to make the long trip across the Bay of Bengal without having any knowledge of sailing or navigating.

Next day they began to examine the engine and found it had seized up. They set their minds on how it could be repaired. They all had limited experience of diesel and petrol motor boats. As stokers, they drove them and occasionally worked with the tiffy in the repair shop to service them. They got Ali to obtain a canful of coconut flushing oil to splash around the rusty cylinders and valve guides, etc. Then they drained the sump of contaminated oil, which was saved for reprocessing by mixing it up with fresh water and scooping off the oil which was floating on the top. This could be used again in an emergency. Then they refilled the sump with flushing oil and left it to soften up the rust and carbon for several days. They then scraped off the four piston tops, cylinder bores, valve guides and valves. They carefully removed all the particles of carbon and rust with an oily rag before trying to turn the crankshaft (which moved, much to their delight). Then they wiped the dust from the cylinder bores again and oiled them before giving the starting handle a series of spins so the crankshaft would throw up the oil to lubricate all the moving parts. Then they drained the sump and replaced the oil with a canful of fresh oil.

Everything was going well until they noticed that two of the exhaust springs, which were tightly packed together, were broken and would be impossible to replace. This rendered the engine useless, which meant altering all of their plans.

After a few days' reflection the trio mentioned the problem with the engine to Ali. He suggested that if they removed the broken springs he would ask at the garage if there were any springs on one of several old engines on the scrapheap which might fit at a pinch. After a struggle they managed to remove the broken springs for Ali to take to the garage.

Nothing further was heard about the springs for several weeks. During this time they had nearly forgotten about them, but Ali had been able to procure two from the mechanic in exchange for a string of fish. They were not quite the same size but would do at a pinch. Also, he was loaned a forked compression tool to squeeze the rings to allow the cotters to be inserted so that they would hold the valves and springs together.

Ben and Charlie cleaned up the valve seats and components, then reassembled them.

The trio decided to look into escaping across the Strait of Malacca, then up the coast of Sumatra to Ceylon, but they hadn't a clue as to what it entailed. They had a yen to find out how their families had fared and wanted to see them again, so they arranged with Ali for them to see his local teacher. They took her a squid and a large crab as a gift and she was able to supply them with a great deal of useful information. She told them that Singapore to Colombo round the tip of Sumatra was 1,566 miles, so that from the tip of Sumatra across the Bay of Bengal to the coast of Ceylon would be in the region of 1,000 to 1,200 miles. The best time to make the attempt would be between May and September, when the south-west trade or monsoon winds blew from their side of the Indian Ocean towards

Ceylon and India over the Bay of Bengal.

She also told them the distance to the tip was about 410 miles, and supplied them with an old atlas as well as an exercise book with tables and measurements on the back cover. She gave them a pencil, and made a white compass card with the four cardinal points on it, and provided an old tobacco tin to keep it in. They thanked her for her kindness and she wished them good luck.

Over the next few days the trio discussed and worked out crudely their chance of escape, They estimated the distance across the Strait of Malacca would be about 100 miles, and would take about a full day to cross. They would have to tack against the wind for 410 miles up the coast at about 4 knots in easy stages, landing ashore in isolated places and keeping topped up with water and any wild fruit they could find. They needed to be at the tip of Sumatra to land on the Isle of Sabang at the end of June to catch the trade winds. They hoped that the trade winds would increase their speed from 4 to 6 knots, so as to be able to cover about 144 miles per day across to the coast of Ceylon. They would then head in a direction seven or eight degrees above the west towards Batticaloa, if possible, to ensure the strong winds and tidal currents did not sweep them off their course so they would not get lost in the vast Indian Ocean. They expected it to take about nine days, if they were lucky, to cover the 1,000 to 1,200 miles, but their estimate turned out to be hopelessly wrong as their clumsy boat was not built for speed.

One of the most important things they would require would be a compass. They carefully added four extra points on the compass card so as to give them a more accurate course, and pushed a drawing pin through the centre for the needle to swing on. Then they hammered out the needle with a piece of hard spring steel until it was shaped with two long points with a dent in the centre to turn on. The needle was magnetised by laying it across the north and south poles of the magnet from the magneto for a month. After this the north pole was marked with a spot of brown paint, then tested with the merest touch of oil on the pivot, which enabled it to swing around to the north. Then they carefully stowed it away in the little tin for future use.

Now they concentrated their efforts on completing the engine. They cleaned up the cylinder head and screwed it down, inserting a new gasket that they found in the shed. They then assembled the carburettor and magneto and had a great deal of trouble resetting the timing. Once done the sparking plugs were cleaned and the leads were connected. Now all that had to be done was to thoroughly clean out the fuel tank, then fill up with a gallon of paraffin and switch on the fuel cock. Now they got excited when swinging the starting handle, but, alas, after half an hour's hard work they were bitterly disappointed as the engine refused to fire. All their hard work had been in vain.

So they forgot about it and started to use their heavy fourteen-foot boat with one man at each oar for an hour each day before sunset. They soon decided they would be unable to keep up rowing for long periods even though their health and strength had improved greatly. As they could in no way rely on the ancient engine, even if they ever got it started, they would have to look into fitting one or two suitable masts to propel them over the large stretch of ocean.

After a day or so the trio went back to see if they could find what was wrong with the engine, and found the sparking plugs were not sparking. They removed the magneto and found it was only producing a weak spark so they gave it to Ali to take to the garage to see if the mechanic could fix it. He found that the slip ring was cracked and the condenser was weak. He was able to change them and set the points so the magneto gave a good fat spark. When it was returned it was bolted back into position, but still the engine refused to start.

After a few days' reflection Ben cast his mind back to one day on the Barbican in Plymouth (from where the Pilgrim Fathers set sail for America in the Mayflower in 1620). He had been taking a trip across the sound to Cawsand in a motor boat with a similar type of engine and the owner was having trouble starting it. A mate shouted down from the jetty to tell him of an idea to get it going, which was to wrap a hot towel around the updraught carburettor and soak it with boiling water. This caused the paraffin, which has a flashpoint below 153°F, to vaporise and rise up through the carburettor into the engine cylinders. The boatman hastened up the steps to his cabin and soon came back with a kettle of boiling water and a towel to heat up the paraffin. Then with one sharp tug of the handle the engine fired and started running. Without further ado the motor boat was cast off to start the trip. Ben tried out the idea with a piece of rag and hot water from a billycan. This did wonders and the engine started up easily, firing on the first tug of the handle.

One day Ali told the trio that a small yacht had grounded on some rocks half a mile from the shore and had been abandoned several miles up the coast. His boss was keen to get it salvaged and if it was not suitable for them he would have it in exchange for making some improvements on their boat — such as fitting it with a suitable sail and mast and raising the bow section one foot to make a short deck with a cabin underneath containing two short bunks. This would protect their bodies from the sun, heavy seas and rain. Also he would give it a lick of black paint and lend them the necessary tackle for the job.

They gathered the tools and rowed out their skiff to dismantle as much as possible, lashing up the sails which had been lowered and were flapping about. Also they dismantled the mast and took down the rigging, then removed the detachable rudder and loaded them onto the skiff. Then they unscrewed a small compass from its mounting and surveyed the vessel to see if it would be worth their effort to salvage it.

They rowed ashore and stowed the mast and sail, etc., then returned to base where they had a long discussion in the cool of the evening, weighing up the yacht against their clumsy old boat. They decided that although the yacht would be several knots faster, it would be too cramped for them to move about and there was no shelter from the sun. Also there was not enough room to stow their food and water. It was narrow and flimsy, and would be a wet boat cutting through the ocean waves and shipping gallons of water instead of riding on the crests of the waves. The sail was rather thin and would tear to shreds in a strong gale. Their own boat would have a little cubbyhole cabin for'ard with two short bunks where two could shelter whilst the other one took a trick at the helm. It was decided to try to salvage the yacht so as to get their own boat improved. It would be a hard job as the bows were grounded on the rocks, and there were two jagged lumps jutting out which would have to be broken down to allow a clear slipway into the water. They borrowed a sledgehammer, a lump hammer and a chisel, then took it in turns to crack lumps off the rocks, starting at dawn when the tide was low. After a couple of hours' thumping, their hands were sore and they had to give up and soak them in their own urine to toughen them up.

They felt like giving up but Arthur spurred them on and after a few days they returned to the rock and began to make some progress. They had levelled the slipway off by the end of the week.

All that remained to be done now was to return the tools along with the mast and fittings. They retained the sledgehammer and borrowed two sturdy planks and wedges to shore up the hull whilst they tried to withdraw the centre board keel, which jammed halfway up. They then removed the jagged edges from the hole and plugged it up with a linen bag stuffed full of rags. This was a similar idea to that used in Nelson's days when a cannonball burst through the ship's side causing a huge jet of water to gush through in a most alarming manner. Several seamen would approach it from one side carrying a hammock, which they forced into the hole to plug it (getting soaked to the skin into the bargain).

All that remained to be done was to wedge the hull up and insert the two long planks — one under the keel and the other supporting the port side. Then they waited for the high tide before wedging the two planks up about a foot under the bows to form a slope for them to slide down. Ben and Charlie pushed and Arthur bounced up and down in the stern to shake it free so it slid down into deep water after a long struggle. Then they gathered all their equipment together and towed it to the boatyard, along with the sails and mast, etc.

The boss was highly delighted and soon set about keeping his side of the bargain when they rowed their boat round next day.

After three weeks their boat had been completed. The hull had been given a lick of black paint, the bows had been raised a foot and a small deck had been fixed over them to form a small cubbyhole. This contained two short four-foot bunks for two of the men to shelter from the elements whilst the other hand steered the boat.

Now they could put the boat to the test to see how it performed. They painstakingly marked off a measured mile between two large stones planted on the beach. By binding two long bamboo canes together they could measure six yards using a small cheap folding yard rule, which Ali had purchased for them in the market. Then they marked off 293 lengths plus two yards to get the distance of a mile so they could carry out some simple tests.

First of all they had to split up a gallon into twentieths, by the use of a coconut. They took the top off then whittled it down until it held twenty pourings of water into a gallon can to make it easy to calculate the small amount of paraffin used over the short run when two pourings of the coconut measure were added to the fuel tank. Two rag flags attached to long canes were positioned well out to sea in deep water and pushed into the sand so they were level with the milestones.

The first test was now ready to be started with Arthur at the helm and Ben, with his battered old watch, on shore ready to give the signal and start timing as soon as the boat was in position by the first flag. Charlie let in the clutch and opened up the throttle wide so the old engine raced away at full speed until the boat was passing the second flag. Arthur raised his hand for Ben to check the timing and for Charlie to stop the engine and cut off the fuel. He then drained the tank into a graduated bottle so as to estimate the amount of fuel used and the miles per gallon (which worked out at ten miles). Ben checked the time taken between the two points (which worked out at 5 mph).

Then they gave the boat a run at half throttle, and the figures worked out at 2½ mph and 14 mpg, which was not going to take them very far. Four 5-gallon drums of paraffin plus two for the tank would take them distances of 220 or 308 miles.

The boat was also tried under sail, but the wind blew in the wrong direction to get any accurate results. They only made a speed of about 3 knots. They also tried rowing the boat with Ben and Charlie at the oars, but the result was even worse — only 2 knots, which they would be unable to keep up in the heat of the sun.

These were disappointing results but they had not realised the mast was only fourteen feet high. The area of the sail was too small for speed, as it had been made for safety with nettles attached to reef the sail in case of a storm. An Arab dhow, on the other hand, carried a huge lateen sail to catch the wind and was well weighted down with a hold full of cargo so it was quite fast and stable.

However, they still hoped for an increase in speed of 5 or even 6 knots when the boat was being pushed along by a steady prevailing south-west wind bellowing into its sail from aft. (In actual fact they only travelled at about 4 to 4½ knots, covering a distance of about 100 miles a day).

They decided to prepare for the trip from the tip of Sumatra across the Bengal Bay (a distance of between 1,000 and 1,200 miles), which could be accomplished in about twelve days if they were lucky and were not blown off course to get lost in the vast Indian Ocean. With all these details in mind they set about preparing for a long voyage of about three weeks.

Ali was consulted about buying the necessary equipment for the voyage as he had some cash in hand from the sales of fresh and dried fish in the market, and the trio could catch plenty more fish if required to sell or barter.

There was quite a number of items required to make the trip possible. First of all six 2-gallon cans were required for freshwater containers, but all he could get were some rusty old petrol cans which needed no end of scouring with sand and water to remove all traces of the smell. The next items needed were four tea chests for the storage of food. They still had their silver-paper linings in them, and three were cut in half to reduce the size. The fourth one was left full size to store thirty coconuts, the milk of which could be drunk in an emergency if the water ration ran out. The others were used as follows: one for dried fish for emergency, another for five pounds of yams to be roasted on a fire when ashore, and the last one for fresh fruit which they would take with them or collect if possible. Other items required were three small tin mugs to help keep the water ration down to three pints a day, a good sharp strong knife and a large tray for gutting fish. They also needed three sun hats and long-sleeved shirts as they would be exposed to the sun for several hours a day. They also needed three towels to dry themselves after the daily dip and a bucket for bailing out.

Other items that they needed to take from the cabin were two old blankets to use for sleeping on the bunks; a Primus stove, a gallon can of paraffin, a pricker and a box of matches in a small watertight box; a pan to heat up the water, used for the carburettor to start up the engine, or to heat up a meal; an old set of oilskins to protect the helmsman from the wet stormy weather; a small rope ladder to be lowered over the side for them to climb up after a swim and a small fishing net and a spear to enable them to catch some fish.

The compass was fixed where it could be seen when steering the boat. The anchor and rope were secured on the small deck for'ard and the oars and rowlocks squeezed in along the sides. They took a bundle of dry kindling wood along with an old magnifying glass to light up a fire when on shore. Also there were some canvas covers to cover up the food and the engine when not in use.

Once the four 5-gallon drums of paraffin and the six water cans had been stowed for'ard there was barely enough room left to sleep on the bunks. The rest of the gear was stowed under the after seats and the remaining space in the centre of the boat left barely enough space to work around and set sail, etc.

All that remained was to collect the fresh goods from Ali, who had been to market to buy the yams, the dried dates, a bunch of bananas, a dozen oranges, a dozen and a half dried fish for an emergency and coconuts.

Before they left they showed Ali where everything was kept, and the best spots for fishing. They were sorry to say farewell as he had been a good friend.

At last everything was ready for the boat to be launched and the fuel tank was topped up with two gallons of paraffin.

At 15.30 they set off, rowing well out before setting the sails.

They headed straight across the Strait of Malacca, arriving on a deserted beach north of Rupat Isle next morning. They rested up until evening before heading northward up the coast of Sumatra to find suitable bays around Kisaran, Belawan and other isolated bays around Langsa and Bireuen. Eventually they landed up on the Isle of Sabang, which was a distance of about 410 miles. Their intention was to spend a night at each isolated bay away from all habitation and to have a swim, and spear some fish to cook over a fire. They intended to have a good look around for anything else edible they could find. Then they destroyed all traces of their visit before settling down to a long siesta and starting off at sunset, providing the coast was clear.

Things didn't work out as planned because, after leaving Kisaran, a violent storm arose. The boat was tossed about in the most alarming manner, threatening to capsize at any moment. The sail had to be reefed to reduce its area so that it didn't tear into shreds. Arthur heaved on the helm to move the rudder to head the bows into the wind to make for a safe haven, whilst Ben and Charlie prepared the engine for use. They soon had it running, which enabled the boat to make steady headway towards the shore, but it kept revving up as the stern lifted. The propeller would come out of the water, and constantly had to be adjusted down and up. However, after a four-hour struggle during which they nearly ran aground on a hidden reef, they reached shelter and safety.

They had all been terrified during the tossing about they had experienced, but were thankful that little damage had been done to the boat. Their biggest job was to tidy up the boat, make everything shipshape, and bail out the water which was lapping over their feet.

Meanwhile they had to wait for the storm to abate so they could continue their journey for the Belawan area to find a small cove and top up with water and anything else useful they could find.

They prepared for an early start next morning, and hadn't gone far before they were alarmed by the rhythmic diesel knock of a large engine. They turned about and dived for cover. Fortunately it was a large Jap merchant ship with its flag fluttering aft from the flagstaff. It plodded on its set course without having any interest in a small boat, so they were able to continue with their daily routine, sailing northward up the coastline towards their next stop as planned.

Everything was going well until the trio were approaching Bireuen. They espied a fast-moving motor boat on the horizon, heading directly towards them, so they turned about and ran for the nearest bay to drop anchor and lower the sail. They lay out of sight so as not to attract any attention. They anxiously waited with bated breath to see what would happen, but they did not have to wait long to hear the engine note gradually begin to fade as the boat sheered off to head in the opposite direction.

They then waited a couple of hours to ensure it was miles out of sight before setting off northward to the Isle of Sabang, completing the first leg of the journey within seven days, sometimes tacking against the wind to make progress.

The trio topped up with water, fresh coconuts and anything they could find. Then they had a good rest, stretched out on the beach and had a hot meal of fish before setting out on the final leg of the journey across the Bay of Bengal on a course 283° west by north, which with luck should have carried them to Batticaloa on a more or less central position along the coast of Ceylon.

With a steady south-west trade wind blowing from behind they hoped they would increase their speed to about 6 knots, but in fact it made little difference on their small sail area. They were moving steadily at about 4 knots and after three days they would have covered about 300 miles, which was quite promising. However, on the fourth and fifth days they were caught in the doldrums. The wind dropped and there was a terrific monsoon storm. The rain came down like stair rods for several hours. They lowered their sail and spread it as far over the boat as it would cover to prevent the boat being completely swamped. They got soaked to the skin collecting the water running off the canvas to replenish their dwindling supply.

Ben espied a hungry shark swimming around the area for the rest of the day. Meantime they bailed out the bilges which had filled up with rainwater. They started to row, carrying on throughout the night, hoping that a puff would fill the sail. Next morning there was no sign of any wind, and the shark had gone so they took a chance and had a swim to catch several fish with their net. They cooked them on the Primus stove, then spent the rest of the day sheltering from the blazing sun, anxiously waiting for the sunset to cool the boat down before starting to row through the night. They hardly made any progress but just before sunrise on the sixth day the wind sprang up, cooling their bodies and filling the sail, much to their relief. They checked their course and continued their voyage, making steady progress without any more alarms. Each evening, an hour before sunset, they lowered the sail to stop the boat and dived over for a swim to loosen up their stiff joints after being cramped up all day in a small space. Also they netted a few fish, which they cooked on their Primus.

On the fourteenth day the water ran out but fortunately they had an emergency supply of coconut milk as thirty had been stored up for such an occasion. Their spirits were raised when they sighted the large lateen sail of an Arab dhow which was sailing in a south-westerly direction. This indicated they were approaching land, so they started up the engine to hasten their journey's end. It ran perfectly until the fuel ran out.

Just before sunset on the fifteenth day Arthur sighted land. Next morning they were rapidly approaching the coast of Ceylon. They changed course and headed for an isolated sandy beach where they anchored in the bay. They stretched out in the shade thanking their lucky stars that they had made it, although they didn't know exactly where they had landed.

The trio then decided to head up northward to Trincomalee, which was about twenty-five miles away. They managed to sell the boat for 200 rupees to buy some clothes and refreshment, then made their way to the naval canteen to contact the liberty men from the submarine repair ship HMS *Adamant*, where they were taken aboard to report to the officer of the day.

He was amazed to hear their story and reported it to the captain, who arranged for them to be billeted aboard. He took their names, ranks and numbers, and also arranged medical check-ups. He then sent a signal to Devonport Barracks with their identity as they were listed as 'missing presumed dead'. Once their identity had been confirmed each received casual payments before being sent on a merchant ship which sailed from Colombo to Durban (barracks) on the first leg of their journey home. Also they were delighted to receive a pile of back mail from home.

Australia

About a fortnight before leaving Durban the killick, Stoker Brennan, found a small piece of white metal from a bearing in the oil filter of the high-pressure air compressor, which was one of the least used machines in the ship. It was in good working order and had probably lain dormant in some nook or cranny ever since the machine had been built and was nothing to worry about. He reported it to the senior engineer, who, much to everybody's amazement, took the decision to renew all the bearings. It was a crazy thing to do because the spare bearings had an eighth of an inch extra on them to allow for any wear taking place and needed machining out to size. Also it would have meant that the 160-pound crankshaft would have to have its journals ground up to be level and it would have to be sent back to the factory, which was out of the question.

Chief ERA Bungy Edwards and ERA Jack Jones had been sent down to scrape out the bearings to size and had removed the cylinders and pistons, etc. to get at the bearings. They tried to scrape the spare ones to size, but this was a very difficult job and in the end they were left for me. It was the hottest compartment in the ship — as hot as the port boiler room where the watch was changed over every two hours to prevent the men getting heat exhaustion. I told the engineer about it and that I would require constant breaks to get in the fresh air. He agreed as my stoker, Jan Yeo, had died of heat exhaustion in the turbogenerating area on the deck above some weeks before.

Now the two men were required to take over their steaming watches in the port and starboard engine rooms and I was required to take their place. Fortunately, I had had a year's experience on crankshafts and bearings on diesel engines, and I had my own set of scrapers, so went down to weigh up the situation after being relieved from my steaming watch down the port engine room by Ted Perkins.

I found that the pistons and cylinders had been removed and that work had been started on the first two spare bearings. I tried them on the first journal, which had been opened up, and spent an hour on each, and found they were nowhere near fitting as only minute amounts could be scraped away at a time. I was already beginning to feel exhausted by my effort in the heat so decided to replace all the spare bearings in their box, then had to climb up four ladders to slake my thirst with a nice cool drink at the fountain. I then went on the upper deck to cool off.

After dinner I climbed down the three ladders into the stifling heat to remove all the bearings in turn and replace any bad ones. This entailed removing all the split pins and unbolting the top bearings to remove them, and then got a split pin to fit in the oil hole so the shaft could be turned to drive the bottom bearing out. After cleaning it up I would use the split pin to turn it back into position, then clean up the top bearing and bolt it back in position and replace the split pins.

I had only been on the job a couple of days when my stoker down the refrigerating plant rang me up on the blower to tell me that the piston-rod glands were beginning to leak. The rods were moving up and down twenty-four hours a day and needed tightening up very slightly. As they were running through white-metal packings and would soon overheat when tightened up, even with plenty of oil splashed onto them, they had to be eased off immediately or else long scores would appear on the rod, causing them to leak gas more badly. Consequently they had to be nursed for several hours until they settled down. I dared not leave them for several hours until they were running cool.

I continued my work down below until Saturday forenoon, and had Saturday afternoon and Sunday off. The rest of the mess were on steaming watch down below and the Fleet Air Arm and repair party carried on with their own routine, which I spent most of my time watching.

On Monday I continued my work below on the main bearings. So far I had found no fault with them.

On Wednesday forenoon there was a message on the blower for me to go down and take over Taff Gunney's watch in the port engine room. His evaporating plant and their copper heating coils had developed a thick coating of brine on them, which reduced the freshwater output. The water to the bathrooms was cut off and we had to use seawater whilst Taff removed the heating coils and replaced them with spare ones. He then started up the evaporators to fill up the water tanks before the water could be restored to the bathrooms. He also had to have the thick layer of brine removed in the coppersmith's shop. The metal was annealed so the brine could be chipped off ready for use next time.

I had three days of watchkeeping for me before returning to my job on Saturday forenoon. On Monday forenoon I went down below to complete my work on the bearings, which they were all to be boxed up and split-pinned. I found they were all in good condition.

At the end of the third week, assistance was required to draw the heavy chain blocks, large spanners and a lump hammer from the engineers' store to take down the three ladders and rig the blocks up so as to lift the cylinders back in position, so rang up the engineer's office for an extra hand, and he sent down Killick Stoker Bert Brennan, and we lifted the gear down the steps.

He was called away to charge up the 4,000-pound high-pressure air bottles with the for'ard air compressor for the Fleet Air Arm repair party to test some component with. He grabbed the starting handle and turned it, and much to his amazement got the shock of his life. There was a blinding flash and he reeled back severely stunned and shaken. This unfortunately destroyed the box and there were no spares. What had happened was there was a small unnoticed water leak from the pipe above the starter cable, which worked its way along the cable through a gland which had not been sealed. It had damped some of the connections in the box and caused a short circuit when the handle was pulled.

Eventually the engineer was informed and rang down to tell me Bert would be unable to work until Monday. He wanted to know how quickly the job could be finished. I told him it should probably be ready on Tuesday if there were no snags, as it was quite a tricky job bolting up the cylinders and lowering the piston in without breaking any of the piston rings. However, we managed to get the cylinders lowered and bolted in position and we lowered the piston in without breaking any of the brittle rings. We then bolted up and split-pinned the big ends, then bolted down the cylinder heads. We secured all the various pipes and gubbins, drained the dirty oil out of the sump and lugged two large heavy cans up the steps so the oil could be disposed of. We then filled the sump with fresh oil. This left us completely knackered with sweat-soaked overalls, so we went up for a nice cool shower.

Next day we started it up with a loud hissing and grunting as it sucked the air in. However, it ran perfectly, except it would only pump the air bottles up to 3,000-pound pressure instead of 4,000 pounds. We soon remedied the situation by fitting a new air filter and cleaning up the inlet valves. Then we started it up again and it was completely successful, pumping up all the bottles to 4,000 pounds. We reported to the engineer that it was OK then returned the tools to the engineers' store.

Then went on the upper deck for a cool off.

Preparations were made to tidy up the ship from stem to stern for a long voyage into the unknown. The pay bob had ordered all the provisions, which had filled up the numerous compartments down below. All the oil-fuel and water tanks, etc. had been topped up to their maximum capacity, all ready for the ship's departure next day.

When leave was piped I slipped ashore for the last time. I paid Marion and Robin a final visit before the departure. Having enjoyed their company, I took them a large box of chocolates as a final gift. Unfortunately my good intentions were ruined when Marion suddenly produced her autograph album, which was something new to me. My mind clammed up and couldn't think of anything suitable to write in it. Eventually all that I could produce were a few inappropriate words, which I felt thoroughly ashamed of — this annoyed me.

At 09.30 I departed, saying goodbye to Marion and Robin, thanking them for all their kindness and wishing them well. The loss of words for their autograph album was still in my mind — so much so that I spent a restless night tossing about in my hammock thinking about them.

Next morning after lashing up and stowing my hammock, I washed, shaved, then dressed and had my breakfast. Then I took a pen, paper and envelope down to the desk in the port engine room. I wrote out a friendly insert for the album, then signed it and popped it in the envelope, which was then sealed and addressed. Then slipped down the gangway to purchase a stamp then post it before going down on watch at 09.00 to prepare the engine for leaving harbour at 13.30.

The cables were cast off and the ship began to ease its way from the jetty out into the harbour with several long hoots from the sirens and cheers from the dockside workers.

After a fortnight in Durban the ship sailed out of harbour bound for an unknown destination. We travelled in an easterly direction, some 4,000 miles across the Indian Ocean, eventually arriving at Fremantle in Western Australia at the mouth of the River Swan, some twelve miles west of Perth, reputed to be the sunniest city in Aussieland.

The ship anchored in the harbour during the forenoon to wait for the tankers to fill her double-bottom tanks up with oil fuel and take on water. The place looked shabby. There was a variety of old buildings that lacked paint, and there were also several small pubs alongside the quay.

We continued our journey along the Australian coastline, passing by Albany, which was the start of the Great Australian Bight, some 1,040 miles across a vast bay. It looked somewhat similar to a bite out of a large slice of bread. It stretched as far as Adelaide. Then we sailed onward through the Bass Strait between Melbourne and Tasmania into the Tasman Sea, passing by Canberra to Sydney, a distance of some 2,480 miles.

We were heading for Sydney, New South Wales, the oldest city in Australia, and the largest. We approached the Heads, which opened up into a large fjord — a vast expanse of water several miles long named Port Jackson — on which Sydney had been built. The excitement on board began to grow as the men looked forward to a spot of shore leave.

As we passed down the harbour a hill came into view covered with eucalyptus trees whose branches drooped down. There were few people about, being a working day, so the ship arrived unwelcomed except for a passing ferry whose passengers gave us a wave and whose captain gave us a friendly hoot on his siren.

Soon we were passing under the giant girder bridge built by Dorman Long in 1932, which was referred to by the locals as the Coathanger. Then we passed by Circular Quay, which was the ferry terminus, with four landing stages where about six ferries ran from. They had been built in the UK and had steamed out from England under their own power. It was a stormy passage for such small craft with shallow draughts.

The ship carried on steaming upstream, veering to port into the docking area of Balmain and over Iron Cove to the Five Docks area. We tied up alongside for a week before entering Cockatoo dry dock in the navy yard run by Vickers. The usual examinations of corrosion strips around the rudder and props were carried out, along with hull scraping and painting.

We were now in Sydney, on the other side of the world from the UK, some 12,500 miles from home. Here there were sunny blue skies with about fourteen hours of sunshine daily, whilst the UK remained in the icy-cold grip of winter, often with grey skies.

After tea, leave was piped from 16.00 to 07.00 next morning, and 07.30 for chiefs and POs for port and starboard watches alternately. This was the routine whilst we remained in Sydney, with weekend leave from 13.30 to 07.30 Saturdays and Sundays.

We were all eager to get ashore with the first liberty boat, having been confined on board for several weeks. Many made a beeline to the nearest pub. Others were more interested in sightseeing, then looking around for a decent café for a good tuck-in as food was still severely rationed on board. I had a ride around the city, then caught the ferry to explore the end of different routes. After returning to the city centre went in search of a promising place for big eats (which usually consisted of tea; bread and butter; and steak, eggs and chips — or steak, eggs and chips with tomatoes — or mixed grill with sausage, mushroom, bacon and egg and fried bread — or sometimes fish and chips). The meals there were usually prepared on a hotplate so one could see them being cooked.

We had now arrived at our new forward base in the vast Pacific Ocean. The American one was Pearl Harbor, Honolulu, only some 2,100 miles from San Francisco on the western seaboard and 3,389 miles from Tokyo, making a total of 5,490 miles or about twenty-three days' steaming to Japan.

Our forward base at Sydney was badly placed with three varying distances from London. The shortest route is through the Suez Canal, a distance of 11,643 miles. Via Panama, the distance is 12,461 miles. The longest distance is around the Cape of Good Hope, a distance of 12,597 miles (forty-eight steaming days). It is 4,520 miles (or about nineteen steaming days) to Japan from Sydney.

The cream of our merchant ships, and many of their valiant crews, lay in watery graves in Davy Jones's locker, along the various trade routes in all the different oceans of the world. They needed replacing with new ships as we were left with mostly old worn-out ships and engines, which occasionally broke down and were painfully slow in arriving and unloading.

Then from Sydney to the battle area around Japan the newly formed fleet train, which consisted of RF auxiliaries, tankers and supply ships, including the *Unicorn,* transported the oil and goods to the fleet at sea.

On 16 January 1945 the East Indian fleet left their advance base in Ceylon to become the British Pacific fleet, later joining up with US Task Force 63. This proved a formidable task as our ships had never been specifically designed for this theatre of war and were only provisioned with one month's supplies. Destroyers and smaller vessels ran out of supplies in half that time.

Consequently Sydney, with its large dry dock, docks and harbour, was the only seaport not in Japan's hands big enough to handle such massive supplies of food, oil fuel, spares and a thousand and one items required to keep the fleet at sea for three months at a time. Also it was able to house a naval transit camp, which could supply any replacements of men required for the fleet.

The *Unicorn*'s potential was unlimited as she was well equipped in her own right, being the fastest vessel in the fleet train, and able to carry spare aircraft up to the speed of 18 knots. The fastest freighters were much slower, travelling at 11 or 12 knots. The *Unicorn,* with her forklift, mobile crane and lifts, and with the Fleet Air Arm handling party, could quickly load or unload aircraft to or from the jetty. The aircraft would be uncrated immediately on being lifted on board, so that at the end of a trip some of them were ready for immediate take-off. They could be catapulted off direct to the nearest airstrip or fleet carrier; or transferred by our aircraft lighter, which could return with a damaged aircraft to be repaired or serviced back to the ship. Thus the numbers of serviceable aircraft were kept up to full strength in the fleet. Also she could carry up to three complete replacement squadrons, fully equipped with pilots, crews and men, to keep the fleet squadrons up to full strength and also to replace anyone sick or injured. In an emergency the ship could give assistance to the odd destroyer, sloop or submarine.

At weekends there were many invitations sent to the ship to go sailing around Port Jackson with all its inlets, bays and beaches. It is a vast sheltered haven contained by the entrance called the Head. To the north is Outer Head Cliff, which is the start of the coastline running north up to Newcastle and Wallsend, then on up the Queensland coast to Brisbane and beyond. Manly Beach is tucked away inside the north harbour mouth. On the south side is the Inner Head, a long finger of land, which, together with Head Cliff, forms the entrance to the harbour.

Around the Inner South Head is Bondi Beach, and Botany Bay is a few miles down the coast. There are many other smaller popular beaches with thickly wooded bays. To name but a few — Palm Beach, Whale Beach, Avalon, Malibu, Collaray and Bronte. Coogee Beach is just along the road from Bondi Beach, which is the most popular. The surfboarders did their balancing acts on the crest of the huge Pacific breakers.

Along with Manly, Bondi was manned by lifeguards with lookout platforms in case any swimmer got into difficulty. The lifeguards were dressed in bathing trunks and red or yellow bathing caps to distinguish them. When a bather got into trouble they would man a long lifeline to drag a person through the powerful surf to safety. Or about a dozen of them would launch the gaily coloured rowing boat through the breakers. If a shark was sighted a whistle was blown, causing everyone in the water to make a mad rush for the shore as fast as they could go, swimming like the clappers.

On Saturday afternoon six of us accepted an invitation for a motor-boat outing around Port Jackson Harbour with a mixed party of young Aussies to nose around the various coves.

These enclosed waters were teeming with all manner of yachts, large, medium and small, all equipped with bright colourful sails. The spinnakers shimmered under a sunny bright-blue sky.

We anchored in one of the many coves, taking off our shoes and stockings to wade ashore. We had a game of rounders on a fine sandy beach before going in for a swim. Afterwards we gathered driftwood for a fire and boiled water in a billy to make tea, then we had a picnic and exchanged yarns. This was a pleasant change after being cooped up aboard ship in the small mess spaces we all knew so well. One would never have known there was still a war on as we relaxed under the sunny blue sky with plenty to eat and no blackout to grope around in at night. At the end of the trip we bade our hosts farewell and thanked them for their splendid hospitality, before going our separate ways.

Invitations were sent to the ship to spend a long weekend, from 12.00 Friday until 12.00 Tuesday, with mostly English settlers. I accepted one to stop with an old Geordie couple, Joe and Anne Lowes. They had emigrated from Durham during the Great Depression of 1926. He had been a miner when the conditions were bad and there was no work to be had.

They lived in a neat little wooden cottage with a colourful English-type garden in the small village of Coledale, near Nowra, which was on the coast road south of Sydney. The coast road passes through Bulli and Wollongong, some fifty-one miles from the city centre, then on past Port Kembla which was the main centre for coal, iron and steel.

Coledale was a quiet mining village. Joe and Anne's children had grown up there, before leaving for the better working conditions in Sydney.

The front and back doors of the cottage had fine mesh cotton screens and extra doors to keep out the blowflies, which would land on a piece of meat and lay their eggs. Within half an hour it would be alive with maggots. Another strange feature was that each morning an ice van called to deliver a large slab of ice, which was inserted into the top of the icebox. This kept the food cool for the rest of the day.

The cat was walking around as if it had been doped. Annie told me that she must have brushed up against some ticks which sank their claws into the flesh then sucked its blood. She examined its body and found two large ticks. She had trouble pulling them out before destroying them.

On Saturday I went shopping with Annie to Wollongong, then bought a length of dress material to send home as clothes were still severely rationed. Then, after a pleasant weekend basking in the sun on a small lawn surrounded by colourful flowers and reminiscing about the hardships and joys of the old country, my brief visit came to an end. I caught the old bus to take me back to the ship after thanking my hosts and bidding them farewell.

As I got to know my way around I developed a routine of going ashore two or three times a week in the evenings when not on duty. Sometimes I would take a bus or train to the various suburbs or walk around the centre or coastline. One evening Syd joined me for a walk around Woolloomooloo Bay to Rushcutters Bay, where we found an ideal spot for bathing and lying on the beach in the rays of the setting sun. We visited that spot several times. Then we walked down the road to Paddington by the old Victoria Barracks where a couple of sentries stood guard at the main gate. The ceremony of Changing the Guard was performed there on Tuesdays at 10.30 a.m., but we never got the chance to see it. Then we went in search of a good meal, which was always one of the most important parts of my going-ashore routine.

Another evening I walked around Circular Quay, pausing to watch two ferries as they manoeuvred away from the jetties. Then I followed a narrow passage, which led to the large open space of Macquarie Place. There, under the shade of a large Moreton Bay fig tree, there was a cannon and anchor from Admiral Philips' first fleet flagship, HMS *Sirius,* an old gas lamp and a drinking fountain dated 1857.

I then passed around Government House to look around the botanical gardens, where in one corner it was marked off to show where the first vegetable patch of the early convicts had been, and then passed by Farm Cove down the side of Woolloomooloo Bay, then down Dowling Street into the Kings Cross area. As food was plentiful and unrationed so went for a good tuck-in of steak, eggs and chips, which one could watch sizzling on the hotplate as the aroma whetted one's appetite.

As I was returning to the ship a kindly lady shook a flaked-out matelot sleeping on a doorstep. He was obviously worse off from a skinful of plonk. She was going to offer him a bed for the night, but he suddenly woke up, letting out a string of mess-deck oaths and curses. She stepped back and nearly overbalanced, being aghast at such foul language. I advised her to let sleeping dogs lie, especially drunken sea dogs. It had been known for odd ones to sleep in strange uncomfortable places — we had one aboard who had slept on a cabbage patch when blotto, even though he was soaked through to the skin with after a heavy shower. After wishing her goodnight we both continued on our separate ways.

Another time there was a make and mend, so went ashore in the afternoon to watch a local cricket match. It turned out to be quite a lively affair, with one batsman knocking up a hundred runs.

One Sunday I went ashore in the afternoon. The city was quiet with most shops shut, so took a book with me to read in Hyde Park. I sat on a bench in the shade near the Anzac Memorial, then got talking to an old chap who had left his home in Dorset, England, some fifty years before. He had been shipwrecked on his way out around the Cape of Good Hope. However, he was lucky to grab hold of a broken spar, which carried him to the shore on the crest of a large wave. He was beachcombing around Cape Town for a month or so when he was lucky to get a passage on another ship, working as a steward, which took him to Melbourne, Victoria. Then he set out to join in the gold rush at Ballarat.

He told me that he had been a shop assistant, saving up £20 for his passage steerage (the aft part of the ship); also that he had to buy his own rations and bring his own bedding. There were about forty immigrants in a small space, all herded together like a flock of sheep. They all shared the cooking utensils to cook on a small coal-fired galley stove, which was a long drawn-out process.

Many were seasick, hardly ever moving from their bunks. These were the weak ones, several of whom never survived. They gave up the ghost, making more room for the tough ones. The conditions were horrific. The hull constantly heaved up and down, combined with sudden jerky rolling movements from side to side, and her timbers groaned in a frightening manner. Also they were battened down in stormy weather, which made the hot atmosphere indescribable as there was a constant smell of fresh vomit along with the overpowering stench of the lapping bilge water down below.

After a couple of weeks at sea the drinking water became foul and had to be boiled before use. The passengers looked forward to mild sunny weather with a light breeze when they were allowed up on deck to watch the flying fishes scudding over the water and the dolphins keeping up with the ship.

He never made a fortune panning gold, but made enough to move on to Sydney with his partner to set up a small greengrocer's shop, which prospered. After a long chat we parted, both going our separate ways.

One evening I visited the local dirt track, but was a bit disappointed. As it was an oval track, instead of being an oblong one like the Belle Vue track at home, it lost most of the thrill of speeding up on the straight bits before going around the corners.

As the ERAs were in three watches for leave we were free for shore leave most Saturdays or Sundays, so Alf Seldon, Willie Franks and myself had several pleasant outings with Madge Hardy (the full-time organiser of the British Fleet Club) and her sister, Phyllis (the secretary for the Dutch forces). They ferried us around in a large Chevrolet saloon car showing us most places of interest around the outskirts of Sydney.

We motored over the Coathanger Bridge to the north side of the city, visiting Taronga Park, which had a small zoo. We walked around then we went on to Manly Beach, which lies on the inside of an isthmus with the North Head Cliff. The beach was swarming with weekend bathers, whom we watched for a while before going on to a picnic area. We made a fire then boiled the water in a billycan to make tea. We wrapped up sausages in large leaves, which were then cooked in the embers. When all was ready we sat down on some logs in the shade to eat the sausages and wash them down with mugs of tea, which was slightly tainted by the woodsmoke.

Another time we visited Botany Bay, which was a hidden inlet around the headland south of Sydney on the east coast five miles away. It had been discovered by Captain Cook of Whitby, Yorkshire, in HMS *Endeavour* in 1770. Its name was derived from the vast variety of flora living there. It was chosen to be the first penal settlement in the colony, but was soon found to be unsuitable as the land tended to be marshy and it was plagued with flies and mosquitoes, so the site was switched to Sydney. However, the governor built an English-style castle nearby. Today Kingsford Smith Airport has been built in the area.

We next moved on to Bondi Beach, a little further along the coast, but we were surprised to find the place completely deserted. The reason was that the sand was crawling with black flies and jellyfish, which had suddenly appeared to take over the whole beach.

We moved on to Parramatta, fifteen miles up the river from the city centre. The settlement was the second to be established in Australia, and had recently been restored to show off its old-type Victorian buildings (fancy doors, ironwork on the balconies, gates and railings).

We finished up at Koala Park where a family of koala bears resided, mostly up tall eucalyptus trees feeding on the fresh shoots and leaves. They are small with grey fur, about the size of a medium teddy bear and just as cuddly. Two of them sat on a table allowing visitors to pick them up to nurse them; but they had to be careful because their extra-long claws could easily scratch them. Like the kangaroo family they carry their young in a pouch for five months (they measure only half an inch when born). Later they often ride on their mothers' backs. As well as koalas there was a herd of grey wallabies, which are like medium-sized kangaroos. They have strongly made back legs and tails, which enable them to hop round at a good speed. One of them had a joey in her pouch with its head and front feet sticking out. Most of them were quite tame. One allowed Alf to stroke it whilst he had his photograph taken.

As the war had been dragging on for four years I was beginning to feel war-weary, having been in it from the first day.

By now the Russians were halting Hitler's blitzkrieg and the Yanks along with the RAF were now hitting German industrial plants and cities with constant waves of day and night bombing. It was encouraging to see our army was now on the attack and the Royal Navy was holding the Jerry U-boat wolf packs at bay with better techniques in locating and depth-charging them.

At last the scene was changing, so I liked to go to the cinema once a week to find out what was happening on all fronts on the Pathé Gazette newsreel — especially in the Pacific where the Yanks were now geared up for a steady advance towards Japan. They were producing one liberty ship every ten days to carry the massive tonnage of armaments, planes and tanks to supply their front lines thousands of miles across the Pacific to fight against the fanatical Jap troops who defended their lines to the last man.

The Last Two Battles of the Leviathans

The monster battleships, *Musashi* and *Yamato,* weighed 72,809 tons fully laden and were 800.5 feet long by 121.1 feet with nine massive 18.1-inch guns and 176 assorted anti-aircraft guns.

At the Battle of Leyte Gulf on 24 October 1944, they were operating together along with the heavy cruiser *Mogami* in the Sibuyan Sea between Mindoro and Luzon in the Philippines without air cover of fighter protection when suddenly they had to manoeuvre at high speed to avoid 120 Yankee bombers and torpedo bombers. Their anti-aircraft guns threw up a massive barrage of flak as their barrels belched out red flames of fire and black puffs of smoke just like Vesuvius erupting. However, like the ill-fated *Prince of Wales* and *Repulse* before them, they were overwhelmed with aircraft.

Musashi was hit for'ard in her unprotected parts by torpedoes. Then a second wave of torpedo bombers slammed three more tin fish home so the *Musashi* lost speed. *Yamato* was hit by two bombs. She developed a slight list, but was able to break off from the action to have her final fight another day. Seven more torpedoes slammed into *Musashi*'s port quarter. She retired at a speed of 5 knots, listing badly, after the Yank's claim of seventeen bomb and nineteen torpedo hits. She was ordered to run aground on the nearest island but never made land. She turned turtle after dusk before sinking out of sight.

The mighty battleship *Yamato,* in the company of a light cruiser squadron and a destroyer squadron (still without air cover), had broken through the Bungo Strait heading for South Okinawa. She intended to blast her way through the Yankee invasion fleet, sending all and sundry to the bottom before running the ship aground, as she had not taken on enough fuel for the return journey. The 2,000 ratings she was carrying were to be sent ashore to supplement the island garrison. This action was to be coupled to a large kamikaze attack, but fortunately on 3 April a massive air strike from the *Enterprise* task force was launched through heavy rains and squalls. For two continuous hours wave after wave of torpedo and dive-bombers struck the helpless leviathan. She was caught unawares by the first wave of kites, which attacked from out of the heavy clouds. She managed to dodge the bombers and torpedo bombers by high-speed manoeuvring. She was able to turn away out of the tracks of the running tin fish; also she opened up fire with every possible gun that could be brought to bear, firing a massive barrage as the attack developed. She damaged and brought down several kites, which plummeted like fireballs from the sky. Several near misses exploded close by her hull, shaking the ship so severely that a turbogenerator was shaken off the switchboard. The circuit breakers tripped out, causing a power cut to black out the after section of the ship. With no lights and no power on the four massive rams which swung the rudder from side to side to steer the ship to port or starboard she was unable to answer her helm.

The loss of power brought some of the after guns to a standstill as they could not be ranged without hydraulic power.

The electrical artisans had to break the switchboard down so as to gradually build up the load before the power aft could be completely restored. Unfortunately for the ship it was never fully accomplished as another wave of torpedo bombers attacked. Suddenly two tin fish struck port and starboard quarters for'ard, beyond the hulking great slabs of 16.1-inch armour plating, creating massive explosions and tearing large jagged holes in her thin plated sides. Several compartments and mess decks were flooded. This let in thousands of tons of water and caused a total blackout inside the ship.

She was able to continue ploughing ahead with her speed reduced to 5 or 6 knots. Her ring main aft was quickly isolated so the electric power could be restored to the rudder, which was quickly brought back into use, but she was sluggish answering the helm. The after guns were brought back into use ready for the next onslaught, whilst the for'ard guns remained silent, standing still like stuffed dummies deprived of power to work them.

The artisans and damage-control parties fought down below decks, sweating like pigs in the hot stuffy atmosphere, to bring back some power to the for'ard section. They rigged up cables in between the bulkheads to join the electrical circuit up by bypassing the piece of damaged cable. This was a job they had to perform groping in the dark as the few emergency lights that were lit up were very few and far between. Several parties tried to rescue their shipmates who had got trapped. Many compartments had been cut off by the wall of water which had suddenly rushed in. Some of the men were injured or burnt by the blast and were taken up to the sickbay for treatment, whilst others lay dead beside them.

The ship was now down by the bows, which increased her draught by several feet; also she developed a moderate list to port. There was a ten-minute lull in the bombing whilst the next wave of kites was prepared for take-off. Soon they were all airborne heading in a beeline for the stricken vessel. They attacked from the bows end of the ship where the guns remained silent. They plastered the decks with bombs and knocked out many of the anti-aircraft guns, which were only lightly shielded by 1-inch armour plate. More tin fish opened up her sides and thousands of tons of water flooded into various compartments causing a terrific list to port.

This increased her draught by ten feet or more on the port side, making her sloping decks hard to climb up, and making it difficult to pass through the long darkened passages below deck with the bulkhead doors harder to open. There was much carnage below where the men had been caught by the blast of the explosion. (It could splatter one's body into little pieces against the bulkhead or wrap it around a stanchion; it could rip one's skin clean off the bone, particularly if the body was bare and unprotected; or it could rip off an arm or leg whilst the face or hands could be seared by the blast; then again, strange to say, the blast could miss a man completely whilst killing his mate standing close by him.)

Stretcher parties were formed to collect the injured. Once again damage-control parties strove to contain the damage to bring the ship back to some semblance of working order. The ship was still moving on an erratic course, making about 15 knots in a large circle, as once again the power had been cut off the steering gear leaving the rudder at 5° to starboard. Also the guns remained silent through lack of power and were all ranged in different directions and elevated at various angles unable to move.

The only guns which could be brought back into use were the main ones, which along with the boiler and engine rooms were all protected by the massive 16.1-inch slabs of armour plating. All was not well in the boiler rooms as some of the double-bottom oil-fuel tanks had sprung leaks so that seawater was seeping into them. This caused contaminated oil to be sucked into the pumps, then forced into the sprayers, which began to splutter in the furnaces. This dropped the steam pressure by 50 pounds and the speed of the ship was reduced another 5 knots. Within half an hour the list increased, causing the main feed pumps to lose suction of water from the main feed tanks. The boilers ran dry owing to the terrific evaporation in the steam drums and also in the water tubes, which began to melt into the furnaces. This brought all the main and auxiliary machinery to a sudden halt, leaving only three of the main engines turning, being driven by the weigh of the ship. The fourth one, with its starboard outer shaft and massive bronze screw, had lifted clear of the water. Soon the ship was wallowing on her side like a wounded sitting duck, with her sloping deck awash with water lapping over the gunwale.

With no steam left in the ship the forced-draught turbofans no longer turned to fill the stokeholds with air pressure. This air was mixed with the fine spray of oil fuel to ignite in the furnaces to generate the heat. Now the position was reversed as the glowing red-hot furnace brickwork and hot boiler drums heated up the stokehold temperatures, causing a rise of above 15°F. It was as hot as hell and extremely uncomfortable. The ladder handrails became too hot to touch with bare hands. Consequently the boiler rooms had to be evacuated and large lumps of waste were used to grab the handrails.

After the long attack many of the crew began to appear on the upper deck from the total darkness of the decks below, leaving many of their trapped and dead shipmates below. The upper deck was now sloping so badly that a human chain was formed so the crew could climb up without slipping to the starboard side where several hundred men had assembled on its nearly level surface. They awaited orders to abandon the doomed ship before she eventually disappeared out of sight in a massive eruption of water. This confirmed that a battleship without a good umbrella of fighter protection was useless. The last knell had sounded for the battleship.

Leyte

We waited in Sydney for around six weeks for a delivery of fifty brand-new gull-wing Corsair fighters from San Francisco in the United States, some 6,467 miles away. All the necessary oils, spares and engines for the Fleet Air Arm had to be shipped some 12,500 miles from England. Finally we stocked the ship for a long voyage, full to capacity with everything we were likely to need. The Yanks supplied twenty bottles of CO_2 gas, which arrived alongside in a landing craft. They were hoisted aboard and brought down to the lower hangar on a lift. Then they were trucked over several decks and lowered down several hatches before arriving at the CO_2-bottle room. Their main feature was that they were smaller and easier to handle, only weighing 140 pounds when full, whereas our bottles weighed 140 pounds when empty. This was a great advantage when manhandling them.

We slipped through Sydney Head into the Pacific Ocean, travelling northward up the coast of New South Wales, passing by Brisbane and the Queensland coast with its attractive Great Barrier Reef which stretches some 1,250 miles.

We were now playing our part in the fleet train to supply our aircraft carriers, which were now operating on the front line in Japanese waters with new or repaired kites.

We steamed on through the Coral Sea with its numerous islands, passed along the top of Papua New Guinea, veered to port into the Solomon Sea and picked our way cautiously through a number of unnamed islands scattered about along our route. We then passed by the large isles of New Britain and New Ireland into the Bismarck Archipelago where we eventually arrived at Manus in the Admiralty Isles. This is a small group of islands 2° below the equator in the Pacific Ocean. The ship nosed her way into a large lagoon where we spent two days at anchor.

Manus is a green island with lush swaying palms, constantly blanketed by a large cloud which produced plenty of rain. It is hot and steamy with a light cooling breeze (the north-west monsoons soaked the island from December until April). It has a large natural blue lagoon which formed an excellent deep harbour for several large ships.

There was plenty of spare time for water polo and swimming. I jumped in the water several times for short dips although I was not a strong swimmer. Two marksmen with rifles were posted at the bows and stern of the upper deck to watch out for and ward off any approaching shark which happened to sneak into the harbour by firing a few rounds of ammunition at it. General MacArthur some months before had sped up his New Guinea campaign (Ariel) with a reconnaissance which had confirmed that Los Negros Island, where the Japs had an airstrip, was weakly defended. It was strategically located some 200 miles off the coast of New Guinea and nestled off the Eastern tip of Manus, the largest island of the Admiralty group. Los Negros had one of the finest anchorages in the South Pacific, ideal to make a convenient supply base. Consequently MacArthur bypassed the battle lines by some 800 miles up the coast of New Guinea to Hollandia, then with only 1,000 men of the US Cavalry Division attacked Los Negros from the rear. They took the Jap defence by surprise and completely off balance, seizing control of the airstrip within minutes of landing without loss to themselves. Within ten days (on 10 March 1944) he was in complete control of the island, occupying it to cut off the Jap retreat from New Guinea. He was able to use it as a base, along with Manus. It was built up to form an advance shipping base, complete with a small town with all mod cons (such as roads, warehouses, offices, living quarters, electricity, lorries, Jeeps and landing craft). He built up supplies for launching new attacks and formed one of the first stepping stones in his gradual advance across the vast Pacific expanse towards Japan.

The time passed quickly and we were soon off to sea again. It was an uneventful trip away from the main sea lanes passing by numerous islets, one of which had a landing craft beached on it to act as a signpost. After about twenty days we arrived at Leyte in the Philippines. We anchored in a large sheltered deserted bay away from all habitation except for the occasional fisherman in a small boat who cast his net upon the pale-blue waters.

Leyte is one of a large group of about 7,000 islands. Most are tiny but there are several large ones — including Luzon, on which stands the capital, Manila. These isles extend some 1,152 miles north and south and 682 miles east and west. They are part of the Malay Archipelago in the South China Sea. Leyte lies south-east of Luzon and is separated from Mindanao by the Surigao Strait. It is 121 miles long by fifty-two miles wide, and had a sparse population of under half a million people.

There were still strong pockets of Japanese troops on some of the islands. The capital, Manila, is only 1,600 miles from Japan and 630 miles from occupied Hong Kong.

The Fleet Air Arm soon got busy, working day and night preparing, unwrapping and degreasing the brand-new Corsair fighters with their gull-wings, which were not greatly favoured by the Yanks. They had cartridge starters, which emitted a sharp crack when turning the engine over by a small explosion. I always remember watching a warrant shipwright attached to the Fleet Air Arm sitting in the cockpit and helping out by starting up the large radial engines. It took nearly a dozen cartridges. They made the engine turn then splutter until it sprang into life with a mighty roar.

Once they were fully prepared and tested, several of our pilots were catapulted off in them to land on an airstrip ashore. The fleet carriers sent several pilots at a time to fly them back on board.

We stopped in the area for about six weeks. The Fleet Air Arm repaired damaged kites, which were brought in from the fleet by a small freighter as deck cargo. They were winched over onto our small aircraft lighter, which was designed to carry one kite, to be brought back alongside our ship and lifted on board by one of the cranes for repair.

One day a small Yankee landing craft with supplies came roaring alongside far too fast under the crane so that it overshot its stopping position. The man for'ard with the boathook engaged in the eyebolt was suddenly dragged off his feet. He let go of the pole to save himself from falling overboard. The officer on duty on our ship shouted down some good advice to the young coxswain, who promptly replied, "If you Limey bastards can do any better, hop down and do it yourself."

After completing our mission successfully we returned to Sydney for more supplies. Our vitals were running low and our oil fuel was getting short. Most tanks were empty and we needed to restock our Fleet Air Arm with new carriers and spares.

Okinawa

At the beginning of 1945 advance bases had been prepared in the sheltered lagoons of Eniwetok, Kwajalein and Ulithi atolls (room for 600 ships). These ring-shaped coral islands were used as massive supply dumps, containing everything from cartridges to torpedoes.

Everything had to be brought over the Pacific Ocean on a massive belt in the form of liberty ships, which were mass-produced. Large sections were welded together and the ship was launched within a month or less. They endlessly churned up the ocean, making about 300 weary miles a day at 12½ knots.

First they brought over gangs of Seabees, who were construction workers, to erect a small town of warehouses, offices and billets from prefabricated sections which arrived with them. They had the job of bolting the sections together to form a small town, complete with electric power and a water main laid on. They also had to construct a large power plant to supply the lighting and power to drive a large refrigerating plant, which had to supply the whole of the armed forces and others working for them. 25,000 tons of frozen food and ice cream were consumed every month. There was also storage for fresh food. The warehouses had shelves and pigeonholes to accommodate gallon cans of oil, live shells, nuts and bolts and all manner of large and small objects. Everything had to be catalogued so that it could be drawn from the store by forklift and truck to be rapidly assembled on the jetty for instant loading onto a supply vessel for delivery to the front line.

Occasionally a ship would receive the wrong orders as the stack of paperwork sometimes got cross shackled. One such liberty boat spent six months plodding around the Pacific islands trying to deliver a boatload of barbed wire which nobody wanted. Eventually the

298

skipper found he had been directed to the wrong ocean and should have crossed over the Atlantic then through the Mediterranean to Naples.

Okinawa was the greatest sea and air offensive of the century. It was a massive undertaking. 183,000 troops, complete with equipment, were required to combat a garrison of 100,000 Jap troops. They were firmly entrenched in an incredible rabbit warren of defences dug into the soft rock. The expedition was under the command of Admiral Spruance, who ordered a massive bombardment of 44,825 5-inch shells, and a similar number of rockets and mortars, prior to the landing on 1 April (All Fools' Day), which was Easter Sunday. The US 10th Army landed on Okinawa, a large island, fifty-six miles long by fourteen miles wide, lying in between Formosa and the tip of Japan. From the tip of Kyushu to Okinawa or the Great Loo Choo Island was a distance of about 350 miles. It was to be the final stepping stone towards Japan.

This was Operation Glacier. 1,300 US transport vessels had manoeuvred off the west coast of Okinawa. The 5th Division assault corps landed in a five-mile arc at Hagushi Beachhead after the terrific bombardment of naval guns. In the first three days 60,000 men, fully equipped with tanks, artillery and tons of supplies, were landed ashore with little interruption. They advanced inland capturing Kadena and Yantan airfields.

Several Yankee destroyers were positioned in between Japan and Okinawa to act as an early warning radar system. This allowed the new defending fighters at Kadena and Yantan to take to the air ready for the oncoming attack, so as to break up the Jap suicide invaders and shoot them down or put them off their aim.

They also alerted the naval ships, allowing them time for their anti-aircraft gun crews and control parties to close up to defend their ships.

On 6 April the Japs launched the first of ten massive attacks of Floating Chrysanthemums (or Kikusui). Until 21 June there were huge attacks of kamikaze pilots, seven or eight hundred planes at a time. Their main object was to destroy all the supply vessels which were anchored in the bay. They had a success rate of 13%, which was a nightmare for Admiral Spruance. He threatened to withdraw the fleet, which was spread over a wide area.

The situation in Japan had become grim as there was a shortage of oil fuel for the warships, and aviation spirit for the aircraft. Quite a large proportion of aircraft carriers had been sunk along with their planes. Also the cream of their pilots were dead and there was no proper training scheme to replace them. The Jap top brass came up with the idea of suicide squads for all the forces, particularly the air force. Pilots were trained just enough for them to take off then crash their planes onto warships, particularly aircraft carriers, and supply and transport ships.

This idea of suicide or kamikaze pilots was submitted to young volunteers who were asked to dedicate their lives to the glory of their emperor and empire. They were given a special ceremonial last supper in their messes. Each pilot had a large bowl of rice, flavoured with soya sauce and a skinful of potent saki to lull them into a pleasant state of mind and give them plenty of Dutch courage to carry out these terrible suicidal attacks.

They were strapped into Zero fighters, which each carried one 500-pound bomb; then they waved farewell before being sent off on their murderous missions. On 19 March they had put the *Wasp* and *Enterprise,* which were brand-new aircraft carriers, out of commission.

Later on another kamikaze dived down out of the mist, smashing through the wooden deck of the heavy aircraft carrier *Franklin,* starting huge fires and badly damaging parked aircraft above and below deck. It instantly burst into a massive fireball, killing 825 crew.

The British Pacific fleet consisted of five carriers (*Illustrious*, *Victorious*, *Formidable*, *Implacable* and *Indefatigable)*, two battleships, five cruisers and fifteen destroyers under the command of Admiral Rawlings on his flagship *King George V*. It was designated Task Force 57, and operated in the Sakishima-Gunto area between Formosa and Okinawa, flying air strikes against the Southern Ryukyu islands.

The fleet suffered several kamikaze attacks. The *Illustrious* was the first one to be damaged (on 6 April), but she was still able to fly-on and fly-off the kites although her top speed was reduced to 19 knots. The *Indefatigable* was patrolling 300 miles south of Okinawa when she was suddenly jumped on by a Jap kamikaze bomber with a 500-pound bomb strapped to it. The bomber suddenly dived down from the height of 5,500 feet, manoeuvred over the flight deck but missed his target. He tried again, landing on the flight deck, leaving a 3-inch dent in the armour, unfortunately with the loss of eight ratings.

On 4 May the *Formidable* was struck by kamikaze bombers. The first one bounced off the deck, doing no damage. The second one caused a bad fire as several kites were blown up on the deck. It was quickly brought under control by the fire and damage-control parties, so she was back in action within the hour.

This was a rather different story to that of the Yankee carrier, *Bunker Hill,* with Task Force 58, which was hit by a kamikaze on 11 May. The Zero penetrated her wooden deck, damaging many kites which were tanked up with aviation spirit. The fuel tanks burst open, causing large balls of flame which developed into a massive inferno. The conflagration was added to by the full aviation-spirit filling lines, which burst open, spilling their contents. (This practice was frowned on by our Admiralty who insisted that all aviation-spirit or petrol lines should be emptied after use.) The fire and damage-control parties fought the blaze valiantly amongst the kites which were fully armed with bombs or torpedoes. The belts of machine-gun bullets occasionally popped off as they became overheated. They had to keep spraying to prevent them blowing up the ship. Eventually the fire was brought under control but the carrier was so badly damaged that it had to limp away with 392 killed and 264 wounded. This clearly illustrated the advantage of Admiralty armour-plated decks and empty aviation-spirit fuel lines over the wooden-deck fire traps with a greater number of aircraft. All our carriers hit by bombs were able to continue the fight without leaving the battle area.

The Yanks had chosen their landing area in the centre of the of the island with great care. It consisted of a large bay to take all their transport ships with a broad stretch of land to obtain a firm foothold, and two useful airstrips into the bargain. The landing had been a complete surprise to the Japs. Hence there was little resistance as the two strong defensive lines lay on the north and south parts of the island. The north was in amongst the hills and the south was on a narrow rocky piece of ground.

After the Japs had recovered from their shock they immediately launched an attack. 100 heavy bombers attacked the naval and transport ships at anchor. Most were shot down by fighter aircraft and anti-aircraft guns for the loss of three destroyers, three tank-landing craft and two ammunition transports, which were all sunk. Five fully loaded kamikaze bombers broke through the defences, crashing on the runways, setting many aircraft and fuel tanks on fire.

The III Amphibian Corps, 6th Marine Division, landed from the East China Sea, struck out north then split up into two parties and advanced up the coastline. One party passed Onna, then split at Nago into three parties. One continued along the coastline to Hedo Point then carried on to meet up with the other coastal parties at Aha. The other two parties headed for the Motobu Peninsula and advanced on either side of it. They met some stiff opposition in the Yee Taki Hills, killing 2,500 Jap defenders at the expense of 218 Yanks killed and 902 wounded. The 1st Marine Division advanced fourteen miles across country in the first week to Chimu Bay and the Katchin Peninsula.

The 7th Infantry Division took the airport at Kadena and Yantan, then split up and swung south to Kuba. They lined up with the 96th Infantry Division, which had swung south down the coastline. In front of them was the main Japanese defence line (which was six miles wide) at Shuri Castle, where all the tanks and artillery had been dug in. This was on the southern third of the island, where the Japs were safe in caves which had been carefully prepared to repel invaders. No amount of bombing and shelling could dislodge them.

The Japs went on the offensive, breaking through the Yankee lines, only to suffer a loss of 5,000 men. Not until 31 May did the Yanks reduce the Shuri Line to rubble, but heavy rains held up the advance, bogging down the tanks and guns in the mud.

On 21 May the Japanese lieutenant general, Ushijima, issued his final orders for his men to fight on in a guerrilla war, then he committed hara-kiri (suicide). The fighting lasted until the end of July when 7,400 Japs surrendered.

Okinawa was the costliest operation in the central Pacific. Half a million men had been involved. Fighting had cost the Yanks 49,000 casualties, of whom 12,500 men died. More than 110,000 Japs had been killed on the island.

The End of the War

After two weeks I was drafted to HMS *Golden Hind,* which was situated at Warwick Farm in the suburbs of Sydney. It was a racecourse which had been converted to a naval transit camp. It had water, electricity and drains already laid on and all that was required was a large number of tents to be erected. I stopped there about three weeks under canvas in a large bell tent along with eight other POs, before being drafted to HMS *Tyne* (a destroyer repair ship) for more experience to resit my exam for chief ERA. She was a grubby old ship, manned by a Chatham crew, with only one chap on board that I knew. He was an enginesmith, Ken Webber from Cornwall, who was in my training class when I first joined.

She was loading up for about a three-week trip before travelling to her new forward base some 2,000 miles from Japan (well out of range of their land-based bombers). She was to be used for repairing destroyers of the British Pacific fleet operating with the Yankee Task Force 63.

Eventually we moved off, outward bound, on her tiny sloop engines at a speed of about 6 knots. I kept watch below on the throttles of a tiny set of saturated-steam turbines, which hummed pleasantly at a deadly monotonous speed, day in day out, as the ship ploughed steadily forward. We travelled in a northerly direction for about 3,000 miles through the Solomon Islands.

On 15 August 1945 the cease-fire signal was flapping from the halyards of Admiral Rawlings' flagship, *King George V,* when a bomber flew close alongside aircraft carrier *Implacable*, dropping its bombs without damage. This put the captain in a quandary whether to order his guns to open fire or not. Then a squadron of Japanese bombers approached the fleet, ditching their bombs in the centre of it, recognising the peace terms, much to everybody's relief. VJ day had been announced, the Japs had surrendered, peace had been officially declared at last.

There was much excitement on board as everyone expected the ship to turn about in her track immediately but we were bitterly disappointed . She kept plodding on until she reached Eniwetok in the mid-Pacific, about 12° off the equator. It was a large coral atoll with a deep lagoon, big enough to hold our ship and to have a flotilla of destroyers tied up alongside for boiler cleaning and repairs. We waited there for about three weeks with little work to do, eagerly awaiting orders to return to Sydney.

Eventually the day arrived for the ship to depart. The motor boats and gangway were secured with everything on deck being left shipshape and Bristol fashion. The boilers were flashed up and steam was raised. The engines were warmed through and ready to start. The anchor was weighed and the propellers started to turn, driving the ship slowly forward through the blue still waters of the lagoon. She headed through the narrow gap in the coral reef on the first leg of the voyage homeward bound.

I settled down to my throttle watchkeeping in the engine room, with the turbines humming pleasantly, turning the prop shaft at 180 rpm. This was recorded on the rev counter, which was part of the Chadburns tachometer. The revs were shown on a large graduated dial by a big black finger and a red finger which kept dropping to zero then rising up to the other finger.

One night I decided to sling my hammock in the starboard waist, which was pleasantly cool with a light sea breeze and sheltered by the deck above. Unfortunately I chose the wrong night as a tropical storm suddenly blew up, causing the outside of the hammock to get soaked, and had a rude awakening after only two hours' sleep as the damp penetrated through and I started to get wet, so beat a hasty retreat down below to the steaming boiler room to spread out my hammock on the handrail above the steaming boiler. Then I left it to dry out whilst I rested on an uncomfortable hard wooden stool for the remainder of the night.

We continued the rest of the journey without incident until the ship passed through the Head into Port Jackson. Then I had another green rub in the form of a note from the jaunty, instructing me to get my bag and hammock packed for a pier-head jump next day, when I would collect a draft chit back to the *Golden Hind*. This was an unexpected bitter pill as I had expected to return home with the ship. (My old ship, *Unicorn*, was already homeward bound, making for Guzz in glorious Devon.)

Whilst the *Tyne* was tied up alongside and starting to take in oil fuel, water and provisions for the long journey home, I waited alongside with my bag and hammock, etc. for transport back to Warwick Farm.

When the lorry arrived a dozen cheerful ratings, bound for civvy street in the UK, dumped their bags and baggage over the tailboard, then marched up the gangway for their passage home. This annoyed me. Feeling very disgruntled I loaded my gear on the back of the lorry. Then climbed aboard for a short trip back to the camp for another spell under canvas in a large bell tent along with eight other POs.

Apparently the reason for my delay home was that many ships were now superfluous and were beginning to tie up alongside the jetties in Sydney and the home ports. A large percentage of officers and men were due to be demobbed so a dozen ships in harbour had been left with skeleton crews until scratch crews could be mustered to steam them back home. Meanwhile about thirty ERAs and other active-service ratings were retained in barracks to be sent down daily to carry out odd repairs aboard these ships so that they would be in good working order to steam home.

Also the sudden exodus of ships from the war zone converging on the naval dockyards caused them to become choc-a-block far beyond their normal capacity. Many ships had been commissioned directly from the shipyards where they were built and had never visited their home ports.

Devonport Dockyard was no exception. It was brimful with ships. A few old battleships, cruisers and destroyers, and a flotilla of smaller vessels, such as frigates, sloops, corvettes, submarines and motor boats, were all tied up alongside one another. Aircraft carriers, tugs, minesweepers, the odd hospital ship and auxiliary merchantmen were anchored in the mouth of the River Tamar, called the Hamoaze, which lay at the back of the barracks and the dockyard.

As soon as each ship arrived home it was tied up or anchored and long leave was given to both port and starboard watches. Any passengers were drafted back to their own barracks. On their return to their ship, which was probably no longer required (indicated by a long thin white pennant flown from the yardarm), they were paid off. As the vast majority of the crew were HO officers and men arrangements had to be made for them to be demobbed.

Each shipload of men was dealt with in order of when the ship entered the port. The barracks was brimful with men going through the demob routine. This took about a week and threw a terrific pressure on the barracks stanchions, who had had a cushy job running and regulating the flow of ratings to and from the various ships throughout the war. Now with this massive influx of HOs to deal with they were overwhelmed and had to get extra help from active-service ratings left on board ship in harbour.

The demob routine consisted of reporting to the regulating office then being directed to the mess and sleeping billets. From there they joined various queues — at the sickbay; at the dentist for a check-up; at the pay office to have the ledger made up for pay and any extra allowances; at the commander's office to have their discharge papers made up; at an office for collecting their medals, if any were due to them, and to return their gas masks (but not their bags and hammocks, which they were allowed to keep).

Finally, after a week they were all ready to be discharged, and they collected their civvy clothing from the drill hall. Next morning they were issued with their final travelling warrant, ration book, and final payment. The natives marched through the main barracks' gate for the last time, whilst the others awaited a train from the barracks' station to connect them up with North Road Station to await a connecting train.

On their return home many men found conditions had drastically changed and were not as rosy as they had expected. Many of their old jobs were no longer there. Factories and offices had been damaged beyond repair or totally destroyed. Many of their homes had been completely flattened or badly damaged. The power cables and gas pipes were often cut off, along with the water mains and drains, owing to huge craters in the streets where they had all been severed. In many cases wives and sweethearts had been forced to leave the area, or, still worse, some had run away with the lodger. On the other hand, some men were much more fortunate and were able to slot back into their old jobs with their houses intact and their wives waiting for them.

Whilst the barracks was bursting at the seams with HOs who could not wait to get out fast enough, the active-service officers and men, left on board the various ships, suddenly found themselves blacked out and short of essential services, such as power to light up the messes, or cooks to provide meals, etc. It was several months before the numbers in barracks had been drastically reduced to a trickle and they could start sorting out the needs of the active-service men. As many ships were tied up in groups alongside one another with shortages of men in all the different branches, the largest ship was fully manned to provide essential services. A temporary link-up provided the others with lighting, heat, water, food, pay and leave, etc. for several months.

Going Home

So from 26 October 1945 I was still feeling cheated out of my long-awaited tropical leave to get married. However, I made the best of the situation by basking in the sun and enjoying the food and fruit which was unrationed, unlike the situation at home where it was rationed more severely than ever.

The disadvantage of living under canvas, especially at night, was that it went quite cold and for several nights there was a touch of frost.

With the return of the Anzacs the trains of an evening were rammed jammed full of passengers so that one could hardly move to get out at one's destination. The naval patrols were kept busy around the town as there were a number of punch-ups caused by fierce arguments, especially in the government-controlled red-light district, which was put out of bounds to our men.

Our daily routine consisted of being transported to and from the docks to carry out any repairs required on the various ships' boilers and engines. Several ERAs, including myself, were sent to work on a whacking big 10,000-ton merchant ship. It was powered by a massive reciprocating steam engine, which was put into reverse by a small auxiliary engine. Although it looked so big it only developed a few thousand h.p. A much smaller destroyer turbine set would develop up to 25,000 h.p.

She was named the *Bonaventure* and her large holds had been converted into workshops and stores so she became a depot ship for carrying small X craft submarines and their crews. The submarines were fitted with 2-ton side charges of Amatex explosive. They were designed to penetrate enemy harbour defences then manoeuvre under battleships and detach their explosive charges, which were set to blow up some hours later. When they went to attack the German battleship *Tirpitz* in a Norwegian fjord most crews were taken prisoner before completing their work.

The *Bonaventure* was to be immediately converted to have her holds stripped of all the Royal Navy fittings so she could resume work as a merchant ship. The majority of the merchant fleet had been sunk, leaving a great shortage of ships. Only a lot of old rusty tubs were left. They had leaking boilers, which were liable to burst, and engines which were ready to pack up in the first gale they encountered.

I was on duty every other day in the camp, standing by for any emergency that might occur, or in case an extra hand was required on board a ship, and would often have a stroll in the surrounding orchards and pastures after tea. One evening I was surprised to see a skeleton of a cow bleached white by the sun, and another carcase covered by a black carpet which turned out to be blowflies busy picking off all the flesh.

Nothing much of interest occurred, until one local report in the paper stated that a shark had swum some miles upriver to Parramatta and it had bitten off the leg of an unsuspecting boy bather, who was rushed to hospital in a critical condition. This had never been known to occur in the river before.

The only other serious item to occur as front page news was a coal strike which caused electricity to be severely rationed. The coal stocks dwindled down to ten days' supply. The electricity was switched off for long periods throughout the day.

At last, on 5 January 1946, I was drafted to the battleship *King George V* to work my passage home. She spent two weeks in Sydney before making the long leisurely trip home via Hobart, Tasmania and Cape Town, South Africa.

I spent a weekend with Norman and his mate. We had a fascinating trip to the Blue Mountains at Katoomba. He said he had booked me a bed at a hostel but on arrival I found there was no bed for me so I had a hard layer's sleep on the deck. We went by train from Sydney, some 109 miles (fare £4.30).

The railway track passed along the old pioneering trail across the Emu Plains, past willow groves and rushing rivers and through rich farmland and rain forest. Then we found out what makes the mountains blue: the droplets of eucalyptus oil caught by the sun rays cause a dark blue hue with a breathtaking effect. We travelled through the domain of exotic birds and we marvelled at the cathedral splendour of the limestone caves which give a turquoise gleam up the Blue Mountain Road to Katoomba, where there is a memorial to the late Charles Kingsford Smith (a famous aviator).

We hired three horses, which we rode to Cooks Crossing, a gorge with a splendid view looking out onto Katoomba Falls, Orphan Rock and Jamieson Valley (where the woods were full of leeches after a fall of rain). On the way back I felt saddle-sore as my new pair of rough serge trousers played havoc with my legs, causing two large rough red patches, so had to dismount and lead the horse about three miles back to the stables.

The night before *King George V* set sail a red-dust storm arose along with a choking heat which became unbearable, especially to those who had gone to the ship's farewell dance.

Next forenoon, on 19 January, the ship steamed out of Sydney Head, veering southward on our long journey home. We called in at Hobart, Tasmania (where I happened to meet a townie from my hometown and knew the exact house where he had lived).

We stopped a week there before continuing our journey to Fremantle. It was a change to steam with our portholes open as throughout the war they remained shut with the deadlights screwed down to darken the ship.

At last we arrived at Fremantle, the port of Perth, and we stopped there for a week. I had a good look round the town and waterfront, which had mostly been built by convict labour. It had become a boom town during the Western Australia gold rush. Founded in 1829 it contained a small number of interesting features: such as the Round House, built with twelve sides (this was the local prison where hanging took place), the Maritime Museum, the esplanade, the market, and the warders' quarters.

Several times I took the train to Perth, which was a modern city well laid out alongside the River Swan, and had a good shufti before going for big eats and a cinema show.

We started off leisurely on our long journey to the Cape, which was some 5,615 miles long. Eventually the ship dropped anchor off Simonstown for a visit to Cape Town to refuel and stock up. The NAAFI took in large quantities of Cape to Cairo fags, Nutty and tinned fruit, including tinned guavas, and snoek (a fish).

As there were several make and mends I went ashore for a bathe on the fine beach, and wandered around the town but found it very quiet in the evening. We didn't get the local welcome we had received on HMS *Edinburgh* as that had been part of the local ladies' war effort, which had ceased now that peace had arrived.

Eventually we set off on the longest leg of the leisurely journey, some 6,000 miles long. We rounded the Cape of Good Hope and proceeded in a northerly direction.

We arrived in Portsmouth in mid-April after just over a six-week journey and there was little pomp or ceremony. There was not even a band to welcome us home — just a handful of spectators. It was a cool spring day with the occasional shower.

We completed our shutting-down watch in the port after engine room, which by now had reached a comfortable temperature for working in. I climbed up the ladder and made for the bathroom for a hot shower as the atmosphere was quite cold. I wasted no time in getting dressed in the rig of the day ready to go ashore after tea, and dug out my greatcoat and gloves from the locker to keep me warm, then made my way across the dockyard, passing by Nelson's *Victory,* then out through the main gate into Portsmouth. It was a new city for me as my home port was Guzz. I groped my way around, passing by a big sombre-looking brick building, which turned out to be the barracks. It looked cold and unattractive compared to our white stone buildings in Guzz.

All the celebrations for peace were long since over and all the demobbed men were picking up the threads of their prewar lives and were struggling to get back to normality.

The city had been heavily bombed by the Luftwaffe. Large lumps of masonry were missing from the upper structure of the most important buildings. Little work had been done to clear up the massive damage, except that the sandbags had been removed from the base of large buildings, along with the barrage balloons and anti-aircraft guns. The huge problems of restoring damaged houses to make them habitable and the connection of essential amenities still needed to be solved. The clearing away of street after street of flattened terraced houses, the filling in of a number of large bomb craters, and the replacement of lamp and telephone poles still had to be tackled.

After 18.00 most of the citizens returned home from work so the city became dead. There was a dearth of buses and even fewer cars about as petrol was severely rationed.

The next job for me was to locate a phone box that had not been damaged so I could make arrangements for my wedding. It was a cloudy night so it soon grew dark and became lost in the many unlit roads. Most of the houses had drawn their curtains, which were still mostly the blackout ones.

On asking a solitary passing civvy if he knew anywhere where there was a working phone he directed me to a small Swiss café in the next road, so made my call then stopped to have a meal. Being quite hungry I ordered plaice and chips. Portions of sausages and bacon were very meagre as meat was still severely rationed (unlike in Aussie where we were served with big helpings).

After paying I went out in the dark and followed a party of boy seamen escorted by a PO. They were marching to the barracks drill hall, lit up by two faint oil lamps carried fore and aft of the rear line. They carried on through the main gate whilst I made my way towards the ship, where there was a pile of mail awaiting me.

I spent a week in Portsmouth and was then drafted back to Devonport, my home base, which I found in an even worse state than Pompey. Half of the terraced houses had been flattened and there was terrific damage around the dockyard. Happily there was little damaged in the barracks and Aggie Weston's The Sailor's Rest was still intact, along with the Torpoint ferry and Saltash railway bridge across the Tamar. All the shopping centre in Plymouth had been flattened. St Andrew's church had lost most of its roof and was completely gutted. The Octagon and Union Street were flattened, but the Barbican and the Hoe had little damage. Drake's statue, the Armada Memorial and Smeaton's Stump were also still intact.